D1171718

The
Medieval World
at War

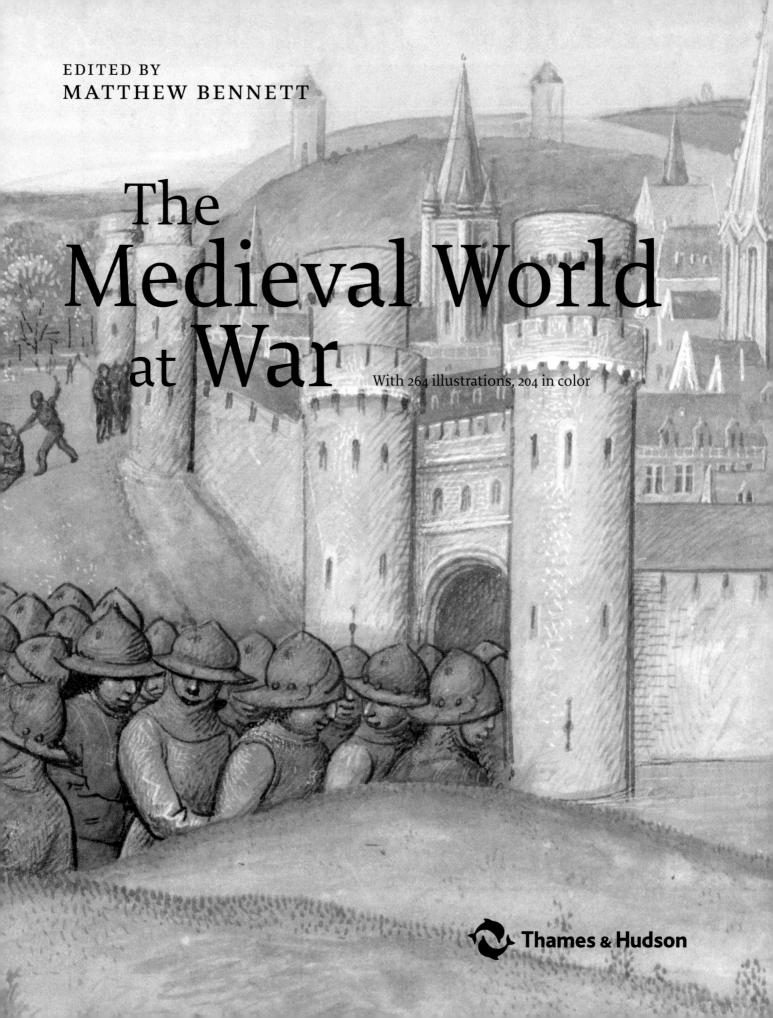

EDITED BY
MATTHEW BENNETT

The
Medieval World
at War

With 264 illustrations, 204 in color

Thames & Hudson

Contents

Half-title: Gold inlaid *kilic* and scabbard made for the Ottoman Sultan Süleyman II, 16th century.

Title page: Louis, Count of Flanders, and the town of Bruges are defeated by Philip van Artevelde and the people of Ghent at the battle of Beverhoutsfeld in 1382; manuscript illumination, 1477.

These pages: Scene from the Bayeux Tapestry showing the decisive moment at the battle of Hastings in 1066 when the Norman cavalry breaks through the English line.

Copyright © 2009 Thames & Hudson Ltd, London

Designed by Ben Cracknell Studios

All Rights Reserved. No part of this publication may be reproduced or transmitted in any form or by any means, electronic or mechanical, including photocopy, recording or any other information storage and retrieval system, without prior permission in writing from the publisher.

First published in 2009 in hardcover in the United States of America by Thames & Hudson Inc., 500 Fifth Avenue, New York, New York 10110

thamesandhudsonusa.com

Library of Congress Catalog Card Number 2008911982

ISBN 978-0-500-25156-0

Printed and bound in China by SNP Leefung Printers Ltd

Introduction:
Change and Continuity in Warfare

Opposite Late 15th-century sword and armour. Medieval warfare in Western Europe is often characterized by knights in armour; but while these warriors played an important role there were many more factors in the pursuit of military success.

Below Stone relief representing Richard I of England, 'Lionheart' (d. 1199), dating from a century after his death. The king was an iconic warrior and it was his leadership on crusade for which he was best remembered, as an example of the perfect Christian warrior.

The Medieval World at War covers a thousand years of military history and reaches from the Atlantic seaboard to the islands of Japan. Although our focus is on Latin Christendom and its responses to external attack, both the internecine conflicts of Western Europe and the remarkable expeditionary campaigns of the Crusades are set in the context of inter-continental operations symbolized by the Mongol world empire. The Muslim world also played a crucial role in bringing new technology and tactics, improved fortresses and siegecraft, to western nations that had lost touch with their Classical military heritage.

Throughout the book there are recurrent themes, many common to societies apparently quite different geographically, culturally or over time. Central to warfare is always the matter of logistics: how to move men and their many accompanying animals over land or sea in order to bring them to a point where they can have the most useful impact in achieving the aims of their commander. The requirements of feeding such forces, particularly specialist animals such as trained warhorses, was usually the most important factor in any military operation. There was also the issue of an exponential increase in baggage animals, required both to carry feed for the cavalry horses and to sustain themselves. Effectively, in the lands of the old Roman empire, this meant that armies of more than 30,000 were almost impossible to support. Even forces of this size might need to travel in separate columns, depending upon the fertility of the territory being traversed. At sea, numbers were even smaller, but transport ships did allow the delivery of the best warriors, such as crusading knights, to exactly where they were needed on the Syrian coast. Almost paradoxically, nomad armies had the advantage that they were their own supply train, their herds of horses simply grazing along their route of march; but even these forces encountered difficulties when the grasslands of the steppe ran out. As a result, few nomad forces penetrated west of the Hungarian plain, or not for long. Further east and in Central Asia, things were different, and the Mongols proved capable of attacking across wide fronts into Europe, the Middle

Dover castle stands above the White Cliffs on England's southern shore guarding the English Channel and the routes from France and the Continent. Known as the 'Key to the Kingdom' it represents the overriding importance of fortifications during the medieval centuries, from the 12th-century keep (top left) to the later medieval gatehouse (bottom right).

East, China and the Far East; but they were in many ways exceptional. Records of Indian and Chinese history do speak of armies in the millions, and while certain areas of these regions were indeed very rich in both resources and people, we should be careful about according total credence to such sources.

Another theme central to the development of warfare over the long millennium that constitutes the medieval era is that of fortification. Although there is nothing to match the Roman or Sasanian *limes* or the Chinese Great Wall (which did remain in use) created in the ancient world, fortifications of all kinds played a crucial role. It is still common to view the period as one dominated by castles, but this is to misunderstand the diversity of fortress types deployed. Indeed, the legacy of the Roman empire in the West was that of fortified cities, best represented by the walls of Constantinople which resisted conquest until overcome by ship-borne crusaders in 1203–04, a conquest which is often forgotten in the light of the final conquest by the Ottoman Turks in 1453, with their new-fangled mighty guns. In the rich societies of the Islamic world, India and China, fortified cities dominated warfare, resulting in the need for expert infantry to support the cavalry elites.

The best hope for success against ports and coastal cities was always provided by naval attacks (as at Constantinople), and played a major part in crusading activities from Portugal to the Holy Land and from the Baltic to North Africa. Fleets played vital roles in the warfare of China and its neighbours too, although the story of their success was often blighted (as in the Mediterranean and its various narrow seas) by the risk of destruction in storms. The Mongol attack on Japan in 1281, crucially undermined

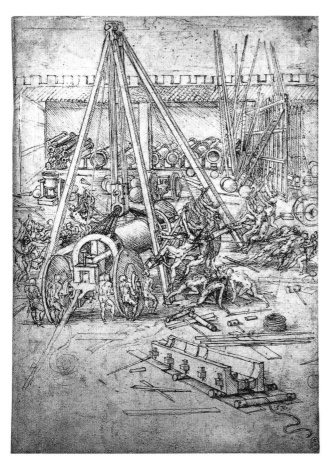

Leonardo da Vinci's drawing of a large cannon being raised onto a carriage. Medieval rulers invested in tall, stone walls because they could successfully repel most assaults. With the development of gunpowder artillery from the mid-14th century onwards, their security was no longer guaranteed.

by the *kamikaze* (Divine Wind), is the most famous case. In many ways, ships became fortresses at sea. The galley type and northern longship, both long and narrow with a low keel-board, dominated until the 12th century, when taller, broader roundships and high-sided cogs were developed in the West. The Chinese had similar vessels; but technological development in the western world took off on an exponential curve from the mid-14th century onwards. It is worth remembering that most of the great inventions prior to the late 18th-century Industrial Revolution – for example, gunpowder and printing – were medieval creations which in turn helped to make the modern world what it became. By the late 15th century, gun-carrying carracks, and in the 16th century galleons, enabled the exploration and exploitation of less technologically advanced nations and the beginning of 'gun-boat' diplomacy that endured until the 20th century. So naval warfare is another important theme when studying medieval warfare.

Finally, there is the issue of how armies (or fleets) actually combated one another on campaign and in open battle. Although it used to be thought by seminal historians like Sir Charles Oman that medieval forces only ever sought battle over other means of defeating the enemy, we now know how far from the truth this was. Small wars of harassment were fought from Scotland to Syria and may be found in Kosovo or Korea during the medieval period. There is no doubt that certain large engagements do still stick in the mind, though, or may be made to represent a typical or crucial encounter between conflicting sides. For example, might the Kingdom of Jerusalem have been maintained had its forces not been defeated by Saladin at Hattin (1187)? Or did the defeat of the Ottoman Sultan by Timur (Tamerlane) at Ankara (1402) dramatically change history? In both cases the answer is probably 'No', since it was ultimately longer term geo-strategic issues that determined the final outcomes; nevertheless, other scholars might take a different view and argue for the retention of the idea of the 'decisive' battle. It is, of course, always possible to win a battle and ultimately lose the war: Agincourt (1415) is a famous example. Battles at sea often produced a longer-term outcome, especially if one fleet was largely destroyed or captured, because the maintenance of war-fleets required such a huge capital outlay in comparison with land forces.

There are many other themes in this book, such as the development of arms and armour and the relationship between different arms in combat, or different forms of tactics. For example, the competition between the development of missile weapons and improved armour can be explored by the history of the rise and fall of the longbow. Eventually, it was to be superseded by gunpowder weapons, even if these were initially unreliable and less than effective on the battlefield. Indeed it was to be cannon and handguns that transformed warfare on land, in sieges, and at sea, helping to create the new warfare of the 16th and 17th centuries – although most of the eternals of warfare described above were unaffected by such developments.

This volume is loosely organized on chronological lines, but it is not possible to maintain the rather deceptively linear narrative of the ancient world (Egyptians, Assyrians, Persians, Greeks, Romans, etc.) simply because what we call the medieval world was a much more diverse place, and is made more so by our quite proper engagement with the Orient, linked via the Mongol empire for hundreds of years.

In his study of Byzantium against Persia and Islam (530–750), James Howard-Johnston explores the development of warfare as the Byzantine empire survived two centuries of assaults from the east and south. Although they called themselves Romans, the armies of the Eastern empire were very different from the infantry legions of the ancient world. They had learnt from the Persians and the steppe cultures, such as the Huns, Avars and Pechenegs, the importance of the cavalry bowman, who became the key soldier in their armies. They did not forget siege techniques, supported by a mastery of logistics. The battle of Dara (530) provides a model for the superiority of Byzantine tactics. In the era of Justinian I, his great general Belisarius was victorious over the Persians and conqueror of the Vandals in Africa and the Goths in Italy. Byzantine professionalism is expressed via military instruction manuals, such as the *Strategicon* of the late 6th century. Another important text, 'On Shadowing', instructed their forces on how to track and then to pounce on Arab raiding parties.

Roy Boss covers the period from the end of the 5th century when the Roman empire in the West collapsed to be replaced by successor states ruled by Germanic tribes, until the empire's reconstitution under Charlemagne. Britain was conquered from across the North Sea; the Franks ruled Gaul, the Visigoths Spain and the Ostrogoths Italy. Their armies were almost entirely collections of war-bands, though urban militias still survived in southern Gaul and south of the Alps. As the Merovingian Franks became the dominant force in the West, their original foot warriors were replaced by an armoured cavalry. Under Charles Martel of the Carolingian dynasty from the mid-8th century onwards, they defeated the Muslims (at Tours, 732), while Charlemagne (768–814) led a campaign of conquest aimed at restoring the Roman empire in the West. After defeating the Lombards in Italy and the Avars in Hungary, Charlemagne had himself crowned emperor in Rome (800). It used to be thought that the stirrup gave the Carolingian armies a decisive advantage, but modern research emphasizes rather their technological mastery in sieges and fortress building that enabled them to conquer the pagan Saxons and Slavs after decades of warfare. Matthew Bennett describes Europe under attack on all fronts by Vikings, Magyars and Muslims (9th to 11th centuries). Although very different in culture and military styles, the forces operated in much the same way. They all used raiding techniques to devastate territory and undermine the defenders' morale. From the lands bordering the southern Mediterranean shore, Muslim fleets and armies set out to terrorize Christian territories. Visigothic Spain fell within a few years of the initial Berber landings near Gibraltar. Raiding forces initially pressed on into southern France, but were held at bay by the Carolingian Franks. Sicily also fell and Muslim bases were established all along the northern shore of the Mediterranean; even Rome was threatened. In the Levant the Byzantines held on by developing a defensive strategy that avoided battle, though

The foot soldier, this one from a late 13th-century drawing by Villard de Honnecourt, made a contribution to medieval warfare that is usually forgotten owing to the celebration of the mounted knight. Men such as these provided essential support on campaign and on the battlefield, playing an especially crucial role in sieges.

this did not prevent several sieges of Constantinople by Arab forces. They faced another threat from whoever ruled the steppe lands to the north, while Slavs had occupied Greece. When these peoples combined they could also besiege Constantinople, almost bringing the empire to its knees.

The Magyars (Hungarians), nomad steppe warriors, devastated central and Western Europe from the 860s until they were decisively defeated by Otto I, the East German emperor, in 955. Christianized by 1000, the Hungarians played a vital role in protecting Europe from further nomadic incursions (and later engaged in crusading operations, which helped to sustain Byzantium even during its final years in the mid-15th century).

Meanwhile, Britain and France suffered from the mid-9th century onwards from attacks by the Vikings, notable sailors whose fleets even reached the Iberian Peninsula and the Mediterranean. They could be defeated only by a combination of blocking their routes upriver and constructing fortifications. In Britain, Alfred the Great led the way in Wessex, creating military and naval forces that proved capable of reconquering the island as far north as Scotland by the mid-10th century, so forging the first true Kingdom of England. Yet the Scandinavians returned, this time in the form of royal expeditions from Denmark, and in a devastating series of campaigns from 1009 to 1016 overran the country and established a new dynasty under Cnut. This conquest was repeated 50 years later by the Norman Duke William, himself of Danish heritage. The forces he brought across the Channel were by then steeped in the French form of cavalry and castle warfare which was to be the Latin Christian hallmark for centuries.

The early crusading era (c. 1050–1250) saw a revival of Latin Christendom, and its pugnacious expansion across the Pyrenees, the Alps and into the eastern Mediterranean lands. John France explores the contrast between the ways of war in Western Europe and the Muslim countries, which possessed a preponderance of wealth and military organization. Turkish warriors, superb horsemen and archers, formed the core of the armies of the competing caliphates of Cairo and Baghdad. The division of the Muslim world undoubtedly helped the crusaders, and against all the odds, western knights and their retainers marched across Europe, Turkey and Syria to capture Jerusalem in 1099. They established several states along the Syrian littoral, of which the

A battle between Timur and Tokhtamysh Khan in 1395, from a 16th-century manuscript. The cavalry traditions of the Turks and Mongols and other originally nomadic nations were very different from the western model, in emphasizing the use of the bow and an altogether more fluid form of warfare.

Kingdom of Jerusalem was the strongest, and protected them with mighty castles, supported by the crucial lifeline of fleets from all over the Christian world. Gradually, the Muslims reorganized, notably under Saladin. He captured Jerusalem in 1187, but crusading warfare continued for centuries. The last great effort in the east was the attack on Egypt in 1248–54 by Louis IX, king of France, although it eventually ended in failure. Like other Frankish rulers he negotiated with the Mongols in an attempt to catch the Muslims between two fires. Indeed, there was long-held hope that somehow a Christian emperor, Prester John, would come from the Far East to rescue Christendom from Muslim encirclement, and the Mongols were cast in this role, unlikely as this may seem today.

Timothy May explains how the great Mongol empire initiated by Chingiz Khan grew to world dominance by the mid-13th century and linked the military spheres of Europe and Asia. To the devastating speed and efficacy of nomad warfare the Mongols brought an additional factor: discipline. Their armies were well organized on a decimal system and supremely co-ordinated on campaign in separate columns that could be brought together at crucial moments. This led their enemies to grossly over-estimate Mongol numbers, which served in turn to terrify any opponent. Although they learnt effective siege techniques, it was the Mongol utter ruthlessness that encouraged cities to surrender rather than risk destruction. Moreover the flexibility of Mongol tactics meant that western armies were outmanoeuvred with ease; Russia and Eastern Europe as far as Vienna had been overrun by 1241. Further advance into Western Europe was prevented not by Christian military effectiveness, but by the death of the Great Khan and the need for Mongol leaders to return to Central Asia in order to elect another.

In contrast, the Egyptian Mamluks proved capable of beating the Mongols at their own game. With lines of command and communication stretching all the way back to the Central Asian steppes, Mongol forces on the western periphery often proved too small to impose their will over the Muslim world. The Mamluks were

Cavalry training exercises, from a *Manual of Horsemanship and Military Practice*, dating to 1371. Such material is hard to parallel in western sources and demonstrates the professional approach of the *faris* and Mamluk troops of Arab rulers.

originally slave soldiers in the service of the Ayyubid sultanate, but in the confusion caused by King Louis of France's crusade, they seized power in 1250. Their generals led armies of skilled, armoured horse archers capable of matching the Mongols in the field. After a victory at Ayn Jalut (Springs of Goliath) near the Sea of Galilee in 1260, the Mamluk sultan Baybars and his successors proved capable of both holding the Mongols at bay and completing the conquest of the crusader states (by 1291, when the key port of Acre fell). In the late 14th century Timur revived the Mongol threat, crushing the Ottoman Turks at Ankara and incidentally providing Constantinople with another 50 years of independent existence. But his empire lasted only as long as his lifetime, until 1405. In the 15th century Mongol rule weakened because of the sheer impossibility of attempting to control lands from Europe to China, with Russia, for example, freeing itself in 1480 and beginning its own trajectory to empire.

In the northern lands of Europe bordering Russia, William Urban demonstrates that the geography and culture of the Baltic Crusades made the region distinctive. Christian missionaries backed by soldiers, mostly non-noble *ministeriales*, enforced conversion among the pagan inhabitants from around 1100 onwards. The military order of the Swordbrothers was created in 1202, and later incorporated into the Teutonic Order. Although defeated by Alexander Nevsky, ruler of Novgorod (and later a Russian hero, although he was at the time a Mongol tributary), in 1242, the Teutonic Knights expanded, their Livonian Order attacking Lithuania. The Poles first attacked Prussia, and from 1226 the Teutonic Knights joined in; but they ended up fighting each other. Winter campaigns dominated in this region, since during that season the many rivers and lakes were frozen, allowing swifter movement. The crusaders constructed a range of fortifications from small towers to huge castles acting as supply dumps, and had a technological superiority over the pagans in respect of ships, siegecraft and crossbows. The conversion of Lithuania around 1400 allowed the formation of an axis with Poland against the German crusaders. At the battle of Tannenberg (1410), the power of the over-mighty Teutonic Order was finally broken. Many of the great brick-built castles of the region have been reconstructed over the last two centuries, with the Nazis playing a major role in the mid-20th century. As a result many sites were damaged during World War II for what they appeared to represent, but are being restored again after the end of the Cold War.

Returning to developments in the heartlands of chivalry, France and the British Isles, Michael Prestwich examines the challenge to the chivalric military system (1275–1475). In the late 13th century King Edward I conquered Wales and built a chain of huge castles to enforce English rule; he was also initially successful in Scotland. Yet at Bannockburn (1314), Robert Bruce led peasant spearmen – or rather they supported his better-quality troops – in order to crush Edward II's much larger army. The Scots then took the war to England, becoming involved in the so-called Hundred Years War between England and France. Great battles included Crécy (1346), Poitiers (1356), Agincourt (1415) and Verneuil (1424), all of which the English won. Yet it was to be the case that the kings of England could win the battles but lose the war. When the French rulers turned to the Fabian tactics of avoiding battle and harassing the *chevauchées* (armed raids) of the English and their allies – rather in the same way as the Byzantines had dealt with Muslim incursions into Asia Minor hundreds of years

At the battle of Verneuil in 1424, an Anglo-Norman army inflicted such a signal defeat on their Franco-Scottish opponents that it became known as a 'Second Agincourt'. This late 15th-century manuscript illustration gives no more than a hint as to how the fighting went, though the English wear red crosses and the French white.

earlier – they gained the upper hand. Even a great commander such as the English King Henry V (d.1422), who conquered Normandy through a series of sieges after his surprise victory at Agincourt, eventually could not prevail against the superior resources and dogged resistance of the French. The inspiring leadership of Joan of Arc turned the tide at the siege of Orléans (1429), which was exploited by the French king Charles VII. He carefully built up a small 'professional' army and invested in a siege train constructed by the artillery entrepreneurs the Bureau Brothers in order to win back territory through overawing the defenders of crucial fortresses and towns. As a result of this strategy, the English were expelled from Normandy by 1450, and decisively defeated in a last-gasp campaign from Bordeaux at Castillon (1453). Confined to their own shores, the English took to fighting among themselves during the sporadic campaigns of the Wars of the Roses between 1455 and 1487. It is also worth remembering that the eventual victor in these wars, Henry VII Tudor, who established a long-lived dynasty, was put on the throne by the support of French troops at Bosworth in 1485.

Meanwhile in Eastern Europe the power of the Ottoman Turks was growing, as Gábor Ágoston shows. They rose from being nomadic raiders to developing Europe's first standing army composed of *spahi* armoured cavalry, a large infantry force of which the Janissary corps provided an elite component and gunpowder artillery used to devastating effect at Çaldıran (Persia, 1514) and Mohács (Hungary, 1526). After the capture of Constantinople (1453) the sultans constructed huge fleets that terrorized the Mediterranean until they were defeated by crusader forces at Lepanto (1571). The strength of the Ottoman forces lay in their organization, which produced armies of over 100,000 men, huge for the time, fiercely loyal to the sultan and displaying discipline which western commentators envied. Together with a ready adoption of firearms as personal weapons and artillery, this made them almost invincible in the field and in sieges.

Michael Prestwich explains the significance of the Gunpowder Revolution (*c.* 1300–*c.* 1500) which underpinned so much successful warfare in the latter part of the Middle Ages. The Chinese were the first to develop gunpowder weapons, *c.* 1200, but the technology to make them truly effective took time to evolve. Developments in metallurgy were required to form an airtight tube to create an explosive projectile. In the West, early cannon were found on land and sea by 1340. By 1440, the French king could terrify towns into submission and by 1494 mobile artillery accompanied the French army in Italy. Personal firearms were only simple handguns in 1400, yet by 1500 a variety of weapons, with the harquebus the most popular, were widely used by foot soldiers. Known as 'shot', these men worked in conjunction with blocks of pike men providing mutual support to create a true infantry that was self-sufficient on the battlefield. Combined with the creation of standing armies in France and Burgundy from the mid-15th century onwards, these weapons wrought a significant change in warfare. Technology knows no frontiers and, as we have seen, non-Europeans such as the Ottoman Turks also used gunpowder to great effect in expanding their empire.

Over the horizon of the medieval world lay India, China and the Far East. T. A. Heathcote shows how Hindu India's huge population produced armies of 100,000 men or larger, combining fast-moving cavalry with elephants and bow-armed infantry. Despite these impressive forces, Mongol attacks in the 13th and 14th centuries proved the system to be a weak one. Notably in 1389, Timur crushed an Indian all-arms force at Delhi. In 1526, his descendant Babur deployed musketeers and artillery behind wagons and stockades to bring modern warfare to the sub-continent.

Peter Lorge explains that China's long history of central rule produced traditions of warfare unmatched elsewhere. Military theorists explored the best way to conduct warfare, and within the seeming continuity there was a great deal of change. Chinese armies faced difficulties in defeating the nomads on their northern frontiers, although the early development of firearms in the 12th century helped in this regard. Chinese warfare was entirely different from that of the West with its many competing kingdoms, being based around huge infantry forces supported by complex bureaucratic logistics systems which ambitious men who would be emperors sought to control in order to rule a unified, centralized empire.

Karl Friday demonstrates how Japanese military tradition developed separately from the mainland even after contact with the Mongols (although this did create the *kamikaze* myth of resistance). The contest was between a centralizing 'emperor' and the centrifugal forces of great warlords. The social elite used the horse and bow, though as the horses were little more than ponies there was no real cavalry, with an emphasis on individual combat. Japanese armour, designed to give maximum mobility to its wearer, became an art form. The samurai were originally mercenary warriors who developed a code of warfare and fought mainly on foot. Fortification played a major role in a series in internecine conflicts, with long wars in the 12th and 14th centuries especially. Around 1500, developments in firearms relegated nobles and samurai alike to a secondary role in war.

In many ways samurai Japan, with its warrior barons, castles and troops of retainers, resembles the emergent West of AD 1000. There are surprising concurrences as well as differences in the warfare of the period before 1500 that we call the medieval world. This is only part of the fascination still exercised by the military history of the era.

1 Byzantium against Persia and Islam, 530–750

Opposite David and Goliath – on one of the nine David Plates, produced in Byzantium between 613 and 629–30. *Right* Justinian is shown triumphant on the Barberini Ivory.

Seldom in the history of warfare have there been changes as revolutionary as those that affected the Romano-Byzantine army at the end of antiquity. At the outset, in the early 6th century, the forces that faced up to the Persian challenge in the Middle East were recognizably Roman, their tactics having evolved gradually from those of the armies that had conquered the Mediterranean for the Republic. By the middle of the 8th century, operating on behalf of a beleaguered Christian state that was the sole vestige of late antiquity in the Mediterranean region, Byzantine commanders had been forced onto the defensive against a vastly superior Muslim adversary and had devised an ultra-elastic form of defence with a pronounced guerrilla character. Of course, faith, memories of an imperial past, a social order reconfigured in an age of crisis, the willing cooperation of civilian and soldier and a fiscal system that continued to function, all made vital contributions to Byzantium's survival. Even more important, though, were a radical modification of the inherited military ethos and the adaptation of traditional fighting methods to new conditions.

EVIDENCE AND SOURCES

There is a reasonable amount of detailed evidence concerning fighting formations and combat from the 6th century. Procopius's *History of the Wars* takes us into the mêlée of battle in the 530s, 540s and early 550s, when the emperor Justinian I (r. 527–65) was striving to recover lost provinces in the central Mediterranean. Procopius, who served in the field with Belisarius, Justinian's most successful general, is the very model of a war reporter, picking out all sorts of incidents of note, above all acts of heroism and gruesome injuries (registered by his colleagues on Belisarius's staff as well as himself). Taken in aggregate, his accounts of warfare on all fronts – in

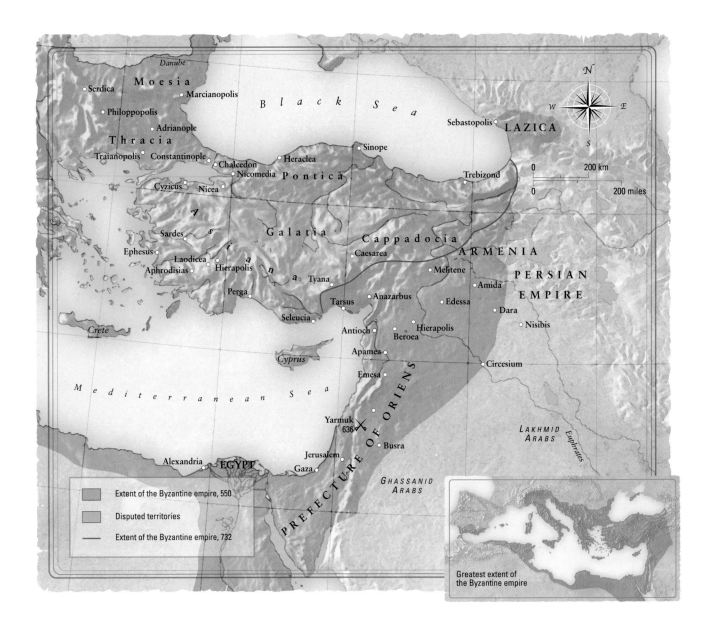

The Middle East on the eve of the Arab invasions.

the west against Vandals, Berbers and Goths, in the Balkans against Kutrigur nomads and Slavs, as well as in the east against Persians - provide a large store of valuable material for the military historian. Surprisingly, the same is true of the histories put together by two of his armchair successors, Agathias and Theophylact Simocatta (both provincials who combined successful legal careers in the capital with writing). Between them they provide full accounts of many important campaigns (in Italy, North Africa, the Balkans and the east) fought in Justinian's later years and under his successors down to Maurice (r. 582–602). They made up for their own lack of direct experience of warfare by quarrying material from sources of the highest possible quality, namely generals' dispatches from the field, or memoirs subsequently penned on the basis of such dispatches.

These historical narratives are, however, left in the shade by a military manual composed at the end of the 6th century. The *Strategicon*, commissioned by the emperor Maurice, is a basic work of reference written in a plain style and intended surely for a wide readership in the officer corps. It presents a succinct, lucid account

> '*Let us be inspired with faith that defeats murder…. The danger is not without recompense: nay, it leads to the eternal life. Let us stand bravely, and the Lord our God will assist us and destroy the enemy.*'

Heraclius's address to his men in Persia, spring 624

of good practice – based partly on recent experience, partly on training manuals – together with instructions for fighting contemporary adversaries. Once subjected to close scrutiny and careful military analysis, it becomes a rich mine of information, unmatched in its range and detail. It makes it easy to conjure up a picture of the Roman army in its last manifestation, or, if you prefer, the Byzantine army in its formative phase.

Thereafter, however, the sources thin out. The bold counter-offensive campaigns of the emperor Heraclius (r. 610–41) against the Persians in the 620s, after the latter had conquered the Roman Middle East (Syria, Palestine and Egypt), can be followed only in outline. Military action can be seen to have been well coordinated with diplomacy and propaganda. It was directed not at the destruction of a powerful enemy, but at the degradation of his resources, the exacerbation of discontent among his subjects and the demoralization of his governing elites. Heraclius proved to be a brilliant strategist, who was prepared to cut loose from home territory. He was also a master of deception. In 624 he attacked in the north where it was least expected, and in 627, as the war approached its climax, managed to rouse baseless suspicion of the shah's commander-in-chief in the west. His forces had been so well trained and were so enthused with religious fervour that they could outmarch and outfight their foes deep into the winter months. Even so, when success came in the form of a virtually bloodless coup d'état

Heraclius is humiliated before Khusro II on this enamel plaque from a cross made in the Meuse Valley, France, c. 1160–70. News of the great drama being played out in the Middle East reached Europe and permanently damaged Byzantium's standing.

The Battle of Nineveh, 12 December 627, as visualized by Piero della Francesca in his fresco cycle of *The Legend of the True Cross* at Arezzo; the figure of Khusro II is kneeling on the right. Heraclius's subsequent advance on the Persian capital precipitated a successful coup against Khusro, who was executed on 28 February 628.

on the night of 23/24 February 628 and the installation of a new Persian government ready to make peace, it was achieved only with the help of the third great power of the time, the Turkish khaganate (empire) which straddled Central Asia. But there is no question of our being able to describe and analyse individual engagements – not even the climactic battle of Nineveh on 12 December 627, memorably illustrated by Piero della Francesca in his fresco cycle *The Legend of the True Cross* – that opened the way for Heraclius's triumphal march on Ctesiphon, the Persian capital.

As for the first, long phase of Byzantium's dour defensive war against Islam (634–750), we have to make do with the few crumbs dropped by two laconic chroniclers writing at the end of the 8th and the beginning of the 9th century. The position is even more dire for the period of acute crisis in the 640s, 650s and 660s, when Byzantium had to reinvigorate its fighting forces and reform its institutions in order to cope with the rampant armies of Islam. There is almost complete silence on the part of metropolitan Byzantine sources concerning the reign of Constans II (r. 641–69), save for the first two years, and they are very sparing with information about the preceding decade and subsequent years down to the first accession of Justinian II (r. 685–95, and again 705–11). Only the sketchiest of outlines of the initial Arab conquests (634–52) can be put together. The same is true of the second wave of attacks during the caliphate of Muawiyah I (r. 661–80). Things improve thereafter. The grand strategy of Caliph 'Abd al-Malik (r. 685–705) and his immediate successors can be reconstructed, from the end of a long civil war (682–92) down to the great siege of Constantinople of 717–18, as can the ebb and flow of warfare in the following decades. But we have to reach forward in time, as late as the 960s, to seize hold of a text that can cast light on the Byzantine defensive strategy that was developed

'When the troops going out to raid have gotten far enough away from the emir's battle formation...then the general should set his own battle line in proper order and launch his attack against that of the emir, now undermanned.'

Nicephorus Phocas (r. 963–69)

and put into action after the repulse of the Arabs from Constantinople in 718. A practical military manual entitled *On Skirmishing* was commissioned by the emperor Nicephorus Phocas (r. 963–69), probably from his younger brother Leo, a distinguished general, to preserve for posterity what was by then an obsolescent guerrilla mode of campaigning. It is a text of the utmost importance, describing as it does the techniques of warfare that helped to secure Byzantium's survival against great odds in its long dark age.

THE CHANGING ARMY

The Roman army of the 6th century was much changed from that of the Republic and early empire. Firstly, large units on the scale of the legion (5,000-plus men) were a thing of the past. By the time of Diocletian, the legion, still the basic component of the army, had been reduced to not much more than 500 men, while the cavalry wing numbered at most 90 men, and may, in some cases, have sunk as low as 30. The legion had, in effect, been broken up into its constituent cohorts, partly perhaps to inculcate a stronger regimental spirit, and partly to tailor fighting units to the size of frontier forts. Secondly, the cavalry had usurped the infantry in the leading role. In the past, the primary functions of mounted units had been to secure the flanks of infantry formations and conduct reconnaissance. In battle, their offensive role had been limited to skirmishing attacks aimed at disrupting the opposing array and to the exploitation of victory by vigorous pursuit of forces broken by the shock tactics of the legion. From the 3rd century cavalry numbers had begun to grow relative to those of the infantry, although infantry remained in the majority.

More important, though, was the gradual shift in offensive capability between the two arms. For Procopius, writing in the 6th century, it was the cavalry who assumed the main burden of battle. Their tasks were to drive off enemy cavalry, and to break up enemy infantry formations by a combination of missile assaults and charges leading to close-order combat; much rested on the psychological impact of the charge. Infantry units evolved into tighter-knit, basically defensive entities. Instead of the extraordinary flexibility given to the legion by its constituent maniples, the infantry of the Late Roman empire acquired many of the characteristics of the Hellenistic phalanx. Their strength lay in their compactness and cohesion. Their prime function was to provide a secure base for the offensive cavalry arm, not only by their ability to hold out in hand-to-hand combat, but also by making full use of their considerably enhanced firepower (arrows, slingshot, lead-weighted darts thrown underarm in volleys to impressive distances, and short, light javelins).

Both infantry and cavalry had become more versatile, capable of engaging the enemy both at a distance as well as close at hand. At the same time there was more specialization than in the past. Heavily armoured units, cataphracts and clibanarii, were formed to improve the penetrative power of cavalry in shock combat. Within the basic infantry unit there were now specialist sub-units: heavy infantry with better armour, who stood in the front ranks with circular or oval shields (smaller than those of the

A 10th-century Armenian carving of a Byzantine heavy infantryman. Such men would have been a major element in the Byzantine army. They wore lamellar armour, consisting of strips or scales of metal sewn onto a fabric or leather base.

Byzantine cavalry in pursuit of routed Arabs, after a victory won by Theophilus (r. 829–42) in northeast Asia Minor in 831, from the 11th-century Madrid manuscript of the History of John Skylitzes. The depiction of cavalry equipment in the many illustrations of combat in this manuscript is generalized and conventional, but an effort has been made to render lamellar armour and stirrups.

legionaries of the Principate), using thrusting spear and slashing sword; lanciarii (javelineers); archers; and artillerymen (ballistarii), in charge of torsion weapons, which in the later Roman period discharged bolts rather than stone missiles. Thus constituted, the fighting unit acquired a collective all-arms capability. Only in the regular cavalry was versatility sought from the individual soldier (as it had been from the legionary in the past). He was trained both as archer and as lancer, the ideal being a mounted soldier adept at handling both weapons.

By the 6th century, then, the basic strengths of the Roman army were the solidity of its infantry formations, a new shock capability in the cavalry, increased firepower in both arms and an ability to vary tactics from light skirmishing operations at one extreme to full-frontal charges at the other. The resulting versatility of fighting units and larger formations enabled them to take advantage of perceived enemy weaknesses and to tailor operational methods to different types of terrain. In addition, there was the traditional high level of discipline,

instilled in the course of rigorous training, and engineering and construction skills that few adversaries could match. The construction of marching camps, with strong perimeter defences and a regulation internal layout, remained a distinguishing feature of the Roman army, as did its bridge- and fort-building capability. Torsion artillery, which required regular maintenance and careful tuning, was brought into action not only in sieges, but also in battle by being mounted on wagons.

AN ARRAY OF ENEMIES

Different enemies posed different problems, and were vulnerable in different ways, to 6th-century Roman forces. The emperor Maurice's *Strategicon* itemized the principal characteristics of four ethnically and militarily distinct adversaries: Persians (whose cavalry, it was noted, was better adapted than the Roman for engagements on irregular terrain and whose archers could fire lighter arrows at a faster rate), steppe nomads (including Avars, who by the end of the 6th century had established their

Battle scenes from a 5th-century illustrated manuscript of the Iliad. Contemporary weaponry and fighting methods are absent from this late antique view of the Homeric past. The temptation of artists was always to retreat into classicizing archaisms.

hegemony over Eastern and Central Europe), Franks and Lombards (picked out from other Germanic peoples as the most powerful, and known for their heroic ethos and the solidarity of their kinship-based units), and finally Slavs (described as a people of the forests, rivers, lakes and marshes, who were adept at light-infantry tactics). It is evident from the main lines of foreign policy in the reigns of Justinian I and his successors that the greatest priority was attached to the eastern front, not surprisingly given that the Persians had imperial pretensions as strong and as well founded as those of the Romans.

Persia was the primary target of Roman offensive action at the beginning of Justinian I's reign. He was exploiting the greatly improved frontier defences resulting from a twenty-year programme – initiated by Anastasius I (r. 491–518) and brought to completion under his uncle Justin I (r. 518–27) – of investment in military infrastructure in the east and of successful diplomatic machinations on both sides of

'When the army is prepared and lined up for battle, do not delay.... Once you get within bowshot make the attack...for any delay in closing with the enemy means that their steady rate of fire will enable them to discharge more missiles.'

Strategicon of Maurice,
on fighting the Persians, late 6th century

the Caucasus. Three field armies were sent into Lazica (western Georgia) in 528, presumably with the objective, once they had joined forces, of striking across the mountains into Persian-controlled Iberia (eastern Georgia). At the same time, with Roman naval assistance, the Ethiopians launched an attack across the Red Sea on the Jewish ruler who had taken control of Yemen with Persian backing a few years earlier. This was the first act in a long-prepared Roman war of revenge, for the Persians had brought some 120 years of virtually uninterrupted peaceful co-existence to an end with an unprovoked massive attack in autumn 502. The spectacular initial capture of the rich and powerfully defended city of Amida in the upper Tigris basin was only reversed by a massive exertion of Roman power in the region in 503 and 504. Justinian's offensive, however, went wrong from the start. The Persians launched a pre-emptive attack of their own, defeated the Roman armies in detail in Lazica, and were thus able to seize the military and diplomatic initiative, which they did not relinquish until they forced Justinian to negotiate a formal, open-ended peace in 532.

These were the first two in a series of five wars fought by the two great powers of the Middle East in the 6th and early 7th centuries, in which the role of aggressor alternated between them – Persia in late 502, East Rome in 528, Persia in 540, East Rome in 572–73 and Persia in 603. There was a perceptible escalation in the scale and intensity of conflict, culminating in nearly thirty years of war (603–30). In the last two wars, both of the aggressors aimed for the annihilation, rather than mere defeat, of the enemy. The Byzantine emperor Justin II (r. 565–78) harboured such a hope between 572 and

Capital showing Khusro II as victorious warrior (*c.* 627), from the unfinished palace complex that he was building at Bisitun (now Taq-i Bustan, Iran). Nearby a huge panel had been prepared on the cliff face above the palace, for the carving of a grandiose scene of triumph.

573 after negotiating an offensive alliance with the Turkish khaganate, a hope that was dashed all too soon by a brilliant defensive strategy devised and executed by the aged shah Khusro I (r. 531–79). His grandson Khusro II (r. 590, then 591–628) resolved, in winter 615/16, to liquidate what remained of the East Roman empire, once he had gained control of its richest provinces (Syria, Palestine and Egypt), and came very close to achieving his goal in 626, in alliance with the Avars.

The tactics of the Roman army in battle against Persian forces can be observed on many occasions, notably in the large-scale defensive action fought outside Dara, very close to the eastern frontier, in 530 (see box on pp. 26–27). A large Persian army, put at 40,000 by Procopius and rising to 50,000 when reinforcements arrived from Nisibis on the other side of the frontier, was faced by 25,000 Roman troops jointly commanded by Belisarius, Master of the Soldiers of the East, and Hermogenes, the Master of Offices. There is less reportage than in many of Procopius's later set-piece narratives, which may indicate that he was not present at the battle. There are also puzzling gaps in his account.

The Battle of Dara, 530

A 25,000-strong army, commanded by Belisarius, the emperor Justinian's favourite general, was established in a strong position outside Dara (in modern Turkey) in June 530, when the Persian king, Kavad II, ordered his forces to invade Roman territory both north and south of the Armenian Taurus. Peroz, commander of the southern invasion army, dared not continue his advance beyond the mouth of the Plain of Dara, since that would have left a potent Roman force in his rear. He turned north to engage the Romans. With a 2:1 numerical advantage, he could be confident of the outcome. Belisarius sought to negate this by digging a trench to shield his battle array and by deploying two contingents of Hunnic cavalry in the angles of the trench, from which they could threaten the flank of a Persian attack on either wing. Despite their small numbers (600 in each contingent), the Huns played a vital part in the fighting when battle was joined two days after an initial skirmish. Twice the Persians gained the upper hand, first when their right wing pushed back the Roman left, later when their left wing, bolstered with crack troops (the Immortals), broke the Roman right.

In each case their attacks were disrupted and repelled when they were caught between the opposing Roman units and lateral attacks by the Huns (both contingents in the second, climactic phase). Further damage was inflicted by 300 Germanic Heruls who emerged from concealment to attack the Persians in the rear in the first phase, and by the Roman reserve that was fully committed in the second.

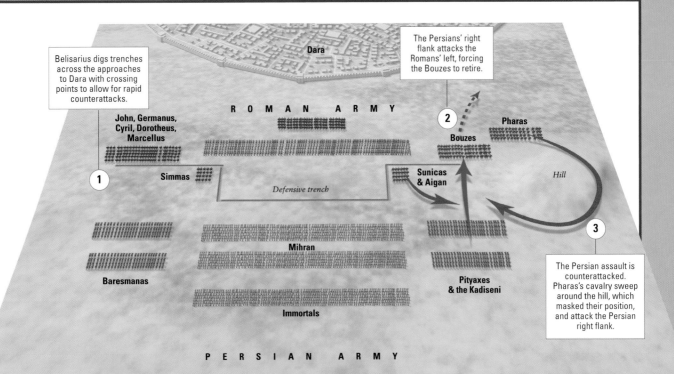

	ROMANS	PERSIANS
COMMANDERS	Belisarius	Peroz
STRENGTH	25,000	50,000
CASUALTIES	Unknown	8,000

This page The battle of Dara: the two main Persian attacks, first (*above*) on the Roman left, second (*below*) on the Roman right are successfully parried.

Opposite above Justinian on horseback, from the reverse of a medallion dating to *c.* 535.

Opposite below Fortifications of Dara. The original defences built in 505–7 were upgraded under Justinian.

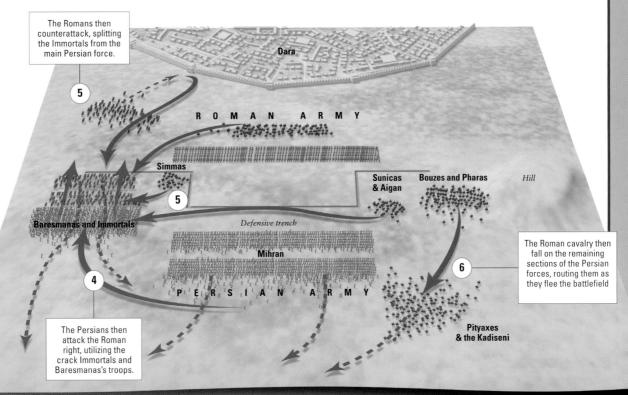

Procopius makes much of a defensive trench that was dug a stone's throw (presumably, the maximum range of an artillery piece) from the city walls, whose function was evidently to act as an outer perimeter defence for the Roman army when arrayed for battle. He gives a careful description of its layout, which was in a straight line except for a short, projecting central section. It was held by the main body of troops, both mounted and foot, backed by a reserve under the personal command of Belisarius and Hermogenes. It was fronted by two Hunnic cavalry forces, each of 600 men, placed outside the trench in the angles of the central projection; these men were assigned the task of reinforcing the wings, and were flanked on both sides by two other purely cavalry forces (including 300 Heruls on the tip of the left wing, who, at their suggestion, were to lie in ambush in the hills and to attack the enemy from the rear). But when the fighting begins on the third day, the trench vanishes from the account. The Persians attack first the Roman left, then the Roman right, in both cases presumably having to negotiate their way through the many gaps in the trench, at the cost of some disruption to their formations. Nothing, though, is said of this, nor of the problems for fleeing troops when each of the attacks is parried with counterthrusts (on the left by the Heruls and the designated 600 Huns, on the right by all 1,200 Huns and the reserve). The only hint comes from the high figures given for Persian casualties in what were limited engagements: 3,000 on the Roman left, 5,000 on the right.

Two features in Procopius's account of the battle deserve to be highlighted, apart from the prominent role of cavalry and the mass discharge of arrows by both sides that preceded the general engagement. The military building programme initiated by Anastasius had endowed the empire with a deep forward defensive zone, which could play an active part in a war of movement. Field army operations on Roman territory were greatly facilitated by the presence of numerous fortresses capable of housing substantial numbers of troops, who might emerge to attack the enemy from the rear or a flank. Such defensive installations, ranging from large urban settlements endowed with barracks and powerful walled circuits to purpose-built military bases, thus acted as the fixed points around which to organize the movements of field forces. The combination of the two could significantly enhance Roman fighting power, or redress a massive numerical imbalance, as happened in 530 not only at Dara, but also in the north at Satala, which commanded the main road from Armenia into northeast Asia Minor. The fronting trench at Dara shielded Belisarius's troops from the full force of a Persian attack, while the city, with its recently upgraded defences, provided a menacing backdrop behind which reserves might be concealed, and which could act as a secure final refuge. At Satala a small Roman army, commanded by Sittas and Dorotheus, succeeded in driving back a 30,000-strong Persian invasion force, after a short engagement in which the Persians were caught between a surprise attack by a small body of cavalry (1,000 men) concealed outside the city and a sally in force from within.

The value of secure, strategically placed bases was fully appreciated by 6th-century Roman generals, so much so that they prioritized their acquisition in the course of offensive campaigns, as demonstrated by Belisarius in the 530s in Italy. By this transformation of a strategic offensive into a series of tactically defensive actions,

Lower register of a monumental Persian relief carving at Naqshi-i Rustam, near Persepolis. Scenes of mounted combat illustrate the victorious prowess of the Sasanian king, or, in this case, the designated heir of Bahram IV (r. 388–99), whose own victory is depicted in the upper register.

he was able to negate the great numerical superiority of the Ostrogoths while maintaining political pressure on the ruling regime.

The war for control of Lazica (western Georgia), which dragged on from 548 to 556 after an armistice came into force in the main west Armenian and north Mesopotamian theatres, was equally, though more conventionally, shaped by manmade fortifications. The Romans, with two secure redoubts in the west (an area known as the Island, with impregnable water defences, and the powerful coastal fortress of Petra), and the Persians, occupying strongholds commanding the fertile plain of Mocheresis in the interior, competed for Laz support and targeted the key intermediary city of Archaeopolis. An even more prominent role was played by fixed emplacements in the penultimate Romano-Persian war (572–91), which, in its later stages (from 578), centred increasingly on Arzanene, a Persian frontier district controlling the southern approaches to the Armenian Taurus. The war of movement, of raid and counter-raid, gave way to a series of local Roman pushes, in which the ground acquired was to be held by well-garrisoned forts in commanding positions.

The second feature to note in Procopius's account of the battle of Dara is a certain fluidity in cavalry tactics. It showed itself on the first day of confrontation, when cavalry on the Roman left feigned retreat and then wheeled round to attack and drive back the Persian force that was pursuing them. This fluidity can be glimpsed

29

Joshua and the Israelites, after crossing the Jordan, on their way to Jericho; an illumination from the mid-10th century Joshua Roll in the Vatican Library, itself copied from a 7th-century archetype. The dress and equipment of the soldiers are rendered in the late antique archaizing style.

again two days later, in the tactics devised to counter a Persian attack, again on the Roman left: a surprise attack from the rear by a Herul ambush, backed by a Hun thrust from the centre. The Huns were masters of flexible cavalry tactics, capable of drawing out the skirmishing preliminaries of battle until the enemy was worn down and ready to crack, thereby transforming the actual engagement into little more than a transitional moment between skirmishing and pursuit of a broken enemy. It was, it may be conjectured, Hun contingents serving in East Roman forces after the disintegration of Attila's empire (after his death in 453) which prompted emulation on the part of the best Roman mounted units. By the end of the 6th century, greater urgency was being put into the upgrading of Roman cavalry performance to a level rather closer to that of steppe nomads (to match the Avars in combat) so that security could return to the Balkans. Far more interest is shown in cavalry than infantry in the *Strategicon*. The principal aims were to improve the fighting capabilities of individual cavalrymen by intensive training, and to boost the cohesion and resilience of formations in skirmishing. The latter was achieved by separating off a third of the men to form a secure defensive line, containing gaps through which the main body might pass before wheeling round, reforming and preparing to engage again.

Even if the instructions issued by the emperor Maurice to his commanders in the late 6th century were put into practice effectively, there would still have been a significant shortfall in the capability of Roman cavalry. Steppe nomads had learnt how to ride, manoeuvre and shoot on horseback in childhood, and were able to operate in looser-knit formations than Roman (or Persian) cavalry. Instead of a small number of large units, they consisted of a large number of small units. This gave them the sort of flexibility that the maniple subunit had given to the classical Roman legion. Only a small proportion of Roman cavalry seems to have been judged capable of operating in such irregular formations. They were to be placed on the extreme left, with the task of disordering and disabling opposing units. A generation or so later, when he was preparing to commit everything to a bold counter-stroke, Heraclius conducted intensive training exercises in Bithynia in northwest Asia Minor. They were intended not only to accustom the men to the face of battle, but above all to train them in mounted skirmishing combat, in the swift and orderly transformation of attack into retreat and of retreat into attack, as well as in the full-frontal charge. It is likely that a higher proportion of troopers mastered the full range of nomad tactics than in the past. The success of what must have seemed to many, at the outset, forlorn campaigns against Persia is attributable mainly to the enhanced fighting capability (of infantry as well as cavalry) resulting from the exercises, together with the conviction, which the emperor sought to inculcate, that they were fighting a holy war (the dead being designated martyrs who gained direct entry to paradise) and the stamina subsequently built up in the course of successive campaigning seasons.

THE RISE OF ISLAM

The last of the Romano-Persian wars fought at the end of antiquity was formally brought to a close when the emperor Heraclius celebrated victory and restored the fragments of the True Cross (purloined in 614 by the Persians) to their proper place in Jerusalem on 21 March 630. Less than four years later a greater conflict broke out when the Arabs, energized by a new religion that sanctified the armed struggle against non-believers, invaded the Holy Land. The Roman authorities were probably aware of what was happening deep in the Arabian interior and the danger this posed, as a large defensive force was barring the route north inland from Gaza. The crushing defeat inflicted by the Arabs on 4 February 634 inaugurated twenty years of victorious advance. Palestine submitted before the year was out. Syria followed suit by the end of 635, after three set-piece battles, the third calamitous. Then, in 636, the Arabs turned their attention to Persian Mesopotamia. Resistance here was stronger, but was overcome after five years' hard fighting. Thereafter the Arabs concentrated their forces in the east, their prime aim being to conquer the Iranian highlands that lowered over Mesopotamia and to destroy what remained of Persian fighting forces. Any action taken in the west was no more than a sideshow. Nonetheless, two such sideshows proved remarkably successful: the Roman authorities in Egypt capitulated after a mere two seasons of campaigning by a small invasion force (641–42), while the Arab governor of Syria, Muawiyah, seized control of the maritime approaches to the Aegean (649–50). When the caliph 'Uthman ibn 'Affan issued orders for his forces to regroup in the west for an attack on Constantinople, the end was plainly nigh for the Romans.

There was no resistance as two armies marched in 654 into the Anatolian core of the rump Roman empire that we customarily call Byzantium, nor were the two fleets, sailing from Egypt as well as Syria, engaged as they sailed north through the Aegean. An authoritative, contemporary source reports that the whole population of Asia Minor – those living on the plains (the interior plateau), in the mountains (that fringe the plateau) and on the coasts – submitted. The shock of defeat in the recent past had clearly undermined the provincials' will to fight, the speed and scale of Arab success perhaps convincing them that God was intervening in human affairs through the agency of the Arabs. However, the imperial government, headed by Heraclius's grandson Constans II, still in his twenties, had not shed its imperial pretensions and made ready to defend the massive redoubt of Constantinople. Storm damage, aided perhaps by the nascent Byzantine navy, saved the city and the state of which it was

Opposite A Persian king out hunting boar, bear and lion, depicted on a gilded silver plate of the 7th or 8th century from Novo Bayazid, near Erevan, Armenia. The crown depicted is not that of a specific king. Note the absence of stirrups, which were first introduced into the Middle East in the late 6th century.

the capital. An invaluable breathing space of five years (656–61) was then granted, when, as if by act of God, the caliph was assassinated and civil war broke out among the Arabs. At last, the leading Christian power of the Mediterranean and the Middle East had a chance to recuperate and to prepare to fight in earnest, not simply for survival, but to reassert its imperial credentials.

We are now deep in the period of silence from Byzantine sources. A great deal of conjecture is required to sketch out the main policy initiatives taken by Constans's regime, on the basis of snippets of information gathered from abroad or inferences from later, better recorded decades. Five developments should probably be dated to this period. All were perforce improvised, but taken together they constituted a remarkably effective response to the crisis facing Byzantium.

First, the army's primary task was now defined as the defence of Asia Minor. All available troops were concentrated there. Four armies were created out of the detritus of those defeated by the Arabs in the Middle East and out of the vestiges of Roman armies elsewhere. Two were lineal descendants of the Eastern and Armenian field armies, relocated far from the old frontier. One, named the Obsequium, was an amalgam of guards regiments and the two old Praesental (central) field armies. The fourth was transferred from Thrace, thereby leaving the Balkans all too exposed.

Secondly, the troops themselves had to be reinvigorated, and given the confidence to face large bodies of jihad-fighters who were ready to die for their faith. Intensive training was required, as it had been for Heraclius's men in 622. We should probably envisage a series of exercises spread over two to three years, involving much religious exhortation. Inspiration was also sought, as it had been by Maurice, from the finest fighting forces known, namely steppe nomad armies and, in particular, the Avars (despite their temporary eclipse after their failed siege of Constantinople in 626). It was not just that various items of equipment had been copied (including cavalry tunics, tents, stirrups and lever artillery – long in use in China) and that Avar tactics were viewed as an ideal at which to aim, but also whole field armies were upgraded in the minds of commanders and men to the Avar level.

Thirdly, Constans's government did not renounce the Roman past in general. It was memory of past imperial rule, together with Christian belief, that gave Byzantium, the most Roman of the sub-Roman successor states, its ultimate purpose. Among the many traditions maintained was fort and fortress construction, both as a way of securing control over terrain and of maximizing the security and fighting efficacy of the armed forces. The dating evidence, which is mainly circumstantial (masonry styles, and coin finds associated with specific building projects), points to a major phase of fortification in the reigns of Constans and his son Constantine IV (r. 669–85), beginning with strategically important cities in the Aegean coastlands (and perhaps the main naval bases on the south coast) and gradually working its way inland. By the middle of the 9th century the whole of Asia Minor was studded with castles and heavily fortified, shrunken Roman cities.

Fourthly, perhaps the most important development – and one which can be credited to Constans's regime – was the build-up of Byzantine naval power, both at the centre and, when Constans moved to Syracuse in Sicily in 663, in the west.

Fifthly, Constans took decisive action to exploit the sudden weakening of his Arab adversary brought about by civil war (656–61). He intervened in Transcaucasia in 660–61,

Egyptian ivory relief, dating to the 6th century, depicting a mounted archer and infantrymen. All wear scale armour and carry round shields. The almond-shaped shield came into use only in the 10th century.

and, through a show of force, obtained the submission of the leading princes, thereby creating a grand anti-Muslim coalition. Two years later, towards the end of 662, he set off for the west to shore up Byzantine power in Italy and to mobilize naval and military forces for a battle for control of the central Mediterranean and of the western approaches to Egypt (664–69). He was conscious of the imperial status of his realm. He was ready to engage the Arabs in conventional warfare on the grandest possible scale, as indeed were his successors down to Tiberius III (r. 698–705).

There were several striking reversals of fortune in the forty years following the caliph Muawiyah's victory in the Arab civil war. He swiftly re-imposed Arab authority on Transcaucasia (662), resumed attacks on Asia Minor and disposed of Constans (assassinated in July 669 in a bathhouse in Syracuse). Constans's death and the political troubles that ensued provided cover for Arab attacks first on North Africa (669) and then, when the main Byzantine fleet had been lured west, on the metropolitan region (670–71). After a pause, the main Muslim offensive was launched in 673, three naval and military expeditionary forces being deployed against the coastlands of Asia Minor. It came to a juddering halt in 674, when one of the expeditionary forces was defeated on land and then annihilated as it withdrew by sea. The pendulum swung in Byzantium's favour even further when, within a year or so, special forces were landed on the Lebanese coast and triggered a Christian insurgency in Syria and Palestine, which grew more dangerous when civil strife broke out once again in the caliphate (682–92). Constans's grandson, Justinian II, was able to extract massive concessions from the new standard-bearer of the Umayyad cause, 'Abd al-Malik, in return for agreeing to withdraw the Byzantine special forces in 686.

It was only a generation or so later that the futility of fighting with conventional means – orthodox tactics, and full-frontal engagements – by land and sea along a front extending from the western shore of the Caspian to Sicily, was finally impressed upon Byzantium. It was quite impossible to match the resources deployed by the new Muslim empire, once it was reunited under 'Abd al-Malik in 692. Counterattacks were still launched into its territory, but Byzantium was again driven out of Transcaucasia, Asia Minor was again raided and Byzantium's major resource base in the west, North Africa, was torn from its control (697–98). A third attack on the metropolitan region took place in 717–18 – by land and sea as in 654, but this time on a larger scale. This convinced the government, now in the hands of an experienced military commander, Leo III (r. 717–41), to jettison any lingering hope of reasserting Roman authority in the Middle East, in the face of a firmly entrenched Muslim power.

THE CHANGING FACE OF WAR

It was probably during these decades that a new defensive strategy was developed, designed to minimize the loss of manpower and resources during Muslim attacks, to prevent the establishment of permanent Muslim bases inside the mountain periphery of Asia Minor and to inflict reverses where terrain and timing maximized the chances of Byzantine success. Roman traditions of fighting were discarded. The risks of orthodox combat were too great, given the Muslims' strength in manpower and morale. Instead of an orderly, disciplined array ready to engage and break the enemy in open battle, a premium was put on intelligence, cunning and the indirect approach. There was to be no attempt to hold the line of frontier mountains against invasion. The enemy would enter Asia Minor, and would be able to roam and ravage at will in the great interior plateau. But he would find it emptied of its population and livestock, since the first task of the defending forces was to evacuate civilians and their movable, self-propelled wealth from threatened regions to secure refuges, either well-defended cities or highland redoubts guarded by castles. Their second task was to shadow and harass the invaders, a task deputed to small, swift-moving, purely cavalry forces, the infantry's role being to hold the strongholds and to prepare to counterattack later, when the enemy was withdrawing through the frontier passes and was perhaps encumbered by booty and disadvantaged by terrain (see box on p. 36).

Early intelligence about enemy objectives was to be gathered by agents and by strategically placed observers and then transmitted by relays of messengers to the regional military command. Good intelligence was vital, if evacuations were to be properly organized. So too were good relations between soldiers and civilians, fostered by awareness of their shared peril. Above all, careful attention had to be paid to the tactical requirements of shadowing the enemy. It was vital to keep in touch with him at all times, by night as well as by day, to follow each and every one of a raiding army's movements and operations, waiting for opportunities when a detachment could be caught and attacked on its own by a numerically superior Byzantine force. The recommended system of pickets, relaying information back to the shadowing commander, is detailed in the handbook commissioned by the emperor Nicephorus Phocas in the 960s, as are the tactics to be employed in surprise attacks. What was advocated was nothing less than an advanced form of guerrilla warfare, designed to make good use of superior mobility (on the part of the shadowing force) and of every advantage offered by terrain. In effect, it was a defensive strategy that relied on breaking down warfare into a series of small engagements, in which the defenders seized the

Byzantine Shadowing Tactics

1. A system of pickets for maintaining contact with an Arab raiding army on the move. Three pairs of troopers, followed by three units of four, shadow the enemy. The defending Byzantine force follows at a distance, messages being relayed along the line of pickets, and thence via the vanguard to the commander.

2. A guerrilla attack on Arab raiders. Before dawn the Byzantine general conceals his force within striking distance of the villages that the enemy is intending to pillage. He allows the enemy foray to leave the main body of the raiding army (the ambush) before launching a surprise attack. He can choose whether to target the depleted ambush or the foray as it engages in its depredations.

3. A more complex plan of attack. A hundred cavalry are stationed in villages close to the road used by the Arabs as they change camp. Their function is to lure the enemy foray into pursuing them and to lead them into a trap on the road ahead, where Byzantine troops are concealed on either side. Meanwhile, the main shadowing army is to launch a surprise attack on the depleted Arab ambush from the front and the rear.

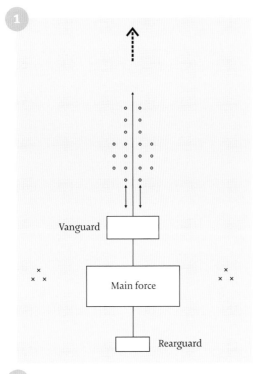

Vanguard

Main force

Rearguard

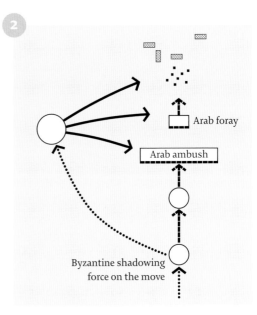

Arab foray

Arab ambush

Byzantine shadowing
force on the move

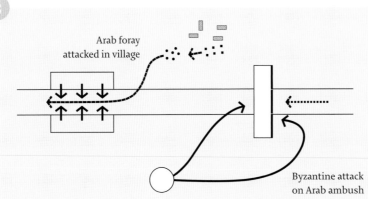

Arab foray
attacked in village

Byzantine attack
on Arab ambush

tactical offensive, with several ulterior purposes: to deter the enemy from dispatching forays to widen the swathe of devastation, to limit his ability to resupply himself through foraging and to chip away at his morale.

Such were the novel tactics adopted by Byzantine commanders when conventional fighting methods had failed, and were acknowledged to have failed. One vital element, the manmade stronghold, had been made a high priority two generations earlier. The military construction programme initiated by Constans II in the mid-7th century was gradually endowing the interior of Asia Minor with secure refuges for civilians. A second element – the shift from orthodox to guerrilla tactics – can be documented on the eve of the great siege of Constantinople. The harassing attacks launched against Muslim forces massed in Bithynia in the winter of 716/17 resembled, we are told, those conducted by the special forces inserted into Lebanon in the 670s. It is likely, then, that the crucial development – that of combining the two elements together to form the core of a defensive strategy – took place around the time of the great Muslim offensive of 716–18, perhaps beforehand, but more probably over the following few years when a highly competent emperor took stock and made preparations for a defensive war which he expected would last for many generations.

> '*The emperor ordered the generals not to fight an open war, but to make the forts secure by stationing garrisons of soldiers in them. He appointed high-ranking officers at each fort and instructed them to take each 3,000 chosen men and to follow the Arabs so as to prevent them from spreading out on pillaging raids, while burning in advance the horses' pasture and whatever other supplies were to be found.*'
>
> Emperor Leo IV's instructions, 779

The new guerrilla mode of fighting went against centuries of Roman military practice and challenged a traditional ethos that prized discipline and courage above all. Cunning and ingenuity now came to the fore. Victory was to be sought by devious means at minimum risk. Fundamental principles were cast aside. Cavalry and infantry were prized apart and given independent assignments (shadowing and harassing as opposed to holding defensive positions and preparing ambushes). Cavalry achieved greater mobility by cutting loose from the road system and substituting the pack animal for the wagon as transport, while infantry affixed themselves more firmly than before to particular places, garrisoning strongholds and holding passes. As before, there was interplay between fortifications and field forces, but it was now at a strategic, rather than a tactical, level.

The society of late 8th-century Byzantium was a world away from that of Justinian's revived empire. It was a society enmeshed from top to bottom in war. Civilians and soldiers were bound together in a common endeavour. Seldom had so high a proportion of able-bodied men in town and country been recruited into the armed forces. Byzantium was probably almost as militarized as the Roman Republic. The army itself had changed out of all recognition, not in its fundamental structures, but in its mode of operation. It was a citizen army defending a beleaguered Christian state on the northwestern flank of the caliphate, the lone great power in early medieval western Eurasia. Gibbon was utterly misguided to envisage Byzantium as a soft, wealthy society that paid others to do its fighting. Byzantium was a guerrilla state, geared to war – a medieval analogue to North Vietnam in the 20th century, save that its struggle lasted ten times as long.

2 From Barbarian Kingdoms to the Carolingian Empire, 500–850

Opposite A Germanic god, depicted as a mounted elite warrior, on the Hornhausen stone.

By 500, the unity of the Western Roman empire had been well and truly fractured. Without exception, new rulers of barbarian descent exercised effective power and the military structures of the Roman army had ceased to operate in their territories. There has been much recent debate about how far this situation represented a real break with the Roman past, or how far it resulted from an evolutionary process. What is clear is that the degree of change between 400 and 500 had been much greater than in any preceding century. An old Europe, in which there had, in effect, been only the Roman empire, gave way to a new Europe of many states under dynastic leadership, in which centripetal regional tendencies conflicted with regular attempts to recreate a dominant central power. In many ways, this conflict has shaped much of European history up until the present day.

A further topic of debate relating to this period focuses on the influence of changing military technology on social organization, in particular the adoption of the stirrup. Was there an increase in the effectiveness and prevalence of the mounted warrior? Furthermore, did the costs of supporting mounted campaigns lead to the introduction of land being held in return for military service, and to a once-free class of peasant soldier being pressed into serfdom?

SUB-ROMAN GAUL

In the last decades of the 5th century Roman Gaul was divided into a number of kingdoms. The Visigothic kingdom, centred on Toulouse, dominated the south and southwest. The Visigoths had settled in this area following a series of victories over Roman armies, most notably at the battle of Adrianople in 378 (where the emperor Valens was killed) and the sack of Rome in 410. Their army had absorbed Roman influences. It was composed of the forces of the nobility, who led groups of bucellarii (dependent warriors to whom the lord issued arms and armour) and a wider levy supported by taxes, plus significant forces from the Gallo-Roman lords (who also had their own bodyguards). In eastern Gaul lay the Burgundian kingdom, allied with local Roman landowners to defend against the encroachments of the Alemanns from across the Rhine. In the north an independent Breton enclave received reinforcement from British migrants, while the remains of the Roman army of Gaul under Flavius Afranius Syagrius was centred on Soissons (northeast of Paris). There were also several groups of Franks who, with Roman agreement, had settled along the lower reaches of the Rhine and were semi-independent.

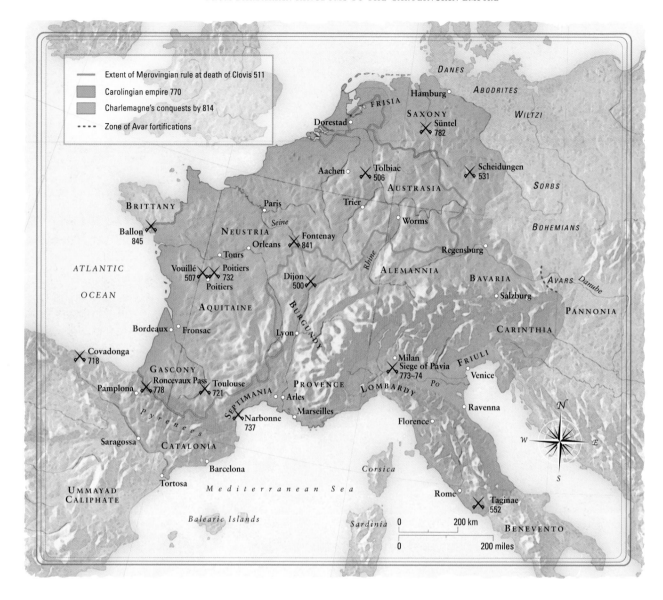

Frankish Europe, showing the main sites and battles discussed in this chapter. The story of this period is of the emergence of the Franks as winners in the construction of states from the debris of the Western Roman empire and the establishment of a common Catholic Christian culture across Western Europe, beyond the old frontiers, cemented by the conquests of Charlemagne.

The Visigoths had spread their power from Gaul to Spain largely in the reign of their aggressive king Euric (r. 466–84). Acting in conjunction with Roman forces, they had defeated the Vandals, crushed the Alans and penned the Suevians into the northeast of the Iberian Peninsula. The Vandals had incorporated the Alans and moved across the straits to Africa, where they established a kingdom that terrorized the Mediterranean with its pirate fleets. However, much of Spain was effectively administered not by barbarians, but by its Roman cities. When imperial control broke down it was replaced by the *civitas* (the city and its surrounding dependent lands). In a highly centralized empire such as the Roman one, there were no provincial governments with provincial armies to resist the outsider. Although the great landowners of the senatorial class held land in several provinces, and might have their own private bodyguards, they could not mobilize larger forces without becoming a competitor for the imperial throne. In a confused situation with no imperial army present, the local dignitaries, and often the bishop, would provide the necessary leadership.

The town walls of Lugo in northern Spain. The successor kingdoms took over a local Roman administration that was based in cities, often with impressive defences. These served as a model for modes of fortification that were to survive into later centuries. The necessity for kings to be able to take such cities demanded that they be competent at besieging and reducing them, and dictated that many campaigns such as those against the Aquitanian dukes involved expeditions over several years. Although restored over the centuries, the walls of Lugo show the power of such fortifications.

ARTHURIAN BRITAIN

Maps are often as deceptive as they are informative in this period, giving an impression of homogeneity of control. In Britain, for example, it is wrong to represent the country as clearly divided, with Celtic kingdoms to the west and Anglo-Saxon kingdoms to the east. In reality, post-Roman Britain consisted of many 'kingdoms', closely resembling the tribal map of Britain before the Roman conquest. One reason for this is that the *civitas* units were originally based on tribes; another is the geography of hills, which divided the administrative units, and rivers, which formed the major communication routes that united them.

One scholar has created a map of forty-three separate political units in the year 500. While there does seem to have been a concept of a high king (vortigern) or acknowledged overlord among the British, it must have been hard for so many small jurisdictions to combine and act together against an aggressive invader. This was no doubt exacerbated by the hiring of these same invaders as mercenaries for use in local wars or against other raiders. However, at least one epic period of united resistance may have given birth to the legend of Arthur, a war leader who was not a king.

In fact, the term 'invasion' reveals a huge misunderstanding of what the arrival of Angles, Saxons, Jutes and others was really like. They first landed as small bands of soldier-settlers. They did not invade as an army and sweep towards the capital of the province seeking a decisive battle, rather they disembarked at many sites along the coast and pushed inland, changing the character and population of the countryside and keeping up a constant pressure under their local leaders. These groups pushed as far as the present-day Welsh border, evolving, by the 8th century, into larger, territorially aggressive kingdoms such as Kent, Mercia, Wessex, Northumbria and East Anglia. The British polities were too small to resist and lacked the will to fight a war of extermination; indeed, many indigenous communities moved west or to Brittany, led by their priests, who, recognizing the aggressive paganism of the Germanic invaders, may have seen emigration as a preferable option. Many of those who were left behind found it convenient to adopt the culture of the newcomers. The Britons became Anglicized, but not vice versa. In the territories to the west the Britons reactivated and garrisoned ancient hill forts, supporting them with bands of armoured horsemen that gathered around the local petty kings. In the 11th century England was assessed as providing 5,000–10,000 mailed horsemen. This suggests that in the disrupted economy of the 6th and 7th centuries a division into twenty or more territories left each one with only a few hundred mounted warriors, with perhaps up to 1,000 more fighting on foot. By the 8th century, the average force available to each of the larger, new kingdoms would have numbered only some 1,500–3,000 warriors.

OSTROGOTHIC ITALY

The conquest of Africa by the Vandals in the 5th century cut off the economic base of the Western Roman empire. In 476 a revolt by the largely barbarian army stationed in Italy under Odoacer, a prince of the Scirii, overthrew the Roman boy-emperor Romulus Augustus. The barbarian leaders wanted land and the Roman elite would not give in to this demand. Although described as 'king', Odoacer's position was not unlike that of 'master of the soldiers' in command of the Roman armies of the West, a role recently held by barbarians. He took over Roman administration, looked to the borders of his kingdom, and, while acting independently, recognized the authority of the East Roman emperor. Some Roman units, such as the guards, continued to exist, but the army was primarily composed of barbarian groups – Scirii, Alans, Heruls and others – who lacked the homogeneity to form a national kingdom.

The Goths who entered Italy in 488 under Theoderic the Amal (later known as 'the Great') consisted of various groups that had been living within the empire, some for up to three or four generations. They had maintained a consciousness of their identity. Perhaps many had served individually in the Roman army; certainly the two main groups had operated as tribal allied contingents under their kings, and both were heavily dependent upon Roman subsidy. Indeed, their mission to Italy was sanctioned by the East Roman emperor, who wished to depose Odoacer and reconquer Italy, and was probably hoping that the opposing barbarians would destroy each other in the process.

This plate decorated the front of the royal helmet of the Lombard king, Agilulf (r. 590–616). It shows Agilulf enthroned with Roman and Christian symbols of regal power, such as the angels derived from winged victories. Legitimacy was an issue for the successor kingdoms, and imperial court ceremonial was adopted to set his nobles at a distance from the king lest they aim for the throne. Agilulf is backed by the temporal power of his guards, armed and wearing plumed versions of the spangenhelm that this plate once adorned.

Between 488 and 493 Theoderic defeated Odoacer in several battles. After a protracted siege and naval blockade at Ravenna, Odoacer eventually surrendered, and was personally executed by Theoderic with a blow that nearly cut his body in two. Following the conquest, the Goths (including subsumed groups from other tribes who made up Theoderic's army) were supported by state taxes and placed in garrisons on the frontiers and at the capital, and their leaders took over the land that Odoacer's men had held. Every year the army (or at least a portion of it) collected at Ravenna to be paid, and to parade and exercise. It was a large army, perhaps up to 30,000 strong. What we know of Gothic social structure suggests that troops were provided in four ways: as followers of the nobles who had a direct service relationship with their lord; as units of free-Goth soldiers, paid from state funds; as the city militia; and as allied barbarians, such as the Suevians and Alemanns on the northern border.

JUSTINIAN'S RECONQUEST (535–54) AND THE LOMBARDS

The Gothic army proved effective in mounting expeditions to rescue its Visigothic neighbours from Frankish aggression and expanding its territories in the Balkans. However, holding Rome proved to be a poisoned chalice for Theoderic's successors. In 535 the East Roman emperor Justinian launched a three-pronged attack on Italy, in a prestigious attempt to recapture the founding city of the empire. His general Flavius Belisarius brought the war to a conclusion in 540, after holding Rome against the Gothic army (which was ruined by the siege), but insisted on total submission rather than Justinian's more limited aims. This led to a resurgence of the conflict until the victory at Taginae under Justinian's general Narses in 552.

The descriptions of these military operations by Roman historians are far superior to anything that would be produced in the West in the 500 years that followed. From them we learn that the Gothic army had a large infantry component consisting of spearmen and archers, and that the Gothic cavalry of mounted lancers and javelineers operated in conjunction with the infantry, advancing by groups to combat and then retiring to the infantry for support, before finally launching a charge when their enemy was weakened by the mêlées. This is not unlike Late Roman tactics and certainly prefigures medieval deployments whereby the infantry were a base of operation and firepower that supported a dominant, mounted arm. The Romans, however, were better at combining all arms to achieve a decisive result. In 552, the Gothic king Totila had too few infantry to face the large army (possibly 25,000 men) that Narses had brought to Italy. So, in the critical battle of Taginae (near Gualdo Tadino in northeast Umbria) he relied upon a massed cavalry charge, but this failed to break the well-designed Roman formation. Narses had stiffened his centre with dismounted barbarian allies and formed his wings from both infantry archers and dismounted cavalry archers, retaining a mounted reserve in hand. Totila, who had won a previous victory with a surprise rear attack, attempted to place a force in the Roman rear, but failed. His last

> '*Whilst both sides were fighting stubbornly, Amalung, a bodyguard of the Lombard king Grimuald, charged violently with his spear held two-handed, struck a certain little Greek, lifted him from the saddle and raised him over his head. When the Byzantine army saw this, it became seized by panic and fled.*'
>
> Paul the Deacon (*c.* 720–*c.* 799) on the battle of Forino, 663

tactical gamble was to mass his cavalry in the centre and attempt to break through. The Roman line held, and the Goths were condemned to making further charges, each of lessening effect as the arrows from either side of the valley took their toll. Totila was fatally wounded and the infantry, too few to protect the rallying cavalry, were swept away in the rout.

Lombard and Saxon shields were decorated with studs and plaques that gave symbolic as well as physical protection. This plaque from the Stabio shield may represent Odin. He is shown in armour, wielding his lance with a two-handed grip, a style of fighting that the Lombards perhaps acquired from their sojourn in the Hungarian plain, where their neighbours were Iranian steppe nomads. Around his waist is a belt with dangling strap ends, another fashion of nomad inspiration.

Roman control in Italy was severely disrupted in 565 by the invasion of the Lombards. This pagan Germanic tribe had been outside the imperial borders, but upon the irruption of the fierce Asiatic Avars into the area of present-day Hungary, they gathered up the remnants of other tribes and invaded Italy. The Lombards conquered the North Italian Plain and founded two duchies – Spoleto and Benevento – further south. They were perhaps distracted from completing their conquest by the early death of their king Alboin and the fragmentation of the tribe into its component clans, each led by a duke. Subsequent kings never had the necessary authority or impetus to evict the Byzantines from Calabria, Liguria, or Sicily and their campaigns against the Byzantine exarchate of Ravenna only led to the creation of the Papal States in 756, as the Franks supported papal ambitions. However, the Lombards did resist major attempts at reconquest from Constantinople. We know from later Lombard laws that the army consisted of mailed, mounted spearmen, unarmoured mounted retainers and dismounted bowmen.

ETSYRIAM SOBAL· ETCONVERTIT

A 9th-century Carolingian count and his mounted retinue preceded by a dragon banner, a military symbol inherited from the Late Roman army, for which the earliest Franks had fought.

THE MEROVINGIAN FRANKS

The Frankish king Clovis (c. 466–511) is regarded as the founder of the Merovingian dynasty, which ruled most of the former Roman province of Gaul until 751. He stands above all others in providing dynamic royal leadership for a state built upon the territories of the Roman empire. In conquering his neighbours and then dividing the subsequent acquisitions between his sons, Clovis was doing what Frankish kings had always done, but was now operating without the sort of limits the former Roman empire had imposed on the flow of power and wealth. He conquered territories within and beyond the former imperial borders, at first bringing other Frankish kings into an alliance before destroying them to create a single source of regal power.

Clovis's father Childeric I (*c.* 440–81) – son of Merovech, from whom the term 'Merovingian' derives – had been a commander of Frankish troops in Roman service and ruler of a tribe around Tournai. In 486 Clovis conquered Soissons, seat of the last Roman commander in Gaul, adding these troops to his own. He then crushed the Alemanns, overran Brittany, cowed the Burgundians and, in 507, destroyed the Visigothic kingdom of Toulouse in a single battle at Vouillé, west of Poitiers, forcing the once mighty Goths into Spain and down the coast of southeast France. Given the depth of Clovis's penetrating strikes and the formation of his army from the bucellarii of several kings, it may be that his expeditionary forces largely comprised mounted troops. Each of these campaigns added to his treasure, increasing his ability to reward his men and remove his rivals.

Clovis left his kingdom to his three sons in a complicated donation that intermingled their holdings and was a source of much trouble to come. Even so, they continued his energetic work, conquering Thuringia, the Burgundian kingdom, Provence, Bavaria and Swabia, and invading Italy twice. Western Europe now had a superstate, stretching from the Pyrenees to Denmark and from the Atlantic to the Great Hungarian Plain. This was tremendously significant, allowing the eventual spread of a common, Frankish culture that incorporated Roman, Christian and German elements.

Most Merovingian warfare was internecine. The creation of three kingdoms in 511 (Neustria, Burgundy and Austrasia), and the kings' habits of having several wives and concubines, spawned disputes over succession as the nobility competed for power and influence. Attempts to conquer Spain, Italy and Pannonia (western Hungary) all failed. The Franks assembled each March for campaigning; indeed, the frequency and savagery of their fighting gave them a considerable advantage in combat. Time and again the sources tell us of severe casualties: in 595, when the Franks put down a rebellion of the Thuringii, 'so many fell that few of that people survived'. In 600, 'Chlotar's army was massacred.' In 612, 'Theuderic won and cut Theudebert's force to pieces.' And in the same year at Zülpich (Germany), 'the carnage on both sides was such that in the fighting line there was no room for the slain to fall down. They stood upright in their ranks.'

There were two models for Frankish warfare: the Germanic, and the Roman. These concepts had already begun to fuse together in the frontier zone in the course of the preceding centuries. The Germanic ideal was centred on heroic behaviour, as evidenced in epic poems such as *Beowulf*, *Fight at Finnsburg* and later *Waldere*, as well as in chronicles. In his *History of the Franks*, Gregory of Tours (538–94) describes the duel arranged between two Frankish Mayors of the Palace (senior noble military commanders). King Chlotar II's mayor Landri was challenged by Theuderic II of Burgundy's mayor Bertoald. Landri refused, but Bertoald, understanding that a general war would ensue, forced Landri to swear on oath that he and Landri would both wear red in the coming battle and would seek each other out. Landri's men would eventually kill Bertoald in battle in 604. In Lombard Italy a question of royal adultery was settled through trial by combat. In England battles frequently resulted

> '*King Guntram...brought together a vast army [and] marched on Poitiers, the inhabitants of which had broken their oath of allegiance.... [They] set light to the buildings and massacred the inhabitants.... In the end the inhabitants had to recognize the king.*'
>
> Gregory of Tours on King Guntram of Burgundy's recapture of Poitiers from the rebel Gundowald, *c.* 584

Above Franciscas, or throwing axes, were widely spread in Germany and were used in Spain and Italy. Such a weapon delivered a powerful, armour-piercing blow and yet was still economical in its use of iron – an important factor in metal-poor societies.

Below The spangenhelm was a popular design of helmet, typically made of six iron plates riveted to a framework of copper or iron. Those associated with elite warriors were silvered and gilded and had flowing plumes. The helmet's origins lie in the east, possibly with steppe warriors. It has been suggested that examples found in Europe were imported from Byzantine workshops, but their variety argues for local manufacture.

in the death of the vanquished commanders. Leadership in war was personal, and courage had to be demonstrated in order to motivate the troops. Nor should we forget the fiercely pagan nature of much of northern Europe throughout this period. There was a strong cult element in Germanic warfare, with veneration of the bear and wolf in the war dances and martial ceremonies of the warrior aristocracy.

Some commentators interpret the rise of knighthood in Europe as a consequence of the cavalry strength of the Goths and Lombards, subsequently transmitted to the Franks. However, this appears unlikely. The Franks of the 6th century were horsemen, but their armies fought mainly as infantry. It is probable that the aristocracy fought dismounted as often as they did mounted. Weapon sets from Frankish graves show two interesting weapons: the ango, and the Frankish axe. The former was a spear about 2 m (7 ft) long; over half of this length consisted of a long, slim, metal sheath with a narrow, barbed head. It was described by a contemporary Greek historian as a mass volley weapon used to pierce the shields of opponents; the Franks would then tread on the shaft of the ango, pulling down the shield and exposing the enemy soldier. However, few angos have been found, and it may be that its purpose has become confused with the Roman pilum. For a barbarian, the amount of metal in the weapon would have made it very expensive, and so the ango should perhaps be seen as a high-status, armour-piercing weapon used by elite warriors against the opposing leaders. The Frankish axe has also been identified as a throwing weapon, although it would have been very difficult to launch it while advancing; it is more likely that javelins were thrown instead, and the axe was used in the hand.

The Roman influence on warfare in the successor kingdoms is clear from an early phase, and understandably so, given that many barbarians had served as contingents in Roman armies on a formal basis. Moreover, nobles of Roman descent served in both Gothic and Frankish armies, and the rule of both was centred on Roman cities, which probably possessed war engines built and operated by the garrisons. Roman textbooks of war were preserved and updated. This does not, of course, mean that many warriors read these works, but when, at the end of the period, Rabanus Maurus produced an updated edition of Vegetius's military manual *De re militari*, we should assume that he had an audience. After his victory over the Visigoths, Clovis performed a triumphal entry into Tours modelled on those of Late Roman generals and wearing insignia sent by the East Roman emperor. Although Clovis had himself publicly baptized in the religion of his Gallo-Roman subjects, when thwarted over the distribution of booty at Soissons he killed the nobleman responsible for the insult with his own axe, in front of the paraded Frankish army and the victim's own men. A Merovingian king had to play to both audiences.

The tactics in Frankish battles are generally related as very simple and direct, with the opposing sides meeting each other, almost by agreement, and joining battle. The Franks made a point of their virility, as compared to their neighbours. The Goths were portrayed as prone to running away, though this may actually represent a rather greater tactical repertoire. For example, a Frankish invasion of Spain was defeated by a feigned flight and subsequent ambush, and on another occasion the Goths feigned a retreat back to a city and then sallied from the walls to defeat their disordered pursuers. As for the Lombards, we know of one occasion when a Frankish force attacked their camp at Asti. The Lombards allowed them to take it, leaving behind their food and wine already set out, but returned at night and won an emphatic victory. Similar incidents are recorded in Procopius's history of the Gothic war.

A contrasting style is demonstrated by King Pepin 'the Short' (714–68), who led the Frankish army into Italy in 754. Only a portion of the army was able to cross the passes and reach the Susa Valley, where the Lombards were waiting for them. Pepin's small force attacked the Lombards frontally and routed them. Yet, the Franks were not entirely devoid of guile, and at one point made a successful night attack on the enemy from behind a screen of branches carried by servants; moreover, their horses were fitted with bells normally attached to grazing animals. Battles were frequent and generally decisive in terms of the campaign, though few campaigns were pushed to a conclusion. It would normally require several attempts before an area was successfully conquered.

One notable feature of Frankish campaigning was the employment of comital forces (i.e. led by counts), operating in several columns. An example of this occurred in 590, when an army with twenty ducal or comital contingents under three generals (and possibly operating in three columns) was sent against the Lombards; it took many towns, but in the end was defeated by dysentery. An attack in 630 upon the Slavic tribes of the Wends (eastern Germany), who were led by Samo (see box overleaf), involved three columns from Austrasia, the eastern Frankish realm, and a column of allied Lombards. In 635, during a revolt of the Gascons (Basques), Dagobert I (King of Neustria and Burgundy) sent an army from Burgundy against them led by Chadoind, a court official and an experienced war leader. The army consisted of the forces of 'ten dukes and many other counts with no dukes over them'. We can deduce that the army was raised by royal officers summoning the counts, rather than working solely through the higher nobility. Such an organization made operation in separate divisions easy, but suffered from divided command.

The obligation to military service was the badge of the free man in Frankish society, yet recruiting an army was more complicated than simply organizing a mass levy, notably because it consisted of the king's household, his court officials (such as the Mayor of the Palace) and their retainers, the dukes and their retainers, and city counts and their men. It also included groups of settlers, such as the Taifals and the Saxons of Bayeux, the retainers of Roman landowners (particularly in the Auvergne and Aquitaine), and in the south the Basques (who acted as mercenary troops). Later Frankish laws refer to equipment requirements graded by wealth; thus, an army with more ducal contingents would have more mounted men and a generally better level of equipment. An army that contained fewer dukes and counts, such as that which invaded Italy in 553, may well have had a much wider levy of poorer men and more infantry – and indeed that is how the forces of the dukes Lothar and Buccelin are portrayed by the East Roman author Agathias Scholasticus (*c.* 536–582/594).

> '[The Franks] all closed their ranks, both infantry and cavalry, and drew themselves up into a compact formation, which, though not deep, was a solid mass of shields regularly flanked by the converging wings of cavalry.'
>
> Agathias Scholasticus (*c.* 536–582/594), on 6th-century Frankish forces in Italy

In terms of size, the Frankish invaders of Italy in the 530s numbered 10,000 strong, and those of 553 were probably even stronger given that they faced a Roman army of 15,000–20,000 men. Numbers are rarely given in the sources, but a force with twenty dukes could well have numbered 10,000 men or more if each duke, or count, had 500 followers. Frankish expeditions were also well equipped with tents and camp gear, for we hear of these being lost in defeats.

The Merovingian polity depended upon a negotiation between the nobility and the monarchs. When the king was weak or still a minor, the nobility advanced their power and struggled to control the throne. When the king was strong, the nobility were involved in campaigns against other Merovingians or external enemies. In the 7th century this balance was upset; more remote areas, such as Aquitaine, Thuringia and Bavaria, gained more independence, and the monarchs became pawns in bitter struggles between palace nobles. Out of this emerged one family, who fought back to claim supreme power, ruled without kings, and then became kings – the dynasty of Pepin of Héristal (*c.* 635–714), destined to become the Carolingians.

David slays Goliath, from the 9th-century Stuttgart Psalter. Goliath carries a white shield with a pointed boss that provided protection to his hand and acted as a battering weapon. His coat is of mail and his helmet of segmented construction. Note the overarm use of the spear in a dual thrusting and throwing stance.

Samo's Kingdom

Samo was a Frankish merchant living among the Wends – Slavic tribes in Bohemia – when they rebelled against their Avar overlords. The latter had used the Slavs as cannon fodder, sending them into battle first to wear down the enemy. Samo acquitted himself well in fighting against the Avars, who were ill adapted to the forests, and the Wends made him their battle leader and king. The Slavs appear in Byzantine sources as loose groupings, but Samo was able to offer leadership based upon a Frankish regnal model. Samo also took twelve Wendish wives, perhaps because they were organized into twelve clans. Once organized the Wends became much more formidable. In 630 some Frankish merchants were killed by Wends, and King Dagobert I sent an embassy to arrange compensation. Samo threw out the ambassadors, so the Franks organized a four-pronged attack. Two of their columns won victories, but Dagobert's forces were defeated in a three-day battle against the excellent Slav light infantry outside the impressive stronghold of Wogastisburg (in the modern Czech Republic). The king fled, leaving his camp to be looted. In the aftermath, other Slav tribes joined with the Wends, and cross-border raids were launched into Frankish Thuringia. The fate of Samo's kingdom after his death in c. 658 remains uncertain, but it is thought that it dissolved with him.

Fortifications of ditches, wooden ramparts and earth banks were common throughout northern Europe where there were no Roman foundations. Such defences could be effectively garrisoned, even by irregular troops, provided there were sufficient numbers.

Based upon several excavations of Slav sites, this reconstruction of the fort at Wogastisburg shows how formidable fortifications that used the contours of the land could be. Reducing such a fortress in forested terrain and within a limited campaigning season would be difficult.

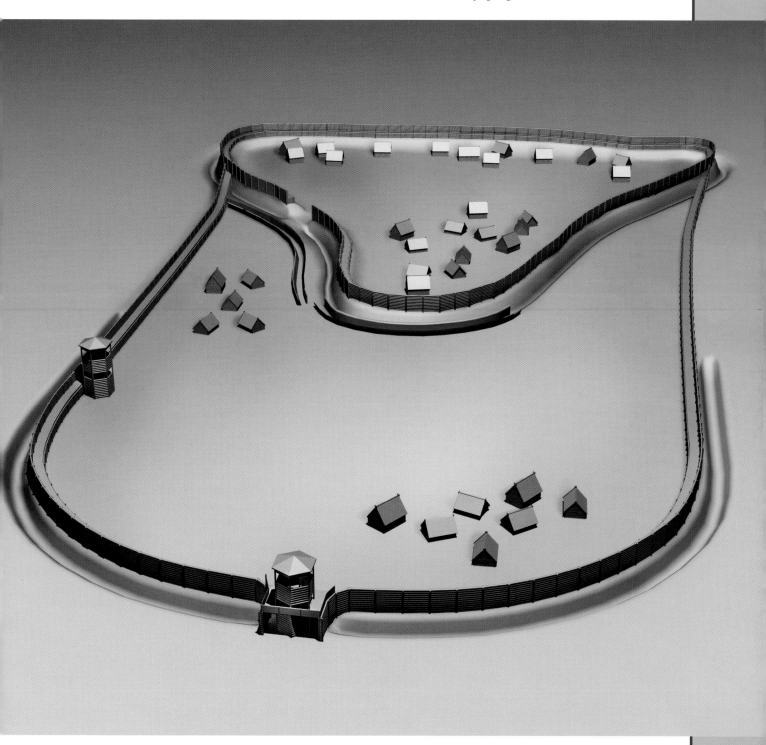

'[Charlemagne] crossed the Rhine at Cologne, advanced through Saxony, reached the River Elbe, and had two bridges constructed, on one of which he built fortifications of wood and earth at both ends. From there he advanced further and subjected the Slavs to his authority.'

Frankish annals, 789

Charlemagne: a near-contemporary representation of the emperor conveys his determination and resolve.

THE CAROLINGIANS

In 724, a Frankish noble called Charles Martel (688–741) achieved more or less unchallenged power through control of the king Theoderic IV (r. 721–37), and set about reincorporating the territories that had drifted out of Frankish control. In a series of campaigns lasting up until 739, he put down a Saxon rebellion, campaigned in Alemannia, Thuringia and Bavaria, and then headed for Aquitaine to bring to heel its wayward Duke Eudo. In 732, Charles rescued Eudo from the Muslims of al-Andalus (southern Spain) and won a great victory against Islamic forces at the battle of Tours (also known as Poitiers) in October of that year (see box overleaf). He then suppressed rebellion in Burgundy and enforced his rule in Frisia (northwest Germany) with a combined land and naval expedition. In 735, following Duke Eudo's death, Charles occupied the whole of Aquitaine. Events in Burgundy required yet another intervention and significantly, in 737, Charles undertook a drive into Provence, where the local duke Maurontus was collaborating with the Muslims of al-Andalus. The Franks retook Avignon by storm and then penetrated Muslim territory, besieging Narbonne, defeating the Saracen relieving army, and burning Nîmes, Agde and Béziers.

What is remarkable about this string of victories is their relentless pace. Frankish armies were on the move from one end of the kingdom to the other, defeating rebels and invaders. Charles's sons inherited his power, and one, Pepin the Short, became king in 751. He warred with the same energy as Charles Martel, invading Italy, subduing Aquitaine, and taking Narbonne.

When Pepin died in 768, the inheritance of Francia was split once again, with Carloman (751–71) sharing power with his brother Charlemagne (747–814). Upon accession they faced the same problem as in previous reigns, as the nobility in peripheral regions made a bid to redefine their relationship to the regnal power. Given that members of the nobility were often interlinked through marriage, these regularly degenerated into family feuds. When Carloman died in 771 Charlemagne excluded his brother's family from power. In the early years of his reign, Charlemagne warred in Aquitaine and reconquered Bavaria. His greatness, though, lay in his extending Frankish claims of lordship over Saxony and Italy into direct rule, and destroying the Avar state that ruled Hungary.

The Saxon Wars lasted from 772 until 804. The Saxons were not Christians and fought hard for their independence. Although there were battles, some of which the Franks lost, the war mainly consisted of sieges and guerrilla actions, with atrocities committed by both sides. In the end it was the ability of the Franks to maintain fortified bases in Saxon territory, to campaign through the winter, and to support separate mobile columns that brought them victory.

In the Italian campaign of 773–74, Charlemagne divided his force into two columns and besieged the Lombard capital of Pavia through the winter, eventually forcing the Lombard king Desiderius to surrender. This was in great contrast to earlier

Frankish invasions, where the Franks had been defeated by the Lombards' ability to retire to their fortified cities and their own inability to remain in the field.

The high-water mark of Carolingian warfare was the conquest of the Avar khaganate (empire), which took the Franks into a land that was geographically very different from their own heartlands. The Avars, who were originally a confederation of Asiatic tribes, had fished in troubled waters by intervening in Italy, perhaps stimulated by Byzantine gold. Their army comprised armoured cavalry (some of which rode armoured horses) equipped with bow and lance, light cavalry armed with bows, and Slav foot soldiers who were employed to wear down their opponents. The Avars operated from large earth and wood fortifications. In 791 Charlemagne campaigned down the River Danube with a large force in three columns, including Slav auxiliaries and with a supporting column from Italy, reducing the Avar border forts. Campaigning was suspended in 792 due to an outbreak of disease among the Frankish horses. In 795 the attack was resumed using a force from Italy under Eric of Friuli – perhaps because Lombardy's horse stock had been less affected. Combined with a major advance from Bavaria in 796, this broke Avar power and brought the capture of fabulous treasure stored in their main fortress known as the 'Ring'. The mopping up process continued until 799. Charlemagne then extended settlements eastwards into Carinthia and Pannonia, colonizing the region with fortifications and settlers. Here, as in Saxony, it took several years of campaigning to reduce the enemy. This was partly because action in other areas distracted the war effort, and partly because the method of warfare was deliberate and relied upon logistical superiority rather than brilliance in battle. In general, the Carolingian empire played to its strengths, and the occasional defeats its forces suffered were due to rash actions. For example, at the defeat inflicted by the Saxons at the battle of the Süntel Mountains in 782 the commanders ignored the advice of Count Theoderic to send forward scouts and instead charged ahead, with disastrous results.

In his *Life of Charlemagne*, Notker the Stammerer provides an interesting description of the advance upon Pavia in 774 of Charlemagne's lavishly equipped and formidable army: 'Then appeared iron Charles, helmeted with an iron helmet, his hands clad in iron gauntlets, his iron chest and broad shoulders protected with an iron coat. An iron spear was raised on high in his left hand, his right always rested on his unconquered sword of iron.... His thighs were clad with plates of iron; his greaves, like the greaves of all the army, were of iron. His shield was furnished in iron; his horse was iron-coloured and iron-hearted. All who went before him, all who marched by his side, all who followed after him, and the whole equipment of the army imitated him as closely as possible. The plains were filled with iron; the rays of the sun reflected the shining iron; a race harder than iron mirrored the hardness of iron.'

The sword of Charlemagne? The hilt is certainly more recent and the sword itself came to prominence when used for the coronation of later French kings. What it does indicate is the power that Charlemagne's example of pan-European power held over the imagination of later generations, and the kings' desire to associate their rule with a genuine northern European imperial tradition.

53

The Battle of Tours, 732

In 720, the Arabs conquered Visigothic Septimania (Languedoc-Roussillon), opening the route into Francia. Initially defeated at Toulouse by Duke Eudo of Aquitaine, in 724 they seized the key gateway town of Carcassonne. In 731, two major raids by Charles Martel into Aquitaine weakened the duchy, leading to a successful invasion by 'Abd ar-Rahman, the governor of al-Andalus. Eudo then appealed to Charles Martel for military aid, as the Arabs headed north to sack the monastery of St Martin at Tours, potentially a huge blow to Frankish prestige. The likely site of the battle is at Moussais, near Vieux-Poitiers, on the Roman road to Tours. Generally this is an area of wide plains, but Charles selected a site between the Vienne and Clain rivers that limited his opponent's ability to manoeuvre. Encumbered with booty, the Arab force could not escape without fighting. The Franks, who were described as being 'immobile as a wall, holding together like a glacier', probably deployed dismounted; in contrast, after such a successful campaign the Andalusians may well have been almost entirely on horseback. Repeated Arab attacks failed to dent the Frankish line, and their leader was killed. They retired to their camp before fleeing back to Spain the following day, leaving all their booty behind, looting the Limousin as they retired. There was no pursuit. Tours was a highly significant battle. Had Charles Martel been defeated, the Muslim conquest of Aquitaine would surely have followed.

	FRANKS	ANDALUSIANS
COMMANDERS	Charles Martel	'Abd ar-Rahman
STRENGTH	12,000	10,000
CASUALTIES	c. 1,000	c. 3,000

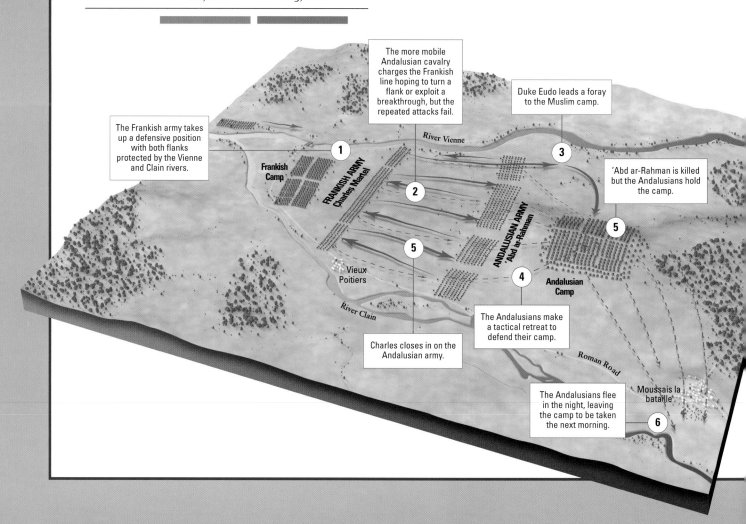

The Frankish army takes up a defensive position with both flanks protected by the Vienne and Clain rivers.

The more mobile Andalusian cavalry charges the Frankish line hoping to turn a flank or exploit a breakthrough, but the repeated attacks fail.

Duke Eudo leads a foray to the Muslim camp.

'Abd ar-Rahman is killed but the Andalusians hold the camp.

The Andalusians make a tactical retreat to defend their camp.

Charles closes in on the Andalusian army.

The Andalusians flee in the night, leaving the camp to be taken the next morning.

River Vienne

River Clain

Roman Road

Frankish Camp

FRANKISH ARMY Charles Martel

ANDALUSIAN ARMY 'Abd ar-Rahman

Andalusian Camp

Vieux Poitiers

Moussais la bataille

Opposite The battle of Tours in 732 marked the high-water mark of Andalusian expansion and yet to the Carolingians it was just an interlude in a series of battles to establish their power over other noble groupings in the Frankish lands. Winning at Tours did not achieve security, but losing could have been disastrous.

Above A 15th-century depiction of the battle of Tours. Although it took many decades to push the Muslims back beyond the Spanish border, in later times the struggle came to be crystallized around this one encounter in which Charles Martel personifies the crusading zeal of French kings.

Opposite Two scenes of battle from the 9th-century Stuttgart Psalter. (*Above*) Armour was rare and expensive in Europe and few could afford the mailshirt of the central figure; most warriors would have carried only a shield and spear and perhaps a knife. A well-armoured warrior had a tremendous advantage. The curved helmet of the middle figure is most likely an artistic convention harking back to Roman illustrations of warriors in plumed helmets. The deep dished shields give a lot of protection to the body. (*Below*) The mounted soldier epitomizes the elite warrior of the Carolingian laws that sought to recruit the maximum number of such men to the army. Note that he rides without stirrups but has a high saddle that holds him securely in the seat.

A Lombard stirrup. Stirrups were introduced by the Avars in the late 6th century, but, as the illustration in the Stuttgart Psalter opposite shows, they were not essential to effective cavalry warfare. We never hear of a battle won because one side had stirrups, but they did make mounting a horse easier and riding less tiring.

THE DOMINANCE OF CAVALRY

It has been suggested that the era of Charles Martel and Charlemagne saw the emergence of a society dominated by the nobility, where the original duty of all free men attending the muster was replaced by military service in return for the use of land. Among the reasons given for this social change are the threat from the Spanish Muslims, which required more mobile forces to be deployed, and the invention of the stirrup, which made mounted warriors so much more effective. However, the Muslim threat is an unlikely cause of change. The Carolingians conquered the areas from whence Andalusian armies might debouch into Gaul using traditional armies and siege warfare. Furthermore, the argument for technological change has been thoroughly deconstructed, notably by Professor Bernard S. Bachrach, who has highlighted the fact that stirrups are rarely mentioned in Carolingian literature, art and archaeology. Moreover, stirrups confer little advantage in combat over a supportive saddle, and we know that saddles that enabled agile manoeuvre and shock charges with the lance had been in use throughout this period. The Frankish historian Nithard's description of cavalry training exercises in the 840s shows clear similarities to Roman cavalry training of the 2nd century AD: 'Teams of equal numbers first rushed forth from both sides and raced at full speed against each other as if they were going to attack. One side would turn back, pretending that they wished to escape from their pursuers to their companions under the protection of their shields. But then they would turn round again and try to pursue those from whom they had been fleeing until finally both kings and all the young men rushed forward with a great shout, brandishing their lances and spurring on their horses pursuing by turns whoever took flight. It was a show worth seeing because of its excellent execution and discipline.'

If there *was* an increase in the proportion of cavalry to infantry, it was more likely driven by the increased distance and duration of campaigns, which placed a premium on horses for both mounted action and transport. We know that the infantry was provided by a general levy from those provinces nearest the area of combat, and that those far from the theatre of war were required to send fewer men than those that were nearer. One way of maximizing the number of cavalry troops was to use the retainers of the dukes and counts, who were provided with horses and war gear by their lords. This meant that the king would be dependent upon the nobility for the cavalry contingents. However, it is more likely that social change was driven by the natural tendency for local lords to aggrandize themselves when the king was weak and to make free men more dependent on their patronage. The edicts of the kings, not only in Francia but in Lombard Italy and England, show them trying to maintain the traditional duties whereby all those of free status should serve or contribute to the support of a soldier. In Visigothic Spain, where the nobility may have been more powerful, the demand was for the lord to bring servants from his estates equipped with 'mail shirts, spears, slings and bows' to the muster. Even there, semipermanent forces garrisoned fortifications in Septimania and the Basque country, giving some indication of the complexity of military provision.

COMPOSITION, TRAINING AND EQUIPMENT

The Franks, both the ruling elite and their dependents, were warriors. Even their cavalry would dismount to fight in the line of battle or at a siege, whenever the tactical situation called for this, as the *Strategicon* – the military manual commissioned by the Byzantine emperor Maurice – notes: 'If they are hard pressed in cavalry actions they dismount at a single prearranged sign and form up on foot.' Indeed, the chronicler remarks on a purely mounted battle that took place in 784 as being an unusual occurrence. The available sources give such brief descriptions of battles that the complexities of Frankish army composition are somewhat opaque. However, some details have been preserved, and we know that forces were recruited from all over the empire. In 803, at the siege of Barcelona, Charlemagne's son Louis led the men of 'Aquitaine, Gascony…. The most prized warriors were the mounted ones.' Large numbers of Gascons served in Aquitanian armies, and these may have provided light infantry and light cavalry – as probably did the allied Slavs who fought on the eastern frontiers. Also, we can deduce that the armies were not simply composed of mounted spearmen, and must have included other types of troops in order to permit tactical flexibility.

> '*Whether on horseback or on foot they draw up for battle, not in fixed formation, or regiments or divisions, but according to tribes, their kinship groupings, and ties of dependency.*'
>
> Strategicon of Maurice, on the Franks and Lombards, late 6th century

Military training was carried out within the households of the duke, count, or king. Youths would join the extended family of their sponsor and take part in horsemanship, weapons training and hunting. Within the royal household there were different grades of guard and the young men would progress through the ranks until they became royal officers with independent roles. Hunting taught many useful military skills, such as conducting a party of mounted men across country, reading terrain and living in the outdoors, not to mention the use of weapons. On festivals and feast days semi-military exercises would take place, a prelude to the major exercises of the general assembly that took place in March or May each year. The *scarae* – cavalry forces that were sent on rapid-reaction missions, such as the three sent against the Slavs in 812 – provided a further training element and helped create a core of experienced troops.

With regard to weaponry and equipment, the Frankish armies of the 8th and 9th centuries were armed with spears, well-made swords and deeply dished round shields; the wealthier members wore coats of ring mail and even armoured protection for their arms and legs. Contemporary illustrations show two-piece helmets as being characteristic; these were probably hemispherical with reinforcing bands around the rim and across the crest. Guard units appear to have sported uniformly coloured cloaks and shields, as well as armour. Frankish bows may have been of the compound variety, and fired special arrowheads that could punch through armour. One edict demanded that 'spear, shield and bow with two strings and twelve arrows' were to be brought by the soldier, and that they were to have

The magnificent late 6th-century Isola Rizza silver dish shows a mounted lancer with a coat of lamellar armour and an elaborate plumed spangenhelm dispatching two unarmoured but expensively dressed figures.

It is almost certainly by a Byzantine artist and was quite possibly a presentation piece to a Byzantine general who had participated in the defeat and death of two Ostrogothic kings, Totila and Teias, in 552.

'coats of mail for the campaigning season'. Another edict specifies that working bows be brought, and not staves – presumably indicating that mere sticks or half-made bows had previously been presented. The 806 mobilization order to Abbot Fulrad of St Quentin calls for 'each horseman to carry shield and spear, long sword and short sword, bow, quivers and arrows and your carts are to contain implements of various kinds – axes and stone-cutting tools, entrenching tools, iron spades…and provisions in the carts for three months' – the later items indicating that engineering and perhaps siege work were envisaged.

We know that the Carolingian armies (and others such as the Visigoths) operated siege engines, as evidenced by Pepin against Bourges, but we know little about the technical specialists who operated them. Presumably they were the same engineers who carried out the extensive bridge building, fabrication of assault boats and canal building that Charlemagne indulged in, notably with the bridge across the Elbe that featured fortified towers at each end. It is possible that the specialists in siege warfare came from the establishments of the major abbeys, and were the audience for updated versions of Vegetius's work on the military art. Later Carolingian armies were highly proficient at logistics and must surely have engaged specialists to keep a large army fed and supplied on such long campaigns in hostile territory. These armies, unlike the 6th-century invaders of Italy, did not starve, though they were affected by disease.

In summary, throughout this period warfare was the career of a professional caste, and it could be very well organized. Once a ruler had secured power, campaigns were frequent and covered large distances. Cooperation with naval forces also took place and worked well. However, incorporating new territories proved difficult to achieve, and military operations focused on sieges and the establishment of fortified bases. Armies needed constant practice to be fully effective and the strategic advantage lay with the aggressor. Once outward expansion stopped, the dynamics of social relationships within the elites meant that conflict became internecine. Continuing external warfare alone guaranteed stability for the successor states of the Roman empire.

'Our troops, burning with yet fiercer rage…beat against the defences of [Nîmes] with continuous attacks, cast crashing showers of rocks, set fire to the gates, and broke through the narrow breaches in the walls.'

Julian of Toledo on the suppression of a rebellion by Wamba, King of the Visigoths, in 673

3 New Invaders of Christendom: Muslims, Vikings, Russians, Magyars and Normans, 800–1066

Opposite A Magyar nobleman with captive; gold bowl, 7th–9th centuries. *Right* Two horsemen engaged in combat, from the highly decorated cart of the Oseberg ship burial, *c.* 800.

The peoples of Christendom – the Latin West and Orthodox East – viewed the attacks on their territory that materialized from 800 onwards as attacks on Christianity itself, launched by the Devil through his agents, the pagans and heretics. Although the product of very different military cultures, the Viking, Muslim and Magyar forces that invaded Europe operated in ways that were similar to each other. The overarching strategy was based on debilitating raids, which enabled the attackers to assess the strength and deployment of the opposition before attempting conquest.

THE MUSLIM THREAT

By 800 the Muslim world was politically fragmented. Although the Abbasid caliphate, based in Baghdad, was still the largest state, it had ceased to be the most aggressive. Rather, it was the new emirates of North Africa and the west that took the offensive. The Muslims had conquered Spain within a few years of the initial invasion in 711, and the Umayyads began to launch attacks on the Balearic Islands from 798 onwards. The Aghlabids, based in Tunisia, were well positioned to raid and conquer southern Italy and the Mediterranean islands. In 823, Andalusian Muslims attacked Crete and took it from the Byzantines. Sicily was conquered between 827 and 831, and expeditions reached Rome in 846 and 875, taking much plunder. Such raiding does not always qualify as military (or naval) activity, since it was endemic and might seem to lack a political objective. However, it helped to set the agenda upon which rulers could make truly strategic decisions, and led to the conquest of territories and the changes of allegiance that moved the frontier to the benefit of Christian or Muslim. This is certainly how contemporaries viewed the situation.

On the Mediterranean coast of France, a group usually described as pirates' themselves up at Fraxinetum (Le Freinet) in Provence

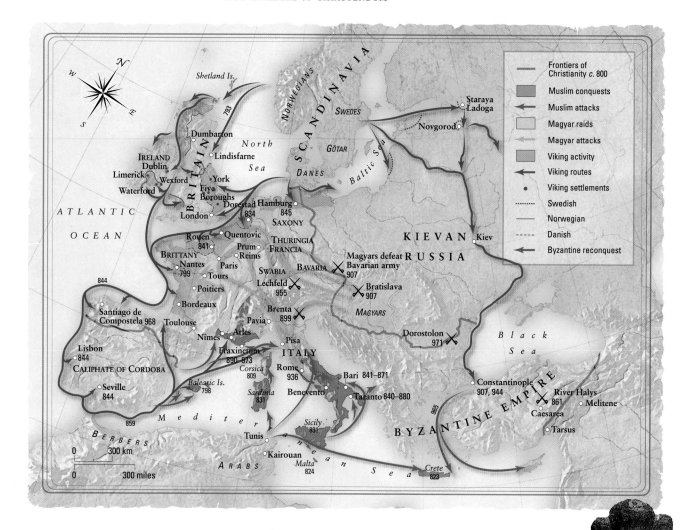

During the invasion period, Christian communities felt themselves besieged by the attacks of non-believers. Apart from the success of Alfred the Great (d. 899), who was precocious in subduing the Vikings in England, the tide did not turn elsewhere in Europe and the Byzantine empire until the second half of the 10th century.

in around 890. Slave-raiding and plundering continued from this base for almost a century, until eventually Count William of Aquitaine was able to expel them in the 970s. It is usually assumed that the Muslim settlement was unable to establish itself permanently, and unable to extend its territories – but this is with the benefit of hindsight. Effectively, until about the mid-9th century, the powers of the southern Mediterranean shore (which happened to be Muslim) held the upper hand over those who controlled the northern coastline. However, Christian Europe, both in the east and west, was reorganizing itself. The Latin kingdoms of France and Germany were beginning to become worthy of the title that they have been accorded by historians. Otto I (936–73) was crowned emperor of the West at Rome in 960, and he and his successors had enough authority over the realm to give the title some weight. Byzantium, having survived a series of attacks from Bulgars, Rus' and Pechenegs, went onto the offensive in the 970s. There was no sense of inevitability about a military and naval revival of the Christian kingdoms (as events of the 11th century were to show), but a strategic line had been drawn across the

Above A group of modern re-enactors simulate the ferocious Viking charge. Only the leader is wealthy enough to afford a mail coat.

Opposite and right Viking swords. These were luxury items of the highest workmanship and only the richer warriors would be able to afford one. The pattern-welding technique of their construction made them light and strong and left a distinctive watery mark along the blade.

Mediterranean that would remain more or less undisturbed until the mid-11th century.

THE FIRST VIKING ASSAULTS

The Vikings came by sea to western Europe, and by the Russian river system to the Black Sea and Aegean. The growth of the Frankish empire in the 8th century presented both a threat and an opportunity to the Vikings. Evidence of the former can be found in the Dannevirke, a ditch and bank built across the neck of the Jutland Peninsula by the Danish king Godfred in 808, together with the fortress of Hedeby, to protect against invasion. The very success of Charlemagne's empire meant that he acquired great wealth (much of which was captured from the Avars in 796), which he disbursed, especially to the Church. It was then conveniently collected together, from the point of view of attackers, into towns and often undefended monasteries. From the 820s, Carolingian aggression waned and political discord flourished. To the maritime peoples of what were to become Norway, Sweden

The prow of the Oseberg ship (c. 800) shows exquisite Scandinavian craftsmanship as well as epitomizing the Viking need for naval conquests.

and Denmark this presented an open invitation for raid and conquest.

In fact, attacks on the settled lands of northern France and England had begun even before Charlemagne's death in 814. According to the *Anglo-Saxon Chronicle,* 'In 793, on 8 June, the ravages of heathen men miserably destroyed God's church on Lindisfarne, with plunder and slaughter.' This piratical destruction of the most important monastery in Northumbria represented the early assaults of what became two centuries of depredations by Scandinavians upon the Christian West. Their English victims called the seaborne raiders 'Vikings', but this broad description conceals a wide variety of military and naval activity. Initially the Vikings arrived in small numbers and disparate groups. By the mid-9th century they had learnt to coordinate themselves into shipborne armies large enough to overcome established kingdoms. In the second Viking phase, around 1000, they were the tools of conquest for powerful monarchs in Denmark and Norway. The Vikings originally came as traders, and as a result learned a great deal about the societies they visited. This made them highly acute at knowing when to attack, choosing feast days when the communities' riches were on display. In addition to simple robbery they demanded protection, took prisoners and even held religious books for ransom, knowing that the faithful would pay to recover the precious texts. All the Christian kingdoms found it hard to defend themselves against the unpredictable assaults of such mobile enemies.

The Vikings' strategic mobility was based upon the vessels known as longships. Surviving examples, comprising ship burials or wrecks, suggest that they varied in size considerably, depending on the numbers of oars they featured. The late 9th-century ship excavated at Gokstad (Norway) is usually taken to be

Above A typical broad-headed axe used by Vikings in combat on both land and sea. Mounted on a handle 1.5 m (5 ft) long, a powerful swing from one of these weapons could remove an enemy's head or limbs, no matter how well-armoured the victim might be.

Below A Viking memorial stone gives a good idea of how warriors were dressed and equipped, and also how the great square sail of the longship carried the raiders far over dangerous seas.

representative of a standard warship. It is 23 m (75 ft) long and shipped thirty-two oars, each with two rowers. Yet the vessel known as Skuldelev 5, dating from *c.* 1000, may be more typical, measuring 18 m (59 ft) long and featuring twenty-four oars. In the 11th century, royal warships were often considerably larger; St Olaf's flagship at the battle of Svold in 1030 had a crew of 100 men – although it may be that more warriors were taken on board when battle was imminent in coastal waters, such as during this encounter. Fleet sizes are also difficult to gauge accurately, since the written accounts of the Vikings' victims may have exaggerated. However, this still meant that forces numbering in the hundreds, and rising to thousands when Viking bands united, were able to roam almost at will in northern waters.

The Vikings' basic strategy was to find an unopposed landing place, often seizing an island as a base. This might be offshore, or could be found by sailing up-river. In France, around 860, Vikings held the island of Jeufosse, just below Paris in the heart of the Carolingian kingdom. In Ireland the fortified sites where the longships were beached were called 'longports' and grew into towns like Dublin, Waterford and Wexford. The subsequent and recent development of Dublin has limited archaeological enquiry, although since the 1980s concerted efforts have been made to recover Viking remains. Fortunately there was no overbuilding on the site of Dunrally Fort (100 km/60 miles up the River Barrow, not far from Kildare), which was excavated in the 1990s. Constructed where the River Glasha entered the Barrow, the longport was 300 m (328 yd) long and defended by a ditch 6 m (20 ft) wide and 2 m (6 ft 6 in.) deep, behind which there was an earthen bank topped by a 2 m (6 ft 6 in.) oak palisade. Inside there was space for twenty to thirty vessels and a citadel surrounded by a similar ditch and a 4 m (13 ft)-high palisade. There was room for as many as 1,000 inhabitants. This made it much larger than the well-excavated site at Repton in Derbyshire (England) built in the winter of 873/74, although a stone-built church formed part of the defences there.

The chronology of the Viking invasions is complex and confusing, not least because there were so many small forces under competing leaders. Until the 840s Ireland suffered most from attack, but the division in 843 of the Carolingian empire between the three heirs of Louis I the Pious (778–840) created an excellent climate for exploitation. In that year a Norwegian fleet established a base at Noirmoutier, in the mouth of the Loire, allowing raiders to strike inland along the river system. In 844 they even reached as far as Toulouse, but most of the attacks were concentrated in the valleys of the Loire and the Seine. Another profitable area for raiding consisted of the trading ports on the Flemish and Frisian coasts. From there it was only a short hop to England, where the offshore Isle of Thanet (Kent) was established as a base in 851. Fleets were also becoming larger; initially numbering only in the tens or twenties, from the 860s onwards groupings of over 100 ships became common. This was also the period of the Great Army, the description given to the large force that invaded England in 865, demonstrating an intention to settle rather than merely raid.

THE GREAT ARMY IN ENGLAND AND FRANCE

Between 865 and 870 the Great Army rode at will throughout the various kingdoms of England. It set up bases, usually for over-wintering, at York (867,

The Oseberg ship, *c. 800*, as she was discovered in 1903. Inside lay the body of a princess – a funerary practice common in pagan times. The ship is nearly 22 m (70 ft) long, with room for 15 pairs of oars.

and between 868 and 869), Nottingham (867–68), Repton (873–74) in Mercia and Thetford in East Anglia (overrun in 869). In 870 its leaders turned their attention to Wessex, winning a great victory at Reading, which became their base. However, Alfred the Great, King of Wessex (r. 871–99), proved able to keep them at bay in a series of nine encounters, during which he twice inflicted significant defeats on the raiders, notably at Ashdown in 871. Eventually, he had to pay tribute to persuade the Vikings to go away. They turned their attention to Mercia, and overran the kingdom in 873. The Great Army returned to Wessex between 875 and 878, setting up a base at Wareham in Dorset, and capturing Exeter, Gloucester and Chippenham. It was from there that it launched an attack during Christmas 877, which completely overwhelmed Alfred's defences and forced him to take refuge in the Somerset marshes. Remarkably, Alfred was able to recover from this setback and defeated the Vikings soundly at Edington (Wiltshire) in June – so soundly that he was able to besiege them at Chippenham and force their leader, Guthrum, to accept a peace treaty. The Great Army then returned to France. This gave Alfred the breathing space he needed to reorganize the defences of

This battle scene comes from the biblical book of the Maccabees, but its representation of 10th-century arms and armour conveys how contemporaries would have understood the defeat of the Magyars by Otto I's East Frankish cavalry.

his kingdom. He made a point of gaining control of London (formerly a Mercian city), and worked on improving his fleet. He built ships that were larger than the Vikings' and manned his fleet with soldiers who were better equipped and motivated by a system of rotation of duties.

The situation on the Continent was much more amenable to the Vikings. The kingdoms of the West and East (German) Franks each had three kings during the 880s, who were often in opposition and keen to pay the Vikings to raid the others' territories. Between 879 and 880 the Vikings ravaged the Low Countries, basing themselves at Ghent in Belgium, then over the next four years, attacked the Rhine Valley, sacked Reims and settled at Amiens. In 884 part of the army returned to England, enabling a combined Frankish force to defeat the remainder at Louvain in 885. But the death of the West Frankish king Carloman allowed the Vikings a free run of the Seine Valley. This was despite the river being blocked by fortified bridges at Pont de l'Arche and Paris itself, to prevent easy communication. In 888 there followed a famous siege of Paris, recorded by its bishop, Abbo. The defenders held out, but had to pay the besiegers to leave.

In 892, the Great Army returned to England. Half of the country, east and north of a frontier running from the Pennines to London, was now under Scandinavian dominance, but Alfred had defended his kingdom well. By establishing a series of fortresses (known as burhs) at strategic locations in Wessex, he was able to restrict the movement of the usually mobile Vikings. First they were pinned to their coastal bases, then, when they did venture inland, they were pursued and harried to prevent them plundering. In 893 Alfred's son Edward defeated the Great Army at Farnham in Hampshire, while Alfred himself relieved the strategically crucial city of Exeter in Devon, which was under siege and blockaded from the sea by the Viking fleet. Vikings still proved capable of taking Chester in the far northwest of England in the autumn, but were unable to stay in Wessex. In 894 they used the rivers Thames and Lea to reach Hertford, but Alfred followed the Frankish model and blocked the Lea with a bridge to contain the raiders. This policy was so successful that the Vikings were forced to disperse to avoid starvation. For the moment their raids were at an end. Alfred died in 899, to be succeeded by Edward the Elder (d. 924).

The Battle of Lechfeld, 955

In July 955 the Magyars under Bulksu launched a major raid into Bavaria. However, they gave up their usual advantage of mobility by besieging Augsburg. Seeing his opportunity, Otto I gathered a small but well-equipped force of heavy cavalry, some 4,000 strong, and sought to offer battle. Fearing the horse-archer tactics of the Hungarians, he gave strict instructions for his order of march to cope with an anticipated ambush, and divided his army into eight divisions for greater flexibility of manoeuvre. He also chose a route of advance through broken country between the rivers Schmutter and Lech, to counteract the Magyars' ability to harass his advancing column with archery fire. As the Frankish force approached Augsburg on 10 August, Bulksu launched an outflanking manoeuvre along the east bank of the River Lech to attack Otto's baggage and the rearguard of Bohemian troops. These were scattered, and the rout spread to the Swabians next in line. The Magyars fell to plundering, allowing Otto to send his Frankish division under Duke Conrad to counterattack and drive them off. Regrouping his forces, Otto then charged the Hungarians to his front. Unable to evade the assault, the more lightly armed horsemen were overrun. Unwilling to flee, Bulksu and his bodyguard were killed or captured.

	EAST FRANCIA	MAGYARS
COMMANDERS	Otto I	Bulksu
STRENGTH	4,000 heavy cavalry 4,000 foot	8,000 light cavalry
CASUALTIES	c. 1,500	c. 2,000 (the rest scattered in flight)

Below The fear induced by nomad raiders is demonstrated in this illustration from the 9th-century Stuttgart Psalter, where the Christian cavalry representing 'Good' overcomes 'Evil' in the shape of horse-archers.

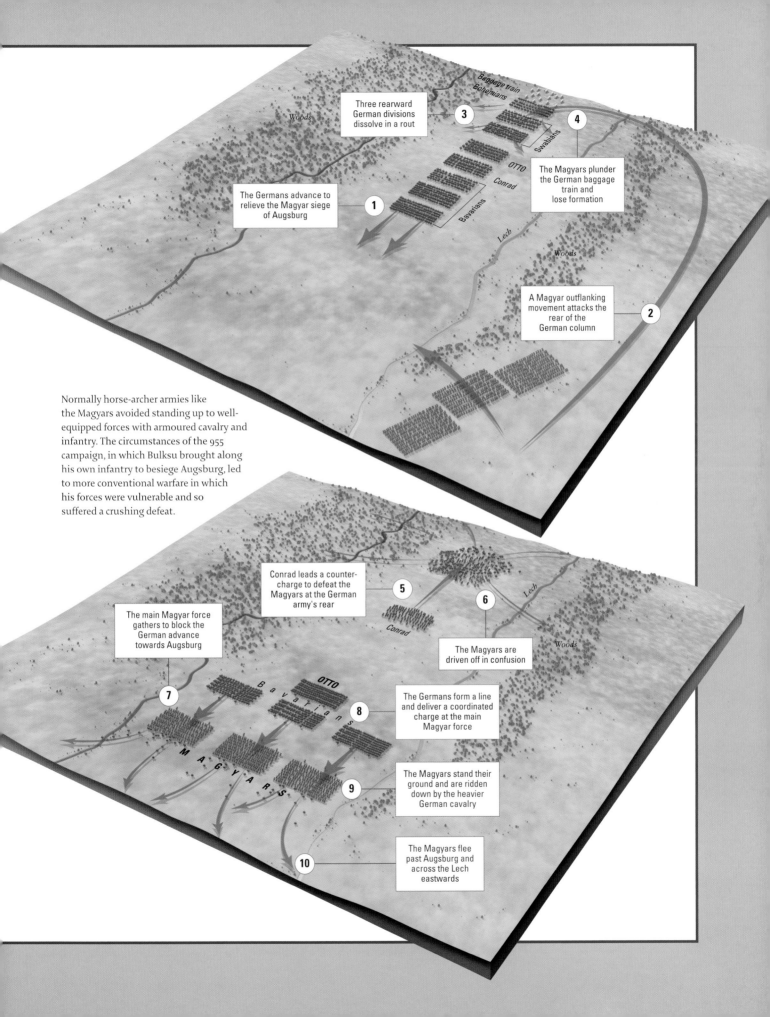

Three rearward German divisions dissolve in a rout

3

Baggage train
Bohemians

4

Woods

Swabians

OTTO

Conrad

The Germans advance to relieve the Magyar siege of Augsburg

1

Bavarians

The Magyars plunder the German baggage train and lose formation

Lech

Woods

A Magyar outflanking movement attacks the rear of the German column

2

Normally horse-archer armies like the Magyars avoided standing up to well-equipped forces with armoured cavalry and infantry. The circumstances of the 955 campaign, in which Bulksu brought along his own infantry to besiege Augsburg, led to more conventional warfare in which his forces were vulnerable and so suffered a crushing defeat.

Conrad leads a counter-charge to defeat the Magyars at the German army's rear

5

6

Lech

The main Magyar force gathers to block the German advance towards Augsburg

Conrad

Woods

7

The Magyars are driven off in confusion

OTTO

Bavarians

The Germans form a line and deliver a coordinated charge at the main Magyar force

8

MAGYARS

The Magyars stand their ground and are ridden down by the heavier German cavalry

9

The Magyars flee past Augsburg and across the Lech eastwards

10

Above The 8th-century Franks Casket from the British Museum provides a rare contemporary depiction of a Viking-style battle-line. The theme of the hero defending his hall is commonly found in Norse saga literature.

Opposite A helmet from the Vendel boat graves in Uppland, Sweden, shows the segmented construction common to this type, together with the eyebrow-band, mask and nose shield. Athough based on a Late Roman model, the animal and human decoration is a distinctive product of the Viking imagination.

THE CREATION OF THE KINGDOM OF ENGLAND

The nature of the conflict now changed to attritional, fortress-based warfare in which Wessex had the upper hand. The heartland of Scandinavian England was York, the area known as the Five Boroughs (Lincoln, Derby, Nottingham, Leicester and Stamford) and East Anglia. Edward of Wessex and Ethelfleda, Lady of the Mercians and daughter of Alfred, now cooperated in campaigns of fortress building and reconquest along the frontier with Danelaw. Burhs were constructed (running south to north) at Hertford (911 and 912), Buckingham (914), Towcester (917), Warwick (914), Tamworth (913), Stafford (913), Thelwall (919) and Manchester (919), together with four more whose locations cannot be identified. They were garrisoned by the king's thegns (retainers), a loyal force that held their lands direct from the king. In 917, after some hard fighting, Edward's campaign in East Anglia brought about the reduction of the Scandinavian burhs and the reconquest of the region. In the following year Leicester submitted to Ethelfleda, who died that year. Edward took over Mercia and soon received the submission of all the Five Boroughs. By 920 Danish settlements as far north as the Humber were seeking English allegiance. Edward died in 924, having effectively created the Kingdom of England, and was succeeded by his son Athelstan (r. 924–39).

Athelstan extended the king's authority further by aggressive campaigning. In 927 he took advantage of the death of the Norse ruler of York to invade that kingdom. Olaf, the young heir, called in support from his uncle Guthfrith, the Viking king of Dublin, but Athelstan defeated them soundly and forced Northumbria to submit. In 934 he demonstrated the range of his growing power by invading Scotland by land and sea. In response, the King of Scots combined with forces of the Dublin Norwegians and Strathclyde Britons to attack deep into England in 937. They were brought to battle and decisively defeated at a place called Brunanburh (the location of which remains uncertain), ending the northern threat. There was a brief revival by Olaf of York following Athelstan's death, during which he recovered both his independence and the Five Boroughs. However, the next English king, Edmund I (r. 939–46), reconquered these territories, forcing York to submit in 944 and invading Strathclyde the following year. Viking raids did not resume until the 980s, by which stage they heralded a much more serious invasion.

This 10th-century Byzantine ivory plaque depicts soldiers around the imperial throne. The shoulder harness was designed to take the weight of the armour. Most of the soldiers wear infantry equipment, but the two messenger figures entering from the right probably represent cavalrymen.

BYZANTIUM: DECLINE AND RECOVERY

After 800, Muslim conquests of the Byzantine empire's Mediterranean possessions continued, with both Crete and Sicily being lost in the 820s. Three imperial expeditions were sent to recover Crete between 827 and 829, with another by the government of Michael III (842–67) following in 843; all failed. Perhaps as a result, the Byzantine navy underwent a revival in the 850s, under the direction of the regent Bardas, its fleet twice raiding Damietta in the Nile mouth, destroying vessels and supplies intended to support the Muslims on Crete.

The civil war that followed the death of the Abbasid caliph al-Mu'tasim ibn Harun in 842 meant that on land the main threat to the Byzantines no longer came from caliphal armies, but from border emirs like Omar, Emir of Melitene (Malatya, eastern Turkey). Supported by the Paulicians (a heretical group), his troops defeated an imperial army in 861 and then invaded the Armeniakon province south of the Black Sea, sacking Amisos. Meanwhile, the Emir of Tarsus led another force northwards through the Cilician Gates. This brushed aside a smaller Byzantine force and advanced to join Omar's troops on the River Halys, creating a combined army of over 15,000 men. The Byzantine general Petronas had been shadowing their advances throughout, and coordinated an attack to surround the invaders. He commanded four units of the *tagmata* (palace troops), together with three bodies of European *themata* (provincial) soldiers, and was joined by other troops from south of the Taurus Mountains and also from the northeastern Armenian territories of the empire. Although actual numbers are unknown, this constituted a formidable army up to 50,000 strong. Omar spurned an opportunity to escape with his force and, as a result,

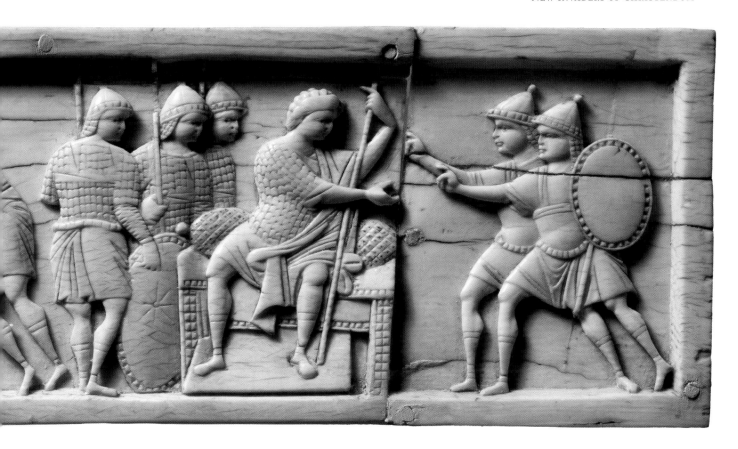

was massacred along with them. Such victories were hard won, but played a significant part in shifting the strategic balance in favour of Byzantium.

The Byzantine revival between 850 and 1025 was made possible by the strategic reorganizations that had been taking place over the previous two centuries. The abandonment of fixed frontiers had thrown regions and localities back upon their own resources, a fact that was recognized by the creation of the *themata* system. Effectively this meant that imperial provinces were grouped together under the protection of a field army (or naval forces on the coast), under the command of a *strategos* (general). Although the *themata* dispositions served the empire well, they were essentially defensive, and they changed over time as Byzantium recovered its strength in comparison to the surrounding powers.

BYZANTIUM AND THE RUS'

The origins of the Rus' people probably date back to the establishment of raider/trader bases in the eastern Baltic lands in the mid-8th century by Scandinavian Vikings, one example being Staraia Ladoga just north of Lake Ladoga. In 838, possibly associated with a raid on northern Asia Minor, a Rus' embassy appeared at Constantinople, representing an unnamed emperor as their ruler. By 860 Novgorod had become the Rus' capital of their semi-legendary leader Rurik. Around the same time, Askold and Dir, two of Rurik's men, seized Kiev. In the same year, a surprise raid on Constantinople supposedly featuring 200 ships rocked the Byzantines; unexpectedly, the Vikings had sailed and carried their craft down the River Dnieper. Around 882 Kiev became the capital of an expanding realm that had advanced almost as far as the Black Sea, and posed a real threat to Byzantium. The Rus' were also in competition with the still powerful nomadic forces of the Khazars and the Volgar Bulgars.

In the 890s the strategic assessment of the Rus' threat by the Byzantine emperor Leo VI (866–912), published in his *Tactica*, was that they were restricted to light craft because of their need to move along rivers. Yet in 907 Prince Oleg of Kiev launched an attack on Constantinople with a large fleet and supported by Slav allies. Although its formidable walls protected the city once again, the Byzantines were shaken enough to make a treaty in 911, and even employ some of the Scandinavians in the imperial guard – the origin of the famous Varangian regiment. In 941 Prince Igor of Kiev launched another naval expedition against Constantinople. Unprepared for this attack, with his fleet and army elsewhere, the emperor Romanus Lecapenus (r. 920–44) had only a few vessels with which to defend the capital. However, these were provided with the Byzantines' secret weapon known as 'Greek fire', a kind of napalm that could be projected by siphons from their ships' prows. The Rus' were caught completely unawares and were driven off, resorting to raiding along the southern shore of the Black Sea, before they were hunted down by the recalled fleet and destroyed. In 944 Igor tried again, creating such a formidable alliance with Pecheneg tribes that Romanus was forced to buy him off.

As the Kievan Rus' became more centrally organized, their ruler Sviatoslav I (c. 945–72) was able to launch an expedition against the formerly powerful Khazars, forcing them to submit. Sviatoslav seems to have envisaged an empire stretching from the Baltic to the Balkans, and he extended his rule over the lower Danube. But in 970 he abandoned his efforts to conquer the Bulgars and turned his attention to the Eurasian steppe lands between the rivers Don and Volga and the Caspian and Black seas. Once again he was successful against the Khazars, besieging and

The beautifully illustrated History of John Skylitzes manuscript is a product of the 11th century but depicts scenes from earlier Byzantine military history. Here, Muslims besiege Constantinople.

Above A funerary scene from the imperial palace features the famous Varangian regiment, recruited from Vikings and Rus' in attendance, many carrying double-handed axes.

Below On more than one occasion Constantinople was saved from naval attack by the Byzantines' 'secret weapon', known as 'Greek fire'. This naphtha-based liquid was projected through a siphon, just like a modern flamethrower.

taking the fortress of Sarkel and sacking and destroying Itil on the Caspian coast, ending Khazar power. Retiring via the Crimea to the Danube lands, Sviatoslav invaded the Byzantine empire, sacking Philippopolis (Thrace) and advancing as far as Adrianople (Edirne, Thrace), within striking distance of the Byzantine capital.

Emperor John I Tzimiskes (r. 969–76) gathered a large army of 30,000 men to oppose the Rus', who may have mustered similar numbers. Sviatoslov's ability to acquire nomad horse-archer allies, who could operate around his core of heavy infantry, made the Rus' a huge threat. The ambush delivered by Byzantine general Bardas Skleros at Arkadiopolis against the Pechenegs in Sviatoslav's force in 970 bought a crucial breathing space for the empire. John went over to the offensive in the following campaigning season and challenged the Rus' in open battle. Sviatoslav chose to defend the fortress of Dorostolon (modern Drista) on the south bank of the river. The defection of his Bulgar subjects had left Sviatoslav without an effective cavalry, yet he was still confident enough to offer battle outside the walls. After three days of fighting the Russians were completely overwhelmed and Sviatoslav had to beg for terms. He was allowed to return home, on the basis of a new trade agreement, but he never made it. As he crossed the Dnieper he fell into a Pecheneg ambush, and was killed along with all his men; his skull was turned into a drinking vessel. The Pechenegs were the new power on the Eurasian steppe, and their aggressive activities had pushed the Magyars westwards from the 860s onwards – a move that would have disastrous consequences for the Frankish kingdoms.

> '*They prefer battles at long range, ambushes, encircling their adversaries, simulated retreats and sudden returns.... When they make their enemies take to flight…they do not let up until they have achieved complete destruction, and employ every means to this end.*'
>
> A Byzantine author on Magyar tactics

MAGYAR RAIDS AND THE CREATION OF HUNGARY

The Magyars established themselves in much the same area as the Avars had occupied up until a century earlier, which in the meantime had been lightly colonized by the Bulgars. Nomadic steppe peoples depended on livestock for their livelihoods and horses for war, and thus required vast tracts of grazing land. This was not to be found further west than the great grasslands known to the Romans as Pannonia (western Hungary). Rather confusingly, because the Magyars were seen as Huns by their Christian enemies, their territories became known as Hungary. Their national creation myth speaks of seven tribes, each with their own chief, but little is known about their early history.

What we do know is how devastating the Magyar attacks were. These took the form of thirty major raids between 898 and 955. Although lightly equipped and incapable of conducting sieges, the rapidity of their movement and rapacity of their actions inflicted great damage, taking booty and slaves and destroying agricultural land. East Francia (Germany) lacked the urban centres found further west and in Italy, and was thus especially vulnerable. Bavaria was ravaged in 900 and Saxony in 906. Between 907 and 910, three Frankish armies attempted to oppose the Magyars, but were defeated, allowing the Magyars to ravage freely. The first attack on Italy took place in 899; a great raid in 936 took the Magyars as far south as Benevento. Raids into France reached

'The Rus' are not accustomed to give in, but would rather die in battle and go to Valhalla.'

Sviatoslav I, ruler of Kiev, at the battle of Dorostolon, 971

westward as far as the Loire, and southward to Nîmes in 924, while Burgundy was regularly pillaged.

The Frankish response was led by the rulers of Germany. Under Henry I 'the Fowler' (r. 919–36) and his son Otto I (r. 936–73), this disparate realm was united and expanded. In 933 a Magyar attack into Saxony was checked at Riade, which signalled the end of their activities there. Henry's strategy was similar to Alfred's in England: construction of fortresses to constrain the raiders' axes of movement, combined with counterattacks by troops of increasingly well-equipped horsemen. In 950 Otto conducted a campaign on Hungarian territory for the first time, dealing out the same kind of punishment as his subjects had been receiving. Four years later a Magyar leader called Bulksu led what turned out to be the last great raid westward. As on earlier occasions, he sought to take advantage of dissension within Germany (Otto's son had rebelled against him in the previous year). When the Magyars returned in 955, they found order restored and a formidable army raised against them. In 933 it was the armoured cavalry that had been credited with the victory, and in the succeeding decades Otto had concentrated in building up this force. One late-10th-century record indicates that the emperor claimed over 2,000 heavy cavalry from the counts and bishops of the southern part of his realm – Otto may have fielded twice as many in 955. Another crucial factor was discipline, for a headlong cavalry charge into a milling mass of horse-archers begged disaster.

Two ivory plaques from the 10th–12th century, showing nomadic horsemen, probably Pechenegs. The right-hand figure is using the 'Parthian shot'.

Invaders of Christendom

The Vikings (a) are best characterized as raider–traders for whom fighting was only one option. Although principally known as sailors, during land campaigns they rode horses to increase their manoeuvrability. Mail coats were hugely expensive items worn only by the wealthiest men. All warriors carried shields, spears or axes and swords when they could afford them. Contrary to myth, helmets were mostly simple bowl shapes, often with a nasal or facemask, a form that originated in far away Sassanid Persia. Horns were only worn on the headdress of shamans.

Islam began in the Arabian Peninsula, but most of the warriors in its armies were not Arabs. Those fighting the Byzantines in Syria probably did wear the Arab-style headcloths and long robes, whereas the invaders of Spain and France were mostly Berbers from the North African Mediterranean coast. Although the 8th-century armies are usually represented as light cavalrymen, the raiders defeated at Tours in 732 would have had a large infantry component (b). Like the Vikings they often stole horses to facilitate more rapid movement.

The Magyars (c) were truly nomadic warriors. Each initially owned a string of horses, which enabled him to fight a fully mobile campaign. Both man and horse were lavishly decorated with precious metals – as nomads, they carried their wealth with them. The Magyars practised the horse-archer tactic of the feigned flight and the rearward facing 'Parthian shot'. By the time of the battle of Lechfeld (955), Magyar cavalry wore armour and were accompanied by an infantry force for the purpose of conducting sieges. In adopting a more conventional style of warfare, however, they made themselves more vulnerable to defeat by the Ottonian German cavalry.

Byzantine cataphracts (d) were heavily armoured cavalrymen, a super-heavy troop type with armour for man and horse that rendered them almost invulnerable to missiles and hand weapons. Even at the height of the empire the state found it difficult to afford the equipment for such men. There were barely 1,000 of them at the battle of Dorostolon (971), yet they provided the decisive blow that defeated the Rus'.

At the battle of Lechfeld that year, Otto's preparations paid off. Marching to relieve the Magyar siege of Augsburg, his force was ambushed, but the Germans proved able to stand up to the Hungarians' horse-archer tactics (see box on pp. 68–69). Otto ordered the Bavarian vanguard to charge at a measured pace and close together, smashing the Magyar line. Unusually, the best-equipped warriors surrounding their leaders stood to fight, instead of taking refuge in flight, and were thus cut down. Otto hanged the prisoners taken, a tactic which decapitated Magyar rule and resulted in two decades of peace on that front. Defeat encouraged the Magyars to take up a more sedentary existence. Their gradual conversion to Christianity and the creation of the kingdom of Hungary under King Stephen I in the early 11th century meant that they had effectively been tamed.

THE DANISH CONQUEST OF ENGLAND

Although the Kingdom of England was far stronger by 980 than it had been a century earlier, it was still a rich target for Viking raids. From across the Irish Sea there came attacks by the Norse settlements in Ireland and on the Isle of Man. In that year Chester was sacked, Anglesey and north Wales were ravaged and raids reached around the coast as far as Southampton. Another great raid in 988 devastated southern Wales and penetrated up the Bristol Channel, although the Vikings were defeated in battle in Somerset. In 991 a fleet of almost 100 ships attacked East Anglia, providing a reminder that the greatest threat still came from across the North Sea. The ealdorman (alderman) Byrhtnoth, responsible for the defence of Essex, challenged the Vikings to battle at Maldon, where they had made an island base. He was killed and his army routed, a signal to the Vikings that England was vulnerable again.

In 994 Swein Forkbeard, King of Denmark, and Olaf, the future king of Norway, led reinforcements into the Thames and launched an attack on London. This was repelled and the leaders returned to Scandinavia, but the Vikings continued to raid along the south coast throughout the 990s. Lacking bases in England, they overwintered in Normandy, originally a Viking state and still sympathetic to the Scandinavian raiders. England was a rich kingdom, but it proved unable to defend itself against this new wave of attacks. Ethelred II 'the Unready' (r. 978–1013, and again 1014–16) resorted to paying tribute. However, although the Danegeld ('Danish tax') bought some respite, it did not prevent the Vikings from returning. In 999 they landed at Sheppey in Kent, defeated an English army at Rochester and, seizing horses to improve their mobility, devastated the southeast. Two years later serious attacks took place along the south coast from Hampshire to Devon. In 1004 a force invaded East Anglia, taking Norwich and Thetford.

Ethelred and his government did not stand idly by, though. In 1001, in order to form diplomatic links with Normandy, he married Emma, the daughter of Duke Richard II. In 1009, the Anglo-Saxon Chronicle asserts, enough money was raised through emergency taxation to construct a large fleet and equip 8,000 men in armour. However, a storm destroyed the fleet, and the English commanders appeared unable to bring the Danes to battle. In the same year the Vikings' chief leader was Thorkell the Tall, who seized the Isle of Wight as a base. In 1010 he moved to Essex, and raided Oxford early the same year. In April he attacked East Anglia, defeating English forces at Ringmer (near Norwich); Viking forces also

Opposite A representation, from the Life of St Aubin, *c.* 1100, of a seaborne invasion shows armoured men crammed into a ship in a purely symbolic manner; but the arms and armour are accurately represented for the Norman invasion period.

sacked Thetford and Cambridge. Towards the end of the year Thorkell's bands again raided westward via Northampton, which was sacked, returning via the Thames Valley. In the circumstances the English government did the only thing possible: it hired him – a highly pragmatic solution to the threat posed. Thorkell served Ethelred loyally for a short time, repelling a Danish attack on London in 1013. However, King Swein returned in 1013, and conducted a campaign that was at the same time a royal progress through the southern and midland shires, taking the submission of Winchester (the capital of Wessex), Oxford and Bath and advancing as far as Lincoln; only London held out against Swein. According to the Anglo-Saxon Chronicle, 'all the nation regarded him as full king'. Ethelred fled with his family to Normandy.

Swein died in early 1014, and the Danes elected his son Cnut as his successor. King Ethelred returned, and it seemed for a time as if the English cause would survive. His son Edmund 'Ironside' took charge of operations, but Cnut now had the support of Edric Streona, ealdorman of Saxon Mercia, and Thorkell. Ethelred died in April 1016, and London had to resist another intense siege. Edmund, who was based in the southwest, went over to the offensive. He chose a battle-seeking strategy, which produced success in two close-fought encounters around Bath, and enabled him to advance to London in the summer, where he defeated Cnut at Brentford. In October 1016, however, Edmund was defeated at Ashingdon in Essex and mortally wounded. Now leaderless, London was forced to submit, and opposition to Cnut ended. There was nothing inevitable about this result, however. Contemporary English commentators blamed Ethelred's poor leadership and the defection of notable Englishmen, such as Edric Streona. Even then it took the Danes fifteen years to conquer England.

Cnut proved himself to be a highly successful ruler of a North Sea empire, and England remained of key importance to his realm. He married Emma, Ethelred's widow, by whom he had a son, Harthacnut (1018–42), who came to the English throne in 1040 and invited his half-brother Edward 'the Confessor' (*c.* 1003–66), son of Ethelred, to return from exile in Normandy. When the young Danish king died unexpectedly in 1042, Edward succeeded him and the old English line was restored. Edward had no heir, however, and on his death in 1066 the crown was seized by Harold Godwinson (*c.* 1022–66), Earl of Wessex, but disputed by his brother Tostig Godwinson (in exile in Flanders), William, Duke of Normandy, and King Harald Sigurdsson of Norway – which resulted in three separate invasions that year.

THE LAST 'VIKING' INVASIONS

Tostig attacked first, in the spring, making landings on the south coast and in Kent. However, he failed to raise enough support for his cause, and after sailing north up the east coast, suffered a repulse and fled to the court of Malcolm Canmore, King of Scots. Meanwhile, in Normandy Duke William was raising a fleet and recruiting soldiers from far and wide to join his attempt. He collected his forces at Dives-sur-Mer, but made no attempt to cross the Channel until late in the summer. This is probably because he was waiting for King Harold to stand down his fleet and coastal garrison, which took place after their customary two months of service on 8 September. As soon as he heard the news, William set sail (12 September), only to

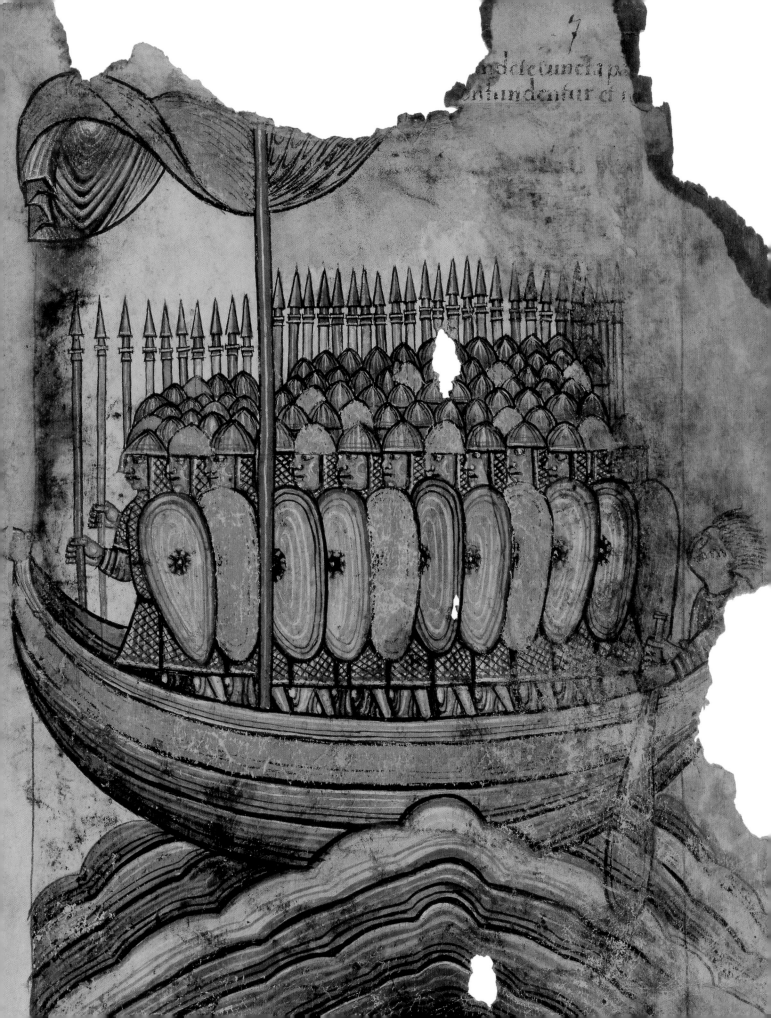

hARO L D REX INTERFEC TVS EST

Above A carved frieze from above a doorway from the church of St Nicholas of Bari, southern Italy (*c.* 1100), shows Norman knights riding off to war, in a style that matches the Bayeux Tapestry.

Opposite The decisive moment of the battle of Hastings, 14 October 1066, as depicted on the Bayeux Tapestry. After fighting all day long the English are overwhelmed by a shower of arrows, one of which strikes King Harold in the eye, and by the final Norman cavalry charge.

encounter a storm that almost wrecked his fleet and drove it into the mouth of the River Somme. Here it was wind-bound for a fortnight, but in fact this worked in William's favour, for during this time Harald Sigurdsson of Norway launched his attack on York, where Tostig joined him. After an initial success against the northern levies at Fulford Gate (20 September), the invaders were surprised and slaughtered at Stamford Bridge (25 September) by King Harold, who had marched up swiftly from the south. This meant that William was able to cross the Channel on the night of 27/28 September unopposed, as the storm that had delayed his fleet had scattered the English one and the English land forces were 480 km (300 miles) to the north. In many ways, William's strategy matched that of his Viking ancestors. He established a base at Hastings on the Sussex coast and awaited Harold's response. Perhaps made over-confident by his success against the Norwegians, Harold rushed south and into battle with William without waiting to collect more than a third of his available forces. The battle was a close-run thing, but ended with Harold's death, resulting in the second conquest of England in fifty years. It took William five years to secure his crown, and he continued to fear Danish attacks for the rest of his reign. Domesday Book, a record of the kingdom's wealth compiled in 1086, was the direct product of a Danish invasion threat the previous year, as the king sought to identify all the available resources with which to defend his realm. The last real Viking attack on England took place in 1098, when Magnus III of Norway (r. 1093–1103) landed in Cheshire and dispersed the local levies, killing the Norman earl of Chester. The age of invasions was by now over, and the next Norwegian king, Sigurd I (r. 1103–30), opted to crusade in the Holy Land instead, matching a wider shift of military priorities for Christian rulers.

So it was that the original attackers of Christianity had become its propagators. The newly Christianized rulers of Scandinavia became fervent supporters of the Northern Crusades. In Hungary, King Stephen I (r. 1001–38) became both the founder of the kingdom and its first saint. Hungary was to be a frontier state of increasing significance throughout the medieval period, especially as Byzantine power waned from 1200 onwards. The global strategic stage was set for a conflict between the Islamic world, spreading from Spain to India, and a newly self-confident and aggressive Latin Christendom. The era of the Crusades was dawning.

4 The Revival of Latin Christendom and the Crusades in the East, 1050–1250

Opposite A heavily armed 13th-century French knight.
Right Crusaders fought to save their souls, so this knight in full armour kneels humbly in prayer.

By 900, the Mediterranean – once the great highway of the Roman empire – was a frontier zone where three civilizations faced one another. The greatest of these was the Islamic world ruled by the caliphs, the most important of which was the Abbasid dynasty, which claimed descent from Muhammad himself. Its capital Baghdad was a fabulously rich city of a million people, and the focus of an empire extending from north India to Spain. Its merchants traded with China, India and the Spice Islands, and it dominated the slave trade of west and east Africa. The oldest civilization of the three was Byzantium, the eastern remnant of the old Roman empire. It dominated Greece, the Balkans and Anatolia and was ruled from Constantinople, a great trading city of 200,000 people. The poorest of this triad was western Europe, where the Roman empire had been replaced by a warring patchwork of petty states whose aristocratic leaders only minimally obeyed those who claimed the title of king. However, what gave western Europe a degree of unity was a common religion, whose supreme authority was the Pope in Rome, and the Latin culture that the church upheld.

THE SITUATION IN WESTERN EUROPE

In western Europe the economy was based around agriculture, standards of living were low in material terms and cities were rare – except in Italy, where Venice with its population of around 10,000 was perhaps the largest. Its constituent states were challenged from all sides – by the Vikings in the north, the Slavs and Hungarians in the east and the forces of Islam in the south. However, such enemies found western Europeans to be tenacious adversaries. In Byzantium and the Islamic territories the aristocrats held land, but both of these ran money economies in which the government collected taxes and provided salaries and patronage, which were far more important to the aristocrats' status. In contrast, in western Europe the aristocratic elite relied purely on land for wealth and status, so that they had no option except to defend it against external enemies and local rivals alike.

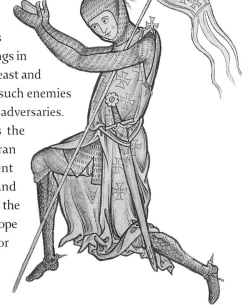

The crusader states on the eve of the battle of Hattin (1187). Although much territory had been lost in the north, the settlements had by this time achieved a degree of stability. The balance of power was radically altered by the union of Syria and Egypt in the 1170s under Saladin.

When European kings failed to provide strong leadership, local warlords stepped in. The result was a highly militarized ruling elite devoted to the warrior ethic. They lived in fortified houses, usually called castles, and recruited knights as their soldiers and administrators. Aristocratic families colonized the Church and even the monasteries, so that ecclesiastical leadership, while vowed to the service of the 'Prince of Peace', shared, or at least were familiar with, the military virtues of the families from which they were drawn. These elites depended so greatly on the land for their wealth and status that they pressed hard upon the peasantry, who were forced to develop more efficient farming systems to satisfy their masters. As a result, western European agriculture became highly progressive and yielded a relatively substantial surplus. In time, these aristocratic leaders began to desire goods that were not local, especially iron for weapons and tools, and thus fostered trade relations. They coveted luxuries from the east – spices, silk and jewels – which were brought in through Italian cities such as Pisa, Genoa and Venice. The process of political fragmentation had allowed such cities to develop as their merchants saw fit, freeing them from the restraints of autocratic rulers. By about 1000, as the external threats were driven back, the high

'Among the Franks – God damn them! – no quality is more highly esteemed in a man than military prowess.... No one else has any prestige in their eyes. They are the men who give counsel, pass judgement and command armies.'
Usama, an Arab from Shaizar, on the importance of knights among the Franks

Above After the Second Crusade the land journey to the east became extremely dangerous, so, despite a widespread fear of the sea, crusaders were compelled to travel in ships, usually provided by the Italian city-states.

Right A crusader sword of the 12th century, just under a metre long. These were finely balanced slashing weapons, symbolic both of knightly prowess and, because of their cross-shaped hilts, of the crusading mission.

productivity of European agriculture had brought about economic expansion and increased political stabilization in this developing society.

THE WESTERN WAY OF WAR

Western Europe was rich in iron, and the techniques of working it were well known, but it was still very expensive. As a result, relatively few (namely the land-owning aristocrats and their knights) had sufficient wealth to own a broad range of the armour and weapons described here. Hauberks were mail shirts extending down to the knee, made of upwards of 15,000 interlocking iron rings, and usually worn over a padded undergarment. Mail provided good protection and did not make excessive demands on the limited metallurgical technology of the period up until the 13th century, which made working with plate difficult. Helmets tended to be pointed iron frameworks into which small triangular plates were fitted. The sword was a cutting weapon, about 80 cm (30.5 in.) long, and being made of fine steel was expensive.

Those who could afford such equipment gradually evolved techniques of fighting on horseback with it. However, suitable horses were also expensive. By 1200 a good warhorse could cost 80 shillings (approximately £5,000 in today's money), while even a riding animal was worth 10 shillings (£600) – by contrast an ox could be bought for between 10 and 13 shillings (£600–£800). European agriculture was based on cereal monoculture, the cultivation of grain across vast areas of the continent. Wherever possible wheat was grown, but even poorer and colder zones were made to yield oats and rye. Upland areas bred cattle and sheep whose meat, leather and wool were valuable. There was, therefore, no room in Europe for the light horse, which in any case could not carry a man and so much metal. So, in Europe warhorses were heavy, stall-fed animals, capable of high speed only over a short distance. Few could afford many mounts to compensate for these limitations.

Opposite Weapons and chain mail armour being prepared for battle in a scene from the Bayeux Tapestry. But note the barrel of wine: provisioning armies with food and drink was as important as arming them.

Cavalry could not fight alone, of course. The infantry were drawn from the more adventurous among the peasant masses, led by a few specialists. Their basic weapon was the spear, but only a few of them would have had shields and iron caps. Many of them were archers and a very few had crossbows, which could pierce any kind of armour. Given that the European landscape was cut by rivers and divided by mountains – terrain in which cavalry was not always at its most effective – such troops were essential. It was an eternal wisdom that cavalry should never risk a frontal assault upon well-formed infantry. But the great limitation was that Europe was too poor to afford standing armies. This meant that peasant masses lacked training and cohesion, which in turn made the infantry less effective. Furthermore, knights lived very local lives around the castles they garrisoned for their masters, so although they were individually well trained and worked well with those they knew, they were not used to working in larger armies. Since commanders were fully aware of the risks of battle, they were usually reluctant to risk such incoherent armies in what might be a chance affair.

This reticence was reinforced by the presence of castles, which dominated the land in Europe. They could serve as refuges for defeated forces – meaning that victory in battle might only lead to the next siege. If land was to be held, capturing castles was essential, and since this was labour intensive any ambitious ruler needed plenty of infantry. It also helped to have engineers, although they were a rare commodity. Many castles were wood and earthwork structures. Ditches and banks in castles were formidable obstacles that required great effort to overcome. We know that William the Conqueror (1027–87) brought a prefabricated tower with him to England in 1066. Besieging archers would keep the garrison pinned down while others mounted ladders to climb over the walls. The archers sometimes carried light wooden panels to give them shelter, and at others sheltered within heavier sheds on wheels, called 'cats'. These could be reinforced and pushed up to the walls to cover battering and picking at the foundations. Deep mines could be dug to create a chamber under the foundations of the wall, supported by props that were later set on fire, causing it to collapse. 'Cats' were sometimes developed into towers on wheels, which would be used to dominate the walls. Another siege machine was the traction trebuchet, a form of catapult that could cast a missile weighing 22.5 kg (50 lbs)

Right The basic protective armour of a knight was the hauberk, a shirt made of iron rings, usually worn over a padded undergarment.

Opposite An illuminated manuscript from Baghdad, dating to 1237, showing the standard bearers of the caliph. Even on the First Crusade the valour of their enemies excited the admiration of the crusaders. An anonymous knight exclaimed: 'What man, however experienced and learned, would dare to write of the skill and prowess and courage of the Turks ... you could not find stronger or braver soldiers.'

up to 120 m (400 ft); leverage was provided by the pulling power of a team of men, as opposed to a counterweight used in later designs. In a siege the defenders enjoyed the advantage of fighting behind fixed defences as well as shelter from the elements. The attackers had to create their own and they also had to find food. The difficulties of siege and the risks of battle meant that invading armies usually waged war by ravaging – which fed their own army and damaged the economic basis of the enemy.

THE EASTERN WAY OF WAR

The great caliphate at Baghdad created a composite army made up of the many peoples over whom it ruled, gathered at need around a professional core that was funded by taxation. We know that Islamic armies were familiar with siege warfare and its machinery; indeed, the trebuchet was a Chinese invention transmitted to the west via Islamic armies.

The Turks of Central Asia were a key element in the caliph's standing army. They were superb light horsemen whose way of life depended on herding and hunting on the steppe; as a result, each man kept a string of horses. On the battlefield they provided long-range movement and sustained speed. Their weapon was the composite bow, whose wooden core was strengthened by layers of bone and sinew,

Right A fragment of a 12th-century Egyptian drawing, showing cavalry attacking a crusader fortress. Taking and holding fortified cities and castles was vital to both sides.

Opposite This 12th-century French map of Jerusalem shows very schematically the main religious sites of the city, which pilgrims came to see. But the portrayal of Christian knights putting the infidel to flight was a reminder of the city's precarious position.

giving it enormous strength and penetrative power. Turkish soldiers became involved with the court factions, whose struggles had, by 1000, reduced the caliph to a nominal ruler and enabled several provinces to break away. Many steppe Turks were converted to Islam, and in 1055 a group led by the Seljuq family invaded the Middle East, leading to the creation of an empire headed by a sultan in Baghdad, who ruled in the name of the caliph. Their way of war depended on fast manoeuvre by horse-archers, whose arrow fire harassed and broke up enemy formations, before engaging in close-quarter battle. Such troops were backed up by heavily armed Persian horsemen, Bedouin light horse and Daylami infantry from the Caspian shore.

The Turks were an alien presence, and this is very evident from the citadels they built in cities such as Damascus in order to overawe the native Arab populations. Other Turks took advantage of the internal problems of the Byzantine empire to defeat its armies at the battle of Manzikert in 1071, and to conquer Anatolia. To overcome their isolation from the native Islamic peoples on whom they depended for tax revenue, the Turks rallied orthodox Sunni opinion for war against the rival Fatimid caliphate of Egypt, which had been established in Cairo in 969.

THE FIRST CRUSADE (1096–99)

The aristocracy of western Europe were devout Christians, whose faith was founded on the terrible fear of hellfire. However, there was clearly a gap between such precepts and their militarized way of life. For example, Fulk Nerra, Count of Anjou (r. 987–1040), had a reputation for great brutality, yet he went on pilgrimage three times to Jerusalem and founded the great abbey of Beaulieu-lès-Loches in central France. The Church was also penetrated by military values and ambition, this time of the papacy, which sought to make good its claim to be a universal directing force in Christendom – as demonstrated by its great quarrel with the German emperors from 1076. The weakness of the papacy lay in its lack of an army, and its claim to universal authority was cast into doubt by eastern Christians, who instead preferred the leadership of a universal council.

Below Gold coin of the emperor Alexius I Comnenus.

During the reign of Pope Urban II (r. 1088–99) events in the east offered a solution to those feeling the tension between heavenly hope and earthly inclination. By 1094 the Seljuq empire had begun to dissolve in a series of wars of succession. The Byzantine emperor Alexius I Comnenus (r. 1081–1118) saw in this an opportunity to recover Asia Minor, but he lacked troops, and so in 1095 he appealed to Urban II for military aid. In return, Urban demanded recognition of his universal authority. Urban understood the mentality of the warrior aristocrats, having been born amongst them. In November 1095, at the Council of Clermont, he appealed for a great expedition to liberate Jerusalem from Islamic rule and to help the Christians of the east. Urban's appeal allowed men to believe that they could find salvation through slaughter. He demanded that 'reputation or monetary gain' should not be the purpose of the journey to the Holy Land, but he did not prohibit participants from profiting; righteous war offered rightful gains. Helping the Christians of the east found some resonance with westerners, who were keenly aware of the menace of Islam in the Iberian Peninsula. Five main armies and many smaller forces were mustered, and marched to rendezvous at Constantinople under the authority of the papal legate Adhemar of Le Puy. The First Crusade had been launched.

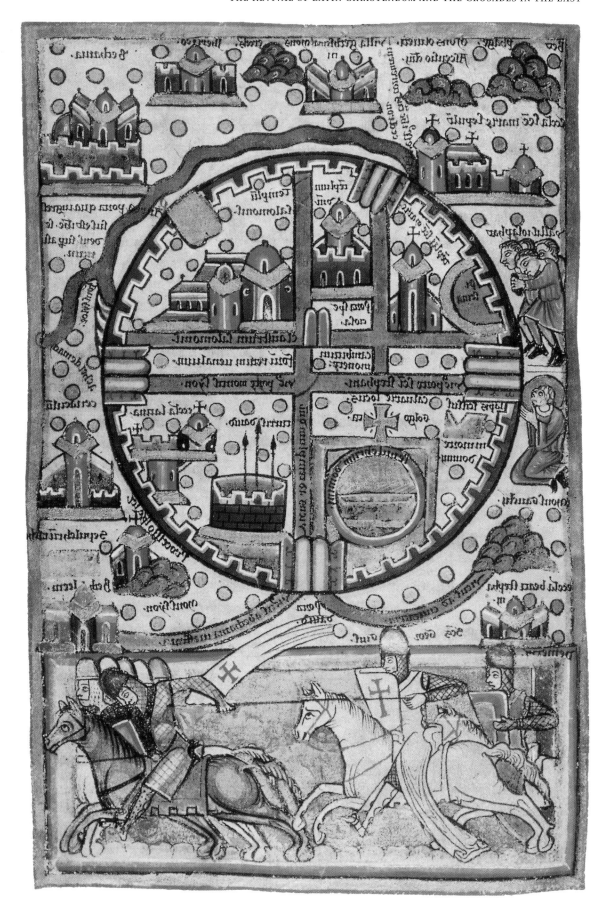

Crusaders bombarding the city of Nicea, from a 13th-century French illuminated manuscript. We know that catapults were used to hurl the heads of dead enemies into the city.

The crusade took the form of an alliance, in which the Byzantine emperor Alexius promised military, naval and logistical support in return for receiving back former Byzantine territories. It was probably through his agency that the crusaders came to an agreement with the Fatimids of Egypt and exploited the presence of strong Christian minorities in the Middle East, such as the Armenians. The campaign turned upon a series of sieges of great cities, which anchored the states of the east. Nicea (Iznik in Turkey), the capital of the sultanate of Rum, had formidable Roman defences, consisting of a wall 10 m (33 ft) high and 4,970 m (16,300 ft) in circumference. It was studded with 114 towers and protected by a double ditch, and its east end abutted Lake Ascania. The first crusader armies reached Nicea on 6 May 1097, but the biggest single force of the Count of Toulouse arrived ten days later, and just in time to repulse an attempt by the sultan to reinforce the garrison. The city was attacked by several 'cats' and trebuchets, and mines were dug. One large siege engine was brought up against the wall, but collapsed when the enemy dropped stones upon it, killing twenty knights. The crusader assault suffered from poor co-ordination between and within the five major armies present. The northern French forces arrived on 14 June, but ultimately it was the presence of Byzantine boats on the lake that

> '*In the Temple and Porch of Solomon, men rode in blood up to their knees and bridle reins. Indeed it was a just and splendid judgement of God that this place should be filled with the blood of unbelievers, since it had suffered so long from their blasphemies.*'
>
> Raymond of Aguilers on the slaughter on the Temple Mount after the fall of Jerusalem, 1099

en celui champ. Dont il
avint q̃ les grec qui te.r̃
notent la cite dantioche
furent mlt espouetes ⁊ re

abatui̇ret les murs iusq̃s
as fundemēs ne onq̃s puis
ne fu habitee cele cite. De
la se partiret ⁊ uindrent

Above The savage fighting of crusader warfare is vividly apparent in this contemporary illustration of fighting during the siege of Antioch (1097–98).

Right The citadel of Antioch, now in ruins, was rebuilt by the crusaders.

Siege towers to overtop the walls of the city were a vital part of the assault on Jerusalem in 1099. This illustration comes from William Tyre's 14th-century *History of Jerusalem*.

isolated the city and forced its surrender on 19 June. The secret terms of the negotiations prevented a crusader sack of the city, which caused many of the crusaders to be suspicious of their Byzantine allies.

The plethora of peoples and princes present in the crusader army mean that it was managed by committee. While this achieved success during the siege of Nicea, field encounters required sharper command. As the army marched eastwards, it became divided into a vanguard and a main force. On 1 July the Turkish sultan of Nicea ambushed the former. Horse-archers struck quickly and encircled the crusader knights, who were forced to fall back on their foot soldiers and accompanying non-combatants. As they did so, close-quarter fighting developed, during which the main crusader force arrived and routed the enemy. Such typical steppe tactics – using speed to catch an enemy off balance and firepower to break up formations – came as a nasty shock to the crusaders. The lesson the crusaders drew from this was that they needed solid formations and rearguards to combat encirclement, and this would inform their field tactics throughout the crusading period. Moreover, the crusaders would appoint a single commander in future.

The crusader siege of Antioch – another large, well-defended city – began in October 1097. Attempts to relieve it were complicated by rivalry between the Seljuq principalities of Damascus and Aleppo. Bohemund I of Otranto (1058–1111) emerged as a formidable leader during the long siege, and it was to him that a traitor turned to betray the city in June 1098. No sooner had the crusaders entered Antioch than they in turn were besieged by a great Muslim army. Again, it was Bohemund who commanded the successful breakout, which forced the Turks to flee. It was on the basis of this that Bohemund seized control of Antioch, despite the protestations of Alexius that it should be returned to him. The violent quarrels of the leaders over this issue caused major rifts in the crusading army, and Bohemund's own force defected from the expedition. The rest of the army managed to maintain a degree of unity and marched south, ending their understanding with the Fatimids of Egypt, who had captured Jerusalem from the Seljuqs in July 1098.

The crusader army besieged Jerusalem on 7 June 1099 and, fearful of an Egyptian attack, attempted an immediate assault on the city on 13 June. The attack failed, and the crusaders settled down to a systematic siege, assisted by the arrival of a Genoese fleet that brought wood and skilled workers. On the vulnerable north wall the French built a ram to batter down the outer wall that covered the defences at this point, opening the way for a great wooden assault tower. On the south, by the Zion Gate, the Count of Toulouse built another tower. These towers were supported by trebuchets and archers, and mantlets were prepared to protect the assault force. The garrison was thus divided, and was wrong-footed when the northern attack was switched from the northwest to the northeast corner of the city. The final assault, launched on 13 July, did not succeed until Friday 15 July, and only after heavy losses. Nevertheless, this was a well-coordinated attack against a formidable target, which indicated how battle-hardened the crusaders had become. An Egyptian relief force gathered at Ascalon, but before it could move the crusaders surprised it in a rapid strike on 12 August. On this occasion the crusaders protected their cavalry with lines of infantry thrown forward and fought off a hasty enemy strike, before devastating them in a great charge.

The Great Citadel at Aleppo (Haleb). The crusaders were a powerful stimulus to the building of fortifications in the Islamic world.

Crac des Chevaliers

'The bone in the throat of Islam' is a literal description of Crac des Chevaliers, standing as it does on a spur of the Nosairi Mountains and dominating the Buqai'ah Plain between this range and the mountains of Lebanon to the south. This narrow 'throat' is the main connection between inland Syria and the Mediterranean coast. Known to the Arabs as Hisn al-Akrad, the 'Castle of the Kurds', the original fortification on the site was captured by the First Crusade in 1099 and subsequently incorporated into the county of Tripoli. In 1144 the area was granted to the Knights Hospitaller, who used it as a base for raiding nearby Muslim Homs and Hama. Following an earthquake in 1202 the castle was rebuilt, assuming its present form.

Crac is a concentric castle whose high inner structure encloses the monastic quarters of the knights, allows enormous storage space and provides a powerful firing platform to support the outer defences. Within both the inner and outer walls there are shooting galleries and box machicolations, giving secure cover for archers and missile men. The wider openings in the inner enceinte are for ballistae (giant catapults). Its position on a spur means that on three sides the land slopes away very steeply, so the fortress can only be approached from the south. Here the

fortifications are at their most formidable, for any assault must seize a high outer wall, cross a deep water-filled cistern and then face the huge sloping mass of the talus which fronts the inner castle.

The prosperity of Crac depended on extorting wealth from Homs and Hama, and after the Mamluks of Egypt seized control of Syria in 1260 this became very difficult. On 3 March 1271 the sultan Baybars attacked the castle from the south with a great army and numerous trebuchets, at a point where the Hospitallers seem to have begun, but never completed, an outwork. The Muslims undermined the walls, an operation probably made possible by deluging the defences with missile fire. On 29 March a breach was opened and the enemy poured in, forcing the capitulation on terms of the inner castle on 8 April. To forestall any attack from this direction the Mamluks rebuilt the south wall massively, and in particular constructed the huge, square 'Baybars Tower' in the middle of the south wall, which was large enough to bear the weight of a mighty trebuchet. What is amazing about Crac is that it is in such superb condition. The surrounding townspeople moved into the castle and lived there until the site was cleared under the French Mandate in the 1920s.

THE CRUSADER EAST AND ITS ENEMIES, 1099–1187

The First Crusade established only bridgeheads in the east with tiny European populations, such as Edessa, an Armenian principality to which Baldwin of Boulogne (c. 1058–1118, later Baldwin I of Jerusalem) had been invited. The new-founded crusader states sought to expand their territories southeast towards the River Euphrates, but in May 1104 they were defeated at the battle of Harran. The capture of Tripoli in 1109 established the last and smallest of the new crusader states. The Kingdom of Jerusalem needed to seize the cities of the coast, and thus launched a series of great sieges that culminated in the capture of Tyre in 1124.

The crusader states appeared tiny compared to their Islamic enemies, but they were actually quite formidable, for a number of reasons. As their populations grew during the 12th century, the European newcomers treated the native Christians well and could thus count on their support. While the quarrel over Antioch had alienated Byzantium and so cut the land bridge to Europe, the Italian city-states had supported the crusade, and their naval power now came to dominate the eastern Mediterranean, particularly the coastal cities, which they helped to capture. The wealth of their trade provided a vital tax base for the kings of Jerusalem. The countryside became increasingly dotted with castles, which, while not individually strong, together constituted a network of strongpoints. As long as there was a field army it would be very difficult for any attacker to besiege a key city. Most importantly of all, the enemy remained divided, and for a long time was demoralized by the defeats suffered.

The Europeans also adapted their military methods. They recognized that the coordinated charge of their heavy cavalry was highly effective and adopted this as the main offensive force in battle. This demanded great forbearance and discipline amongst the knights. It was a lethal instrument against light cavalry, which formed the backbone of all Islamic armies. Given that light cavalry could harass and disorder western European horsemen, they developed the habit of lining up their infantry in front of the knights, preventing enemy archers from picking off knights and horses and thus weakening the eventual charge. On occasion they formed a column of march that resembled a moving fortress, with the knights enclosed by infantry. The crusaders were innovative too, employing Turcopoles (native light horse) to harass the enemy. The military orders of the Templars and Hospitallers were created. These armed monks formed a fanatical hard core of the crusader army, numbering perhaps 600 knights in all, and employing infantry and Turcopoles at need.

The Turks of Syria remained divided and failed to coordinate their attacks on the enemy with (heretical) Shi'ite Egypt. Their leaders needed to stand as champions of Islam to persuade the Arab townspeople and traders to support their jihad against the enemy, and the first to achieve this was Zengi (c. 1085–1146), the atabeg of Mosul, who took over faction-ridden Aleppo in 1128. He spent most of his time fighting other Turks, but in 1144 seized crusader Edessa, provoking the Second Crusade

'[King Louis VII] enacted laws necessary for securing peace and other requirements on the journey, which the leaders confirmed by solemn oath. But because they did not observe them well, I have not preserved them either.'

Odo of Deuil (d. 1162) on indiscipline in the Second Crusade

(1145–49). The Middle Eastern expedition was led by Louis VII of France (r. 1137–80) and Conrad III of Germany (r. 1138–52), who failed to cooperate and were defeated separately in Anatolia. The Kingdom of Jerusalem had not been consulted about the new crusade and was divided as to what it could best do. In the end the army besieged Damascus, but was not strong enough to face the relief force led by Zengi's son Nur al-Din (1118–74) and the crusade collapsed.

Nur al-Din cultivated his image as a champion of Islam against the crusaders, which brought Damascus to agree to government by him in 1154. Fatimid Egypt, meanwhile, had become so weakened by factional infighting that both the Kingdom of Jerusalem and Nur al-Din sought to conquer it. The latter succeeded in doing so in 1169, but was facing rebellion by his Kurdish Muslim governor Saladin (c. 1138–93) at the time of his death in 1174. Saladin was then able to unite Syria and Egypt and to copy his predecessor by posing as the champion of Islam, though he spent more of his time fighting fellow Muslims than western settlers. By this time Jerusalem seemed to be well established, and, together with the principalities of Tripoli and Antioch, to have become a permanent feature of Mediterranean politics. But the increasing resurgence of Islam was a grave threat to which the crusaders adapted at first by alliance with Byzantium, until its defeat at the battle of Myriocephalum in September 1176 by the Seljuq Turks of Anatolia reduced its power. Appeals to western rulers for support became frequent, but this diplomatic effort produced only limited help.

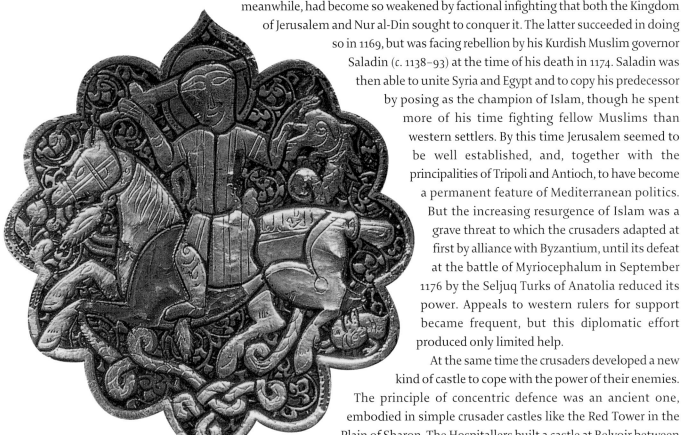

Saladin, here represented on a silver vessel from Syria of about 1230, was a hero to his own people, but also highly regarded in the West as a chivalric leader.

At the same time the crusaders developed a new kind of castle to cope with the power of their enemies. The principle of concentric defence was an ancient one, embodied in simple crusader castles like the Red Tower in the Plain of Sharon. The Hospitallers built a castle at Belvoir between 1168 and 1170, whose massive walls were set with towers at the corners and in the middle of each side. Around the walls ran a vaulted passage featuring loopholes to cover the defenders from enemy fire. There was also a higher, inner fortress that mimicked the outer defences, to which it was sufficiently close for archers to support those defending the outer wall. The whole compound was defended by a deep and wide dry moat. This mighty fortress would defy siege by Saladin for nearly two years after 1187. It set the pattern that culminated in mighty Crac des Chevaliers (see box on pp. 98–99) and Margat. Both of these date from the 13th century and, significantly, both belonged to the religious orders.

The accession of thirteen-year-old Baldwin IV (r. 1174–85) precipitated a grave crisis in the affairs of the Kingdom of Jerusalem. He was a leper, and thus was unlikely to produce an heir, which meant that the marriage of his sisters would be crucial. Inevitably there were tensions between the great lords of the kingdom. Saladin tried to profit from this by attacking Jerusalem from Egypt in 1177, but, as his army

Opposite The fortress of Belvoir, on the Naphtali plateau, overlooking the Jordan River, was the first truly concentric castle. Built by the Hospitallers in 1168–70, its massive double walls defied Saladin for nearly two years after the battle of Hattin. Such powerful fortresses were rare largely because they were extraordinarily expensive to build.

scattered to ravage, Baldwin IV crushed it at the battle of Montgisard that November. In 1179 Saladin scored a great triumph by destroying the new Templar castle of Jacob's Ford (in Syria). The outcome of the bitter power struggle within the Kingdom of Jerusalem was the accession of the newcomer Guy of Lusignan (c. 1150–94) as king in 1186.

Saladin saw this as a crucial moment to attack, and he raised a mighty army with some 30,000 horsemen, supported by infantry. Most of these were Turkish mounted bowmen, but there was a hard core of heavily armed warriors able to take on the western knights at close quarters. Saladin's army crossed the Jordan and laid siege to the isolated city of Tiberias on the Sea of Galilee, while Guy gathered his army 26 km (16 miles) to the west at Saffuriyah. Saladin's purpose was very clear: to lure the Europeans away from their water and strong position by inviting them to relieve Tiberias. For his part, Guy had mustered a mighty army of 20,000 men, including about 1,200 knights. Both leaders needed a success - Saladin because he had achieved so little against the infidels, and Guy because he had to convince his nobles of his worth. We do not know why Guy sallied out with his army on the eastward march through dry land; he presumably planned to bring Saladin to battle. He succeeded all too well, but on Saladin's terms. The Franks formed into three divisions of cavalry,

Conceptual weapons from a treatise on arms and armour written for Saladin after the siege of Jerusalem in 1187: a shield-cum-bow (*above*) and a spear combined with a crossbow (*right*).

Fantastical Turkish knights with lurid devices on their shields ride out to battle in this scene from *Le Roman de Godefroi de Bouillon*, 1337.

each surrounded by infantry, who held the horse-archers at a distance. But Saladin had huge numbers of light cavalry, and he attacked the southern flank of the crusaders and, most savagely, their rear squadron. The crusaders dared not charge the swirling mass of light horse, because Saladin held the mass of his cavalry far away enough to be out of reach yet near enough to destroy any spent Frankish charge. The crusaders spent the night without water, and the next day their exhausted infantry broke ranks, exposing the whole army to destruction at the Horns of Hattin (the name of a nearby double hill) on 4 July 1187. Guy was captured, and so heavy was the loss of life that Saladin was able to overrun the whole kingdom, including Jerusalem, very quickly.

RICHARD THE LIONHEART AND THE THIRD CRUSADE (1189–92)

In his moment of triumph, Saladin's sense of strategy deserted him. He recoiled before Tyre, where the Europeans had rallied under the command of Conrad of Montferrat and found support from western fleets. Instead of pressing the siege Saladin turned north against Antioch, doing little real damage, while aid began to flow in from Europe. In an attempt to divide his enemies he released Guy of Lusignan, who duly quarrelled with Conrad.

By the summer of 1189 substantial western forces had arrived, and Guy led them to the siege of Acre, buoyed up by news that the Holy Roman emperor Frederick Barbarossa (r. 1152–90), Philip II of France (r. 1180–1223) and Richard I of England ('the Lionheart', r. 1189–99) had all taken the cross. In the event the great German army, after enormous success, broke up when the emperor Frederick died suddenly,

'Two days after the victory, the Sultan sought out the Templars and Hospitallers who had been captured.... He ordered that they should be beheaded, choosing to have them dead rather than in prison.'

Saladin's slaughter of the Templar and Hospitaller prisoners after the battle of Hattin, 1187

while Richard and Philip were deeply suspicious of one another and did not arrive until 1191, Richard being further delayed by his conquest of Cyprus. By this time Acre was surrounded by double lines of investment, the inner against the city and the outer against Saladin's attempts at relief. The long siege was sustained by western naval power, which destroyed the Egyptian fleet Saladin had taken such pains to build up. Richard revitalized the siege, bringing into action great counterweight trebuchets; unlike traction trebuchets, these relied on heavy weights of earth and stone to provide leverage, and could hurl bigger stones with greater accuracy. Saladin had dithered in his relief efforts, and on 12 July 1191 the garrison surrendered on terms of their being ransomed. Saladin again delayed, and all 2,700 surviving members of the garrison and their families were massacred.

On 22 August Richard marched south down the coastal road to establish a base at Jaffa, from where he could strike at Jerusalem. His status as a great captain is confirmed by his mastery of eastern tactics. He formed his cavalry into three divisions and ranged infantry and archers along the left side, which was exposed to enemy attack. However, these foot soldiers were rotated so that they could rest from battle on the seaward side, where the army enjoyed the support of a fleet carrying food, water and supplies. Saladin hurled his light horse troops at Richard's column, slowing but never stopping its progress. On 7 September, near Arsuf, Saladin staged a major effort, concentrating especially on Richard's rearguard and allowing his troops to fight at close quarters. Richard wanted the enemy to become so committed that a mass charge would destroy them, but his rearguard were so provoked that they charged prematurely. The result was a great crusader victory that dispelled Saladin's aura of invincibility, but left his army intact (see box on pp. 106–07).

Richard fortified Jaffa, and in November and December, despite terrible weather, advanced almost to Jerusalem. However, a siege in the presence of a strong enemy field army was clearly unwise, and the military orders pointed out that once the crusaders left Jerusalem could not be held. Thus, Richard retired and moved south to rebuild Ascalon, threatening Saladin's communications with Egypt. In May 1192 Richard seized Darun and with this control of the coast, and made another attempt upon Jerusalem before retreating once again. The armies of both sides were creating problems for their leaders. Tension arose between the French and English elements, and Richard was worried by events in Europe. Saladin's troops were tired after continuous campaigning since 1187. The result was a treaty in September 1192, which left Jerusalem in Muslim hands, but recreated the Kingdom of Jerusalem as a coastal strip with Acre as its capital.

This scene from the 14th-century *Chroniques de France ou de St Denis* conveys something of the savagery and fanaticism of the long siege of Acre (1189–91) during the Third Crusade.

Following the surrender of Acre to the crusaders on 12 July 1191, Philip II returned to his native France, leaving Richard I of England as undisputed leader of the Third Crusade. As the recovery of Jerusalem was the objective, the army moved south to establish a good seaport base at Jaffa. This necessitated a fighting march in the presence of a major enemy army, a manoeuvre familiar to the Latins of the east but a novelty for a western commander. Richard marshalled his heterogeneous army very skilfully, taking advantage of the simple fact that the road southwards kept very close to the sea so that he could be supplied from the accompanying fleet. The mounted knights formed the strike force whose concerted assault could shatter the light cavalry of the Turks, but if the charge was mistimed or misdirected the mounted men and their exhausted horses could be isolated and destroyed. They formed three squadrons, which the mounted bowmen of the Turks would seek to harass and weaken, especially by injuring horses.

Richard formed his fighting march by protecting their left flank with a screen of footmen and archers to keep the Turkish mounted bowmen out of range. The baggage train moved on the right side of the cavalry, close to the sea, and infantry formations

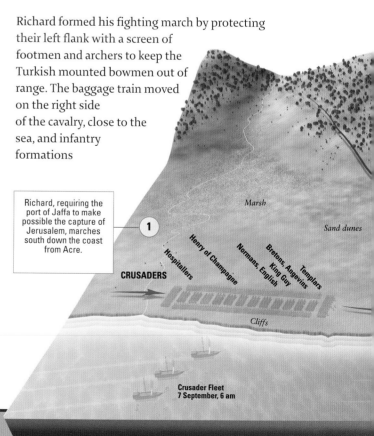

Richard, requiring the port of Jaffa to make possible the capture of Jerusalem, marches south down the coast from Acre.

1

Marsh

Sand dunes

Hospitallers

Henry of Champagne

Normans English

Bretons Angevins

King Guy

Templars

CRUSADERS

Cliffs

Crusader Fleet
7 September, 6 am

were rotated among them to give them rest. The army thus resembled a moving fortress.

It took time for this formation to adapt to this, and on the very first day (22 August) Richard had to rescue his forces when they were penetrated by the enemy. However, after some further difficulties, Richard imposed himself upon the army, which, accordingly, kept its formation despite constant harassing attacks. For much of the time the narrowness of the coastal plain or the presence of woods made it difficult for Saladin to mount a full-scale attack. However, on 7 September Richard's army approached Arsuf where there was ample room to manoeuvre, and here Saladin resolved to force a battle. Saladin repeated the tactic used at Hattin in 1187 of focusing his assaults on the division of the Hospitallers at the rear. Richard, in the centre squadron, refused all requests for aid from them, because he wanted to lure the enemy into a position where they could be destroyed by a single cavalry charge. In the end the Hospitallers charged and Richard was forced to summon the rest of the cavalry to support them. The resultant charge did terrible damage to Saladin's army, but failed to destroy it, and Saladin was able to rally his men to resume their attacks the next day. The result was thus inconclusive. Christian prestige was restored and Jaffa was seized, but Saladin's army remained in being, making any Christian attack on Jerusalem problematic.

	CRUSADERS	MUSLIMS
COMMANDERS	Richard I	Saladin
STRENGTH	20,000 knights, sergeants light cavalry, others	20,000 mainly light cavalry
CASUALTIES	c. 700	c. 5,000–7,000 including 32 emirs

Opposite A 13th-century decorated tile, featuring Richard I and Saladin, from Chertsey Abbey in Britain.

Below In their bid to take the crusade south to Jerusalem, Richard's army met the Muslim forces outside Arsuf. Although the crusaders put Saladin's army to flight, their victory was not decisive.

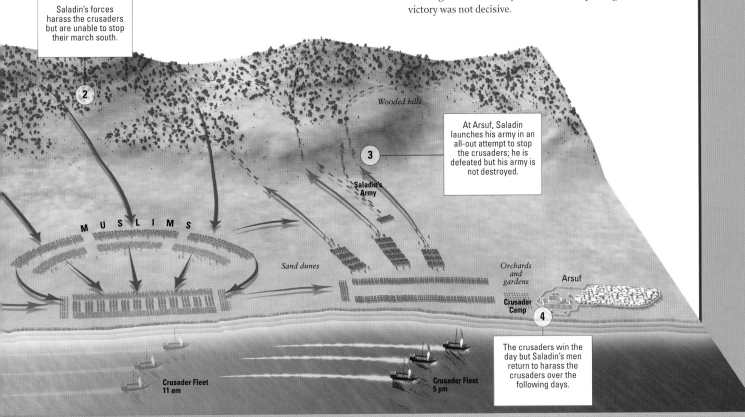

Saladin's forces harass the crusaders but are unable to stop their march south.

2

Wooded hills

At Arsuf, Saladin launches his army in an all-out attempt to stop the crusaders; he is defeated but his army is not destroyed.

3

Saladin's Army

M U S L I M S

Sand dunes

Orchards and gardens

Arsuf

Crusader Camp

4

The crusaders win the day but Saladin's men return to harass the crusaders over the following days.

Crusader Fleet 11 am

Crusader Fleet 5 pm

THE 13TH CENTURY

Richard had wanted to regain Jerusalem by striking at Egypt, but his fellow crusaders remained focused on Jerusalem. It is a mark of his wisdom that all subsequent crusades adopted Richard's strategy. After Saladin's death in 1193 the empire was split between members of his Ayyubid family in Syria and Egypt. The period between 1187 and 1250 was the zenith of the crusading movement, with unprecedented numbers of expeditions arriving in the east. No king chose to join the Fourth Crusade (1202–04), which left its noble French leaders with the task of raising money to pay for a fleet. It is a sign of the maritime ascendancy of the Italian city-states that they were confident of raising a fleet and striking at Egypt by sea. The leaders arranged for a Venetian fleet to convey the expected 35,000 troops to the east, at enormous cost. The main military interest of the Fourth Crusade was that the Venetians used their fleet to mount a successful attack on the walls of Constantinople in 1204, enabling the crusaders to sack the city and establish the Latin Empire of Constantinople, which would last until 1261, diverting considerable aid from the Holy Land. The launching of the Fifth Crusade (1217–21) was carefully prepared by Pope Innocent III (r. 1198–1216), who used the Fourth Lateran Council of 1215 to canvas support. A substantial expedition was sent to the Holy Land. Realizing that the Seljuq ruler of Anatolia's attack on Ayyubid Syria would divert enemy forces, the crusaders attacked Damietta in Egypt on 29 May 1218. The city was well defended, and the siege dragged on until November 1219. During this time disease ravaged the crusader army, while contingents came and went, apparently moved by the belief that spending a year on crusade was a discharge of their vow. This weakened leadership, and command was effectively assumed by the papal legate Pelagius. He refused offers by the sultan to exchange Damietta for Jerusalem, perhaps because he expected the soon to be Holy Roman emperor Frederick II (r. 1220–50), who had taken the cross in 1215, would come. After the fall of Damietta the crusader army hesitated, and only finally marched on Cairo in 1221. By this time the Anatolian assault on Syria had ended, and the crusaders became trapped by the flooding of the Nile. The price of the crusaders' freedom was the surrender of Damietta. The crusade had failed, once again through a lack of

Below This Venetian manuscipt illustration, dating to *c.* 1330, shows crusaders arriving at the city of Constantinople in 1204.

coherence and unified command. However, Egypt was clearly vulnerable and western command of the sea remained unchallenged.

Below Richard, Earl of Cornwall, went on crusade in 1240–41 and refortified Ascalon. He is shown in this seal wearing cutting-edge equipment for a knight of his era: hauberk and pothelm.

In 1225 Frederick II married the heiress of Jerusalem, Yolande, and three years later he arrived in the kingdom with a substantial army, launching the Sixth Crusade (1228–29). He manipulated the quarrels of the Ayyubids to such a degree that in 1229 he agreed a ten-year truce with Egypt, as part of which Jerusalem was restored to the kingdom. This should have opened a way to recovery, but Frederick was excommunicated as a result of his quarrels with the Pope. Frederick's insistence on an absolute monarchy, which the barons resisted, plunged the Kingdom of Jerusalem into a long civil war. Preoccupied with European concerns, Frederick never returned to Jerusalem after 1229. Ultimately the rebels triumphed, but only at the price of weakening the kingdom; it was a monarchy in name only, and power resided with the military orders and the Italian city-states.

In 1239, with the end of Frederick's ten-year truce imminent, Theobald I, the French king of Navarre, arrived in the east with a strong army. The bitterness between the Ayyubids in Syria and Egypt was such that, despite several defeats and the internal quarrels within the kingdom, Theobald was able to reoccupy Jerusalem and increase the size of the

A 14th-century illustration showing Louis IX, king of France, as a prisoner in April 1250. He was released in return for the surrender of Damietta to the Egyptians. The rest of his army was held against an enormous ransom, and many died before it could be paid.

kingdom. Theobald left in 1241, when another western force under Richard, Earl of Cornwall, arrived. By negotiation, Richard was able to secure the return of virtually the whole Kingdom of Jerusalem west of the Jordan. However, the barons, the military orders and the Italians remained hopelessly disunited.

In 1244 the Egyptians took into their service the Turkish Khwarezmians, soldiers of a state destroyed by the Mongols in the 1220s. They ravaged Syria and sacked Jerusalem before joining their Egyptian allies at Gaza. The rulers of Damascus and Homs offered alliance to the westerners, whose army at Acre had been increased by the arrival of further pilgrims. This opportunity to crush the Egyptians prompted an unusual degree of unity, and a substantial army of perhaps 1,200 knights and some 5,000 infantry troops joined up with about 4,000 Syrian allies. At La Forbie (Herbiya, near Gaza) they faced up to a force of 5,000 Egyptian troops supported by 20,000 Khwarezmians. The Syrians, and many in the Christian camp, urged caution, hoping that the Khwarezmians might well be drawn into a premature attack. However, it was decided to launch an assault on the Egyptians using the Christian troops, while the Syrians took on the Khwarezmians. The former became bogged down in the sand dunes; having scattered the Syrians, the Khwarezmians outflanked and slaughtered the Christian army. As a result of this defeat, the Kingdom of Jerusalem lost Ascalon, and was reduced to a rump state. Its very existence now depended on outside forces.

Louis IX of France (r. 1226–70), later canonized, was seen as the very epitome of Christian kingship, so it was hardly surprising that he participated in the Seventh Crusade (1248–54). This was the most carefully prepared of all the crusades, and was an almost entirely French affair, which greatly improved leadership. Louis established a new base at Aigues-Mortes (near Montpellier) on the Mediterranean and built up massive stocks of food. An army of about 15,000 men accompanied the king to Cyprus in 1248. On 5 June 1249 they stormed ashore at Damietta using specially built flat-bottomed boats, and occupied the city the following day. Louis awaited reinforcements, and, rejecting an attack on Alexandria, in November marched his army on Cairo. His troops were halted at Mansoura in December, though, and it was

'The good Comte de Soissons, hard put to it as we were at that moment, made joke of it and said to me gaily: "Seneschal, let these dogs howl as they will. By God's bonnet... we shall talk of this day yet, you and I, sitting at home with our ladies!"'

Jean de Joinville on crusader humour during the battle of Mansoura, February 1250

A curious late 13th-century decorative jug in the form of a crusading knight.

not until 8 February 1250 that they were able to cross the Nile. After that, good luck deserted his army. Having reached Cairo, the forces under the king's brother, Robert of Artois, made a successful attack on the enemy camp, but were then massacred in the narrow streets of the city. The Egyptians then cut off the crusaders' retreat. The price of Louis's own freedom was the surrender of Damietta, and an enormous ransom was also paid to free the rest of his army.

Louis remained in the Holy Land until 1254. He exploited quarrels between Syria and Egypt with some success, and unsuccessfully sought an alliance with the Mongols, before returning to France. The Kingdom of Jerusalem, divided and weak, survived for a little longer, largely because Egypt, now under a highly militarized Mamluk regime, was distracted by Mongol attack. Once the latter had been defeated and Egyptian power over Syria had been reasserted, the Mamluks returned to the offensive. In 1265 Caesarea, Arsuf and Haifa fell, and Antioch followed in 1268. In 1289 Tripoli was captured and in 1291 Acre surrendered to a huge Mamluk army equipped with 100 siege engines. Tyre and Sidon swiftly capitulated, leaving Cyprus as the only crusader possession in the east. It eventually surrendered to the Turks in 1573.

The crusades were fuelled solely by religious dogma; none of the European powers that took part had any vested interests in the capture of the Holy Land. They also precipitated a contest for control of the Middle East between two sets of invaders, Christian and Turkish, and by the turn of the 14th century this area was firmly under the latter's rule. Western soldiers, inspired by religion, were brave and capable, but religious enthusiasm alone could not indefinitely sustain their cause – and as a result they suffered from a lack of reinforcements. The Turks were never numerous, and indeed continued to draw fighting men directly from the steppe, but their leaders played the hand of jihad to consolidate their own power. In military terms both sides developed siege warfare more or less equally, though crusader developments in castle architecture were very advanced. In field warfare the crusades presented a fascinating clash between two very different styles of warfare. The westerners relied on slow and deliberate movement in disciplined mass, while the Turks developed speed and manoeuvre. Both sides produced generals of distinction, notably Richard I 'Lionheart' and the Mamluk sultan Baybars (1223–77), who defeated King Louis IX of France. In the end the Turks were successful because they could tap into greater riches than the crusaders, and their power bases in Egypt and Syria were closer to the scene of action. However, the prospects for the westerners were not without hope. Christians still formed a significant minority of the population throughout the Middle East, even in Egypt, and the maritime supremacy of the Italian city-states in the eastern Mediterranean would last until the 16th century.

5 Nomads Triumphant: Mongols, Mamluks and the Later Crusades, 1250–1400

Opposite Persian miniature depicting Chingiz Khan's campaigns in China. *Right* Yuan dynasty portrait of Chingiz Khan in his later years.

On 9 April 1241 a hastily assembled army – comprising Teutonic Knights, Polish forces led by King Henry II of Silesia (r. 1238–41), German miners, Templars and Hospitallers and others – assembled at Liegnitz (Legnica, Poland) to face 20,000 Mongol invaders under the command of Baidar and Kadan. Although the Europeans outnumbered the Mongols by approximately 5,000 men, they were facing a style of warfare they had not encountered before, and of which they had little understanding. In contrast, having ravaged Poland since February, the Mongols had developed an understanding of European methods of warfare and had adapted their tactics accordingly. Aware that a large army led by King Wenceslaus I of Bohemia (r. 1230–53) was approaching fast, Baidar and Kadan decided to seek battle, before overwhelming numbers negated their mobility.

The Mongols began to move forward in eerie silence, firing their powerful bows. Henry's Silesian cavalry advanced, only to be repulsed by volleys of well-targeted arrows. Henry then ordered the rest of the Polish and Teutonic knights to attack. The Mongols retreated before them, but in an orderly fashion. Not wanting to miss the destruction of the barbarian enemy, Henry advanced with the remaining cavalry, including the Templars and Hospitallers, leaving the infantry behind to serve as a rallying point. The retreating Mongols began to break formation and flee, as did the knights, who had by now moved a considerable distance away from their infantry, in their eagerness to pursue. However, additional Mongol cavalry began to appear on their flanks, carrying pots that spewed noxious clouds of smoke, who rode between the rear of the knights and the infantry. As the knights continued their pursuit, the Mongols unleashed a storm of arrows upon them. The infantry vainly tried to peer through the smoke, as they listened to the distant din of battle and the screams of the wounded and dying.

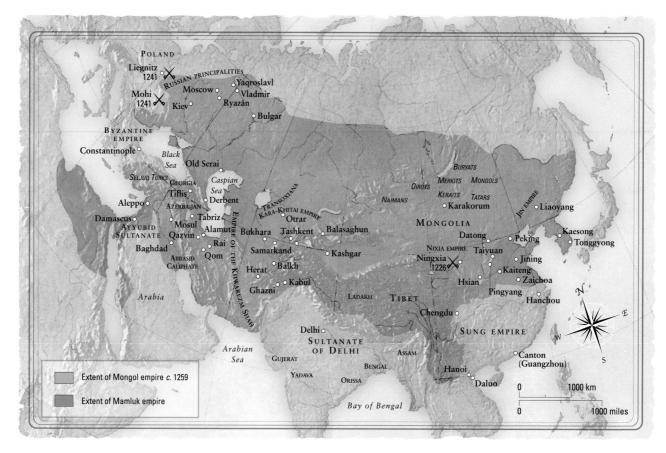

POLAND
Liegnitz ✕
1241
Mohi ✕
1241
Kiev
RUSSIAN PRINCIPALITIES
Moscow
Yaqroslavl
Vladmir
Ryazàn
Bulgar
BYZANTINE EMPIRE
Constantinople
Black Sea
Old Serai
SELJUQ TURKS
GEORGIA
Tiflis
Aleppo
AZERBAIJAN
Damascus
Tabriz
AYYUBID SULTANATE
Mosul
Alamut
Qazvin
BAGHDAD
ABBASID CALIPHATE
Rai
Qom
Caspian Sea
Derbent
Empire of the Khwarezm Shah
TRANSOXIANA
KARA-KHITAI EMPIRE
Otrar
Bukhara
Tashkent
Samarkand
Balasaghun
Kashgar
Herat
Balkh
Ghazni
Kabul
Arabia
Arabian Sea
GUJERAT
Delhi
SULTANATE OF DELHI
YADAVA
ORISSA
BENGAL
ASSAM
LADAKH
TIBET
Chengdu
Hanoi
Daluo
Bay of Bengal
BURYATS
OIROTS
MERKITS
MONGOLS
KERAITS
TATARS
NAIMANS
Karakorum
MONGOLIA
NIXIA EMPIRE
Ningxia ✕
1226
Datong
Taiyuan
Hsian
Hsian
JIN EMPIRE
Liaoyang
Peking
Jining
Kaiteng
Pingyang
Zaichoa
Hanchou
SUNG EMPIRE
Kaesong
Tonggyong
Canton
(Guangzhou)

☐ Extent of Mongol empire c. 1259
☐ Extent of Mamluk empire

0   1000 km
0   1000 miles

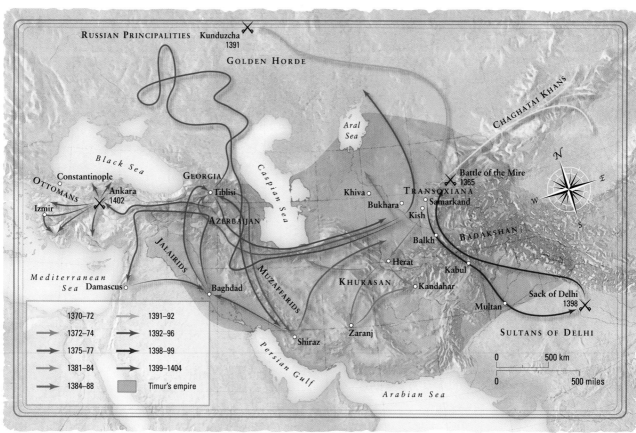

RUSSIAN PRINCIPALITIES   Kunduzcha ✕
1391
GOLDEN HORDE
CHAGHATAI KHANS
Aral Sea
Black Sea
OTTOMANS
Constantinople
Ankara ✕
1402
Izmir
GEORGIA
Tiblisi
Caspian Sea
Khiva
TRANSOXIANA
Battle of the Mire ✕
1365
Samarkand
Kish
AZERBAIJAN
Bukhara
BADAKSHAN
Balkh
JALAIRIDS
Herat
Kabul
Mediterranean Sea
Damascus
MUZAFFARIDS
Baghdad
KHURASAN
Kandahar
Multan
Sack of Delhi ✕
1398
Shiraz
Zaranj
SULTANS OF DELHI
Persian Gulf
Arabian Sea

→ 1370–72	→ 1391–92
→ 1372–74	→ 1392–96
→ 1375–77	→ 1398–99
→ 1381–84	→ 1399–1404
→ 1384–88	☐ Timur's empire

0   500 km
0   500 miles

Opposite above The Mongol empire was the largest contiguous empire in world history and even grew after 1258 with Kublai Khan's conquest of the Sung empire in 1276. The empire may even have stretched further north into Siberia, but the sources are unclear on the extent of Mongol control in the north.

Opposite below Timur dreamed of re-establishing the Mongol empire, and it appeared that his dream could be realized after he defeated the Golden Horde, the Ottomans, the Mamluks and the Sultanate of Delhi. He was marching on the Ming empire in China when he died in 1405. Although his campaigns went well beyond his borders, Timur only ever claimed the territory between the River Euphrates in the Middle East and the Syr Darya, which emptied into the Aral Sea.

Below Mongols eating captives while their horse strips the leaves from a tree, as illustrated in the *Chronica Majora* by Matthew Paris. One of the rumours propagated by Matthew Paris, an English monk, was that the Mongols practised cannibalism. He, and others, also noted that Mongol horses did not eat fodder but only grazed or would eat the bark and leaves of trees if no grass was available.

Suddenly, the lines of infantry were struck by a hail of arrows, before a mass of Mongol horsemen and frantically fleeing knights broke through the smoke. The infantry were quickly encircled and annihilated. King Henry attempted to escape, but the Mongols hunted him down, first killing his horse and then dispatching him as he fled on foot, his head being impaled on a Mongol lance. The bodies of the Teutonic Knights and Polish troops strewn across the battlefield suffered similar indignities, as the Mongol soldiers collected trophies by cutting off an ear from each of the corpses. Baidar and Kadan carried nine large sacks of these back to the overall commanders of the European invasion, Sübedei (1176–1248) and Batu Khan (c. 1205–55). By the time King Wenceslaus arrived, the Mongols had disappeared.

THE RISE OF CHINGIZ KHAN AND THE MONGOLS

The rise of the Mongols was not meteoric. Their first state arose from the turmoil of tribal warfare in the steppes north of China, in which the Mongols were only one of a dozen or so players. In the early 13th century a young chieftain named Temüjin emerged victorious and united the various tribes of the Mongolian steppes under his control. In 1206 his supporters recognized him as Chingiz (or Genghis) Khan (c. 1165–1227), meaning 'firm and resolute ruler'. Chingiz Khan did not merely form a tribal confederation, as had been done for hundreds of years. Instead, he completely altered the social organization of Mongolia, and thus can be seen as its founding father.

Throughout the Mongol wars of unification, Chingiz Khan eliminated the leadership of the tribes he conquered and assimilated those he defeated. While the allies of the Mongols maintained their own structure, conquered enemies were dispersed among his followers. Mongol society was divided into units of a thousand people, known as mingans. This was the basic unit for administering the new civil state and the military. All of society was structured for war, as Chingiz Khan still had plans to expand his state. In many regards, the creation of the empire was somewhat accidental, as Chingiz Khan was more concerned with stabilizing his new

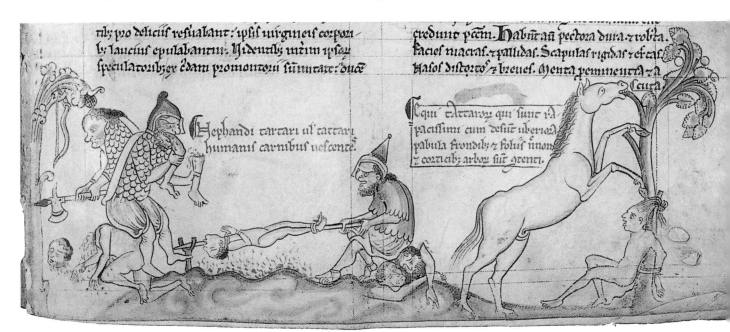

state than conquering new territories. First he hunted down nomadic leaders who had fled Mongolia rather than submit to his rule. The pursuit of these led to incursions into Western Xia in northwest China and into Central Asia, where the Uigurs and other smaller polities voluntarily submitted in 1209. Chingiz Khan's primary intent was to secure goods for his followers, mainly through plundering, as well as to prevent his newly formed state from unravelling. But, having seen how easy it was to conquer the territories he raided, his thoughts soon turned to empire building.

'The Mongols...accustomed their people [to fight as] a single squadron of cavalry, so that they struggled together against the enemy. Retiring [from the battle] and returning [to it] was denied to each of them. They gained from this great experience, which was not [duplicated] by others.'

al-Awsi al-Ansari on Mongol warfare

From 1211, Chingiz Khan released his armies against the kingdom of Western Xia and the Jin empire in northern China, conquering much territory, although the fall of the Jin was delayed until after his death. In the middle of these campaigns, Chingiz Khan marched over 1,600 km (1,000 miles) to deal with a new threat. The pursuit of fleeing nomads into Central Asia had brought the Mongols to the borders of another powerful state, the Khwarezmian empire, extending over much of Turkmenistan, Uzbekistan, Afghanistan and Iran. Its ruler, Sultan Muhammad II (r. 1200–20), viewed himself as a second Alexander the Great. Thus, when one of his governors accused a Mongol-sponsored expedition of espionage (which was probably true) and put them to the sword in Otrar, Muhammad was not alarmed. He knew of the war against the Jin and doubted that the Mongols would open a second front. Indeed, Chingiz Khan attempted to resolve the matter peacefully and diplomatically, but it was not to be. Chingiz Khan left his general Muqali in charge of the campaign against the Jin and marched with almost 150,000 troops from Mongolia to the Syr Darya River, arriving in 1220. After sacking Otrar, the Mongol army divided and struck the Khwarezmians from multiple directions; this included Chingiz Khan marching through the Kizil Kum desert to

A 14th-century miniature depicting Mongol warriors. The primary weapon of the Mongols was always the bow, a weapon that possessed a pull of 100 to an extreme maximum of 160 pounds. John de Plano Carpini, a Franciscan monk who journeyed to the Mongol court in the 1240s, recommended that European knights should wear two coats of mail to protect against the Mongols' armour-piercing arrows.

A special detachment of the Mongolian army serves as the army of Chingiz Khan for ceremonial purposes, wearing equipment appropriate to the medieval era.

sack the great city of Bukhara from the rear. Samarkand fell quickly after that. Mongol armies then pursued Khwarezmian forces into Iran and Afghanistan, defeating all who opposed them. Muhammad II narrowly escaped the Mongols by fleeing to an island in the Caspian Sea, where he died. His son Jalal al-Din fought on, but was defeated by Chingiz Khan in 1121 at the Indus River. By 1225 the war was over, and the Mongol empire now stretched from Manchuria to the Amu Darya River. In 1223 a rebellion broke out in Western Xia following the death of Muqali, and so Chingiz Khan withdrew from Iran and led his forces first to Mongolia and then to Western Xia. He died there in 1227 by falling from his horse while hunting. His sons, however, quelled the rebellion, and forever removed Western Xia from the map.

THE MONGOL EXPANSION INTO RUSSIA AND THE MIDDLE EAST

In 1230, Ögödei, the third son of Chingiz Khan, succeeded his father on the imperial throne. He had developed an ideology of conquest, based upon what he saw as a decree of 'Blue Eternal Heaven', which stated that the Mongols were destined to rule the world. If any prince did not submit to Mongol rule, it would be against heaven's will.

In 1230, Ögödei dispatched his general Chormaqan with 30,000 men to deal with the unrest in Persia caused by the return of Jalal al-Din. Chormaqan marshalled his troops near Bukhara and crossed the Amu Darya River, initially encountering little opposition. While Chormaqan proceeded to subdue Iran, he dispatched a lieutenant named Taimas to hunt down Jalal al-Din. Taimas caught him near the city of Amid, and in a surprise attack the Mongols crushed the Khwarezmians. Jalal al-Din escaped yet again, before eventually being killed by Kurdish troops in 1231. In 1232 Chormaqan moved westwards from the city of Ray and arrived in Azerbaijan the following year. He then invaded Armenia and Georgia, beginning in 1234 (see box on p. 114). The Mongol generals Sübedei and Jebe had led 20,000 troops on a reconnaissance of the western lands in the 1220s. They rode through Iraq and into Transcaucasia, defeating a sizeable Georgian army, before crossing the Caucasus Mountains and defeating

'They show no mercy to those who rebel against them, reject the yoke of their domination or oppose them in the field. They receive messengers with kindness, expedite their business, and send them back again.'

Matthew Paris, an English monk, on Mongol strategy

an allied army of Kipchak and Alan nomads. The routed Kipchaks sought help from the southern Russian princes, who complied, as marriage ties existed between the two. The combined Kipchak and Russian army pursued the Mongols, but then fell to an ambush at the Kalka River in 1224. Thus, mindful of their defeat at the hands of these two formidable Mongol generals, the Armenians and Georgians did not offer battle in 1234.

By 1239 all of Armenia and most of Georgia had submitted to the Mongols. Meanwhile, a massive Mongol army of 150,000 men led by Batu (a grandson of Chingiz Khan) and Sübedei marched west across the steppes towards the Volga River in 1236. As they marched, the Mongols dealt with the nomadic Kipchak Turks. One section of the army marched against the trading city-state of Bulgar, near modern Kazan. By early 1237 the Mongols controlled the Volga–Ural region.

In the winter of 1237/38, the Mongols invaded the Rus' principalities. Ryazan fell first, shortly before Christmas 1237. Then the Mongol army broke into smaller units, spread out and began to threaten all of northern Russia. Grand Prince Yuri II of Vladimir retreated to the Sit River, hoping to force the Mongols to give battle. Instead of complying, Sübedei merely sent an observation force, while he led the main armies against the city of Vladimir on 3 February 1238, capturing it in five days. Other cities fell to the roving Mongol columns. Now surrounded and cut off from all assistance, Yuri was defeated and killed by troops under the Mongol general Burundai on 4 March 1238. From here, the Mongols proceeded towards Novgorod, but were probably halted by the spring thaw. Other Rus' cities fell one by one, as the traditional rivalries of the princes and concern for their own lands prevented the Russians from presenting a unified defence. After regrouping in the southern steppe along the Don River, Batu moved against the southern cities between 1238 and 1239. These fell quickly, until only Kiev remained. The great city was attacked with catapults and battering rams by Sübedei and Burundai over the course of several days, and finally fell on 6 December 1240.

In 1241 the Mongols, led by Batu and Sübedei, entered Central Europe, with two *tümen* (each of 10,000 men) invading Poland and the main force invading Hungary. The Mongols were pursuing fleeing Kipchak tribes, who sought safety with the Hungarian king Bela IV (1206–70). The Hungarians had foreseen the threat, and formed an anti-Mongol alliance with the Bulgarians. After destroying the Hungarians at the battle of Mohi in April 1241, the Mongols marched towards Buda and Pest. The latter fell after a brief siege, and the Mongols massacred the population and burned the city. They then occupied the Great Hungarian Plain. Meanwhile, Mongol forces pursed King Bela to Split on the Adriatic coast, from where he

The Tower of Izborsk, a Russian castle near Pskov. Although Izborsk featured as an important site in the struggle between Novgorod and Teutonic Knights, including being captured by the Germans in 1233, it was also sacked by the Mongols in 1238.

At the battle of Mohi the Mongol army, led by Batu Khan and the famous general Sübedei, defeated the Hungarian army of King Bela. The Mongols captured the bridge crossing the Sajo River with a rolling barrage from catapults and archers, accompanied by a cavalry charge. Meanwhile Sübedei also approached the Hungarians from behind after finding a ford several miles away.

escaped to the island city of Trogir. During the course of their return to Hungary, the Mongols also secured the submission of the Bulgarian emperor Ivan Asen II.

With the majority of Hungary now in the hands of the Mongols and Poland devastated, the Holy Roman Empire appeared to be the next target. A cry for a crusade echoed throughout Europe, focused on the defence of German territory. Fate intervened with the death of Ögödei in 1241, resulting in the recall of the Mongol princes to their homeland to choose a successor. The Mongol retreat from Hungary was anything but disorganized, however. Raiding forces were sent into Austria and perhaps even into regions of Germany, preventing European attacks on the main body of the Mongols as they withdrew into Russia.

HÜLEGÜ AND THE CRUSADERS

Between 1241 and 1256 the Mongols were relatively quiet. Baiju, the commander of the Mongols in the Middle East after the death of Chormaqan in 1241, conquered the Seljuq sultanate in Anatolia and occasionally threatened Baghdad, but otherwise only periodic border raids occurred. This changed with the ascension of Möngke (c. 1208–59), grandson of Chingiz Khan, to the throne. After stabilizing his rule, he renewed the period of conquest, invading southern China together with his brother Kublai (the future khan), while Hülegü (c. 1217–65) – another brother – marched into the Middle East at the head of 150,000 men. Hülegü faced

The siege of Baghdad in 1258, as depicted in a Persian miniature. Although Caliph Mustasim attempted to resist the Mongol attacks, the effective use of siege equipment proved too much for the defences of Baghdad. Desultory sallies by the defenders had minimal results. After a brief siege, the Abbasid caliphate existed no more.

three opponents: the Ismailis (also known as the Assassins), the Abbasid caliphate and the Ayyubids. Hülegü's efforts in the Middle East differed from previous Mongol operations in the region, and the primary catalyst for this change was manpower. Whereas the Mongols had been limited by manpower and focused on mobility and strategy, Hülegü crossed the Amu Darya with an army that allowed overwhelming force – although the Mongols did not abandon their traditional tactics and strategies.

The Ismailis were the first to feel the wrath of the Mongols; their mountain fortresses were attacked even before Hülegü arrived with the main army in 1256. The Mongols attempted diplomacy, albeit on terms of absolute submission to them, but this failed. One by one the fortresses surrendered, although the Ismailis attempted to renew negotiations. The Mongols, however, insisted that all fortifications had to be razed. Eventually, Khwurshah, the leader of the Ismailis, submitted. To ensure that the Ismailis never became a problem, Hülegü executed most members of the leading families.

Hülegü turned his attention to the Abbasid caliphate, which was by now a power in decline. Nonetheless, its capital Baghdad still retained regional and international prestige. Unfortunately, this deluded the caliph al-Mu'tasim Billah (1213–58) into

'If by chance they did spare any who begged for their lives, they compelled them, as slaves of the lowest condition, to fight in front of them against their own kindred.'

Matthew Paris on the
Mongol–Saracen wars

Kublai Khan (r. 1260–94), the brother of Hülegü and the fifth Great Khan, as depicted on a hanging scroll by the court painter Liu Kuan-tao. Kublai rose to power in a civil war against his brother Ariq Böke, after the death of Möngke Khan, their elder brother and the fourth Great Khan. Möngke died in 1259 while fighting in southern China.

thinking that he still wielded great power, especially as his forces had driven off previous Mongol attacks. He did not quite understand that these had been raids for plunder, not attempts at conquest. Indeed, Caliph al-Mu'tasim Billah ignored evidence of the impending attack, and even of treachery amongst his advisors, and his capital was thus woefully prepared for the attack. After routing Baghdad's army on 29 January 1258, the Mongols captured the city and pillaged it for thirty-four days. Hülegü executed most of its notable figures, and eventually ordered the caliph to be rolled up in a carpet and trampled to death – a traditional execution for royalty.

Hülegü retired to Azerbaijan, where he received the vassal leaders of client states and began planning for an invasion of Syria. Although terms were offered to the city of Aleppo, its governor, al-Muazzam Turanshah, refused them. The siege began on 19 January 1260. The Mongols concentrated twenty mangonels on the Iraq Gate, and broke through after six days. Five days of pillaging ensued, before the Mongols razed the walls. The city's formidable citadel held out for a further month. Hülegü returned to Azerbaijan after learning of Möngke's death. In the meantime the Mongols, led by Ket-Buqa, advanced across Syria; as they did so, its cities submitted one by one, the slaughter at Baghdad and Aleppo having convinced many of the futility of resistance. The news of Aleppo's destruction stunned the ruler of Damascus, the Ayyubid prince al-Nasir Yusuf. Although the latter had gathered a sizeable force, his advisers recommended that he retreat to Gaza and join forces with the Mamluks of Egypt. He agreed, and Damascus promptly surrendered to the Mongols in March 1260. Meanwhile, a Mongol force pursued al-Nasir and defeated him at Nablus, which was also captured. Furthermore, the Mongols were in de facto control of the rest of Palestine, with the exception of the crusader states, who were too weak to take advantage of the misfortunes of the Ayyubids. The Mongols also controlled most of the area around Mount Lebanon, including the Biqa Valley, which served as Ket-Buqa's headquarters. Ket-Buqa personally received al-Nasir's surrender at the siege of Ajlun (in Jordan). The terms were generous, guaranteeing al-Nasir's safety; the prince was sent to Hülegü in Tabriz. Ket-Buqa stationed himself in the Biqa Valley, which provided pasture for his horses, and allowed him to monitor the threat from the Kingdom of Jerusalem and impose his will over the northern territories. He stationed another force at Gaza, which monitored the southern borders of the Kingdom of Jerusalem and the Mamluk sultanate in Egypt.

Above Qala'at al-Rabad near Ajlun, Jordan, was one of many fortresses built in 1184–85 near the Jordan and Yarmuk rivers in northern Jordan to guard against marauders from the crusader state of the Kingdom of Jerusalem. With the Mongol invasion of Syria in 1260 it fell to the Mongols.

Opposite Two 14th-century Mamluk swords. Although the scimitar is the weapon usually attributed to Middle Eastern armies, the straight sword was long used.

In 1257, the Mongols sent envoys to the Franks in Palestine requesting their submission. However, Julian, Count of Sidon (r. 1239–60) raided the Biqa Valley and ambushed a Mongol patrol in 1260, killing Ket-Buqa's nephew. In retaliation, Ket-Buqa attacked Sidon, burning much of the city and destroying part of the walls. Later that year, John II, Lord of Beirut (r. 1254–64), and some Templars raided into Galilee. The Mongols destroyed this force and captured John, whom they later ransomed. The crusaders could not hope to hold out against a concentrated Mongol attack on their territories unless reinforcements came from Europe. A steady, though meagre, supply of troops reached the Holy Land, but this was not enough to allow the Franks to take action against the Mongols. The presence of the latter made the Franks increasingly anxious, especially after the sack of Sidon.

ENTER THE MAMLUKS

Of more concern to the Mongols was the nascent Mamluk sultanate in Egypt, formed in the aftermath of King Louis IX's ill-fated Seventh Crusade (1248–54). Although the Mamluks had established their own state, it was internally unstable, but the arrival of the Mongols allowed it to coalesce through fear of the common enemy. When the envoys from the Mongols asked for Egypt's submission or risk destruction, the sultan Qutuz executed them – a clear declaration of war. Qutuz chose his time perfectly and struck while Hülegü was occupied in Azerbaijan awaiting a decision on the succession. Meanwhile, Ket-Buqa secured Syria with a force of some 10,000 troops –sufficiently large to ensure order in Syria, but inadequate for dealing with any external threats. Qutuz chose this time to invade.

The Mamluk invasion of Syria began by defeating the Mongols stationed at Gaza. Afterwards, Qutuz successfully negotiated with the Franks of Acre to obtain safe passage through their territory. The decisive battle for control over Syria took place at Ayn Jalut in the Jezreel Valley on 3 September 1260, with the Mamluks emerging victorious and effectively ending Mongol control of Syria (see box on pp. 124–25). The Mongols tried once again to reestablish their supremacy, but were halted on 11 December 1260 at Hims. Unperturbed, Hülegü deemed this a momentary setback to be rectified after the election of a new khan. Unfortunately for the Mongols civil war broke out in east Asia, with Kublai Khan (1215–94) emerging as the victor in 1265. In the meantime the rest of the empire began to drift apart, with states giving only token recognition to the new khan, before returning to their own rivalries and warring with each other.

Qutuz died in 1260, murdered in a palace coup led by Rukn al-Din Baybars (1223–77), who commanded the vanguard at Ayn Jalut. Baybars resisted the temptation to strike at the Mongols across the Euphrates River, which formed the new border. Instead, he spent his first weeks as sultan securing a power base in Syria, rebuilding many of the fortifications that the Mongols had razed and burning the grasslands near the border to deny the Mongols any pasture. The absence of pasture forced the Mongols to rely on their vassals in Antioch and Cilicia, and raids by King Hethum of Cilicia and Prince Bohemund VI of Antioch continued until 1266.

Hülegü died in 1265. While he was alive, Baybars had maintained a defensive posture, not willing to risk the wrath of the Mongol prince. But now Baybars was emboldened to act, and in 1266 he invaded Cilicia. Abaqa (1234–82), the new il-khan (or 'sub-khan'), as the rulers of the Mongol Middle East became known, failed to assist King Hethum, as he was engaged in a civil war with the Mongols of the Golden Horde (in Russia) and Central Asia. Baybars's attack was so destructive that Cilicia ceased to be an effective military power. King Hethum's sons were captured and ransomed at great cost, and most of Cilicia's fortifications were destroyed. Baybars turned his attention to Prince Bohemund of Antioch in 1268, again while Abaqa was dealing with other Mongol threats, storming Antioch while Bohemund was absent.

Baybars did not forget the other Latin territories in Palestine. He routinely made peace treaties with individual nobles - and abided by them for the most part - which allowed him to isolate fortresses and capture them one by one. The Franks were slow to wake up to what he was doing; in the past the Ayyubids had routinely made

The Battle of Ayn Jalut, 3 September 1260

The Mongols advanced from the Biqa Valley in modern Lebanon, gathering troops along the way, as many of them were dispersed throughout Syria for grazing purposes. Ket-Buqa's forces also included contingents of Armenians, Georgians and some Ayyubid troops. In total, his forces numbered between 10,000 and 12,000 men. They arrived at Ayn Jalut ('the Well of Goliath') first, and camped on a hill. The Mamluks, under Baybars and Qutuz, advanced with similar numbers, with Baybars in the vanguard. As the Mamluks approached, Baybars skirmished

with the Mongols and drove back the advance Mongol elements. When he arrived at Ayn Jalut, Baybars advanced up either Gilboa or Mount Moreh, but retreated when the Mongols began their advance towards his position.

The real battle began on 3 September 1260 with the Mamluks advancing from the northwest in the Jezreel Valley; the fighting took place near the springs. The Mongols advanced rapidly and their right flank defeated the Mamluk left flank. The Mongol advantage was lost when their Ayyubid vassal al-Ashraf Musa deserted with his men on their left flank. This allowed

Late 13th- or early 14th-century Mongol heavy cavalry armour. Lamellar armour, which provided better protection against arrows than chain mail, could be made either of leather or, as in this example, metal.

Qutuz to counterattack, and it almost broke the Mongols, but Ket-Buqa rallied his men and launched his own attack. With his army on the brink of defeat, Qutuz rallied his troops with cries of 'Oh Islam! Oh Allah, help your servant Qutuz against the Mongols.' His desperate frontal attack succeeded. During the battle Ket-Buqa was killed, preventing the Mongols from rallying again. The remaining Mongols fled Syria, but most were pursued and killed by a force led by Baybars or by locals who rose up in rebellion.

The battle of Ayn Julut in 1260 showed the limits of Mongol military power. The Mongol defeat had far-reaching consequences. Not only did it prevent Mongol domination of Syria, but it led to the creation of the Mamluk sultanate and the ultimate demise of the crusader states in the Levant.

	MAMLUKS	MONGOLS
COMMANDERS	Baybars, Qutuz	Ket-Buqa
STRENGTH	c. 10,000–12,000	c. 10,000–12,000
CASUALTIES	Heavy	Very heavy

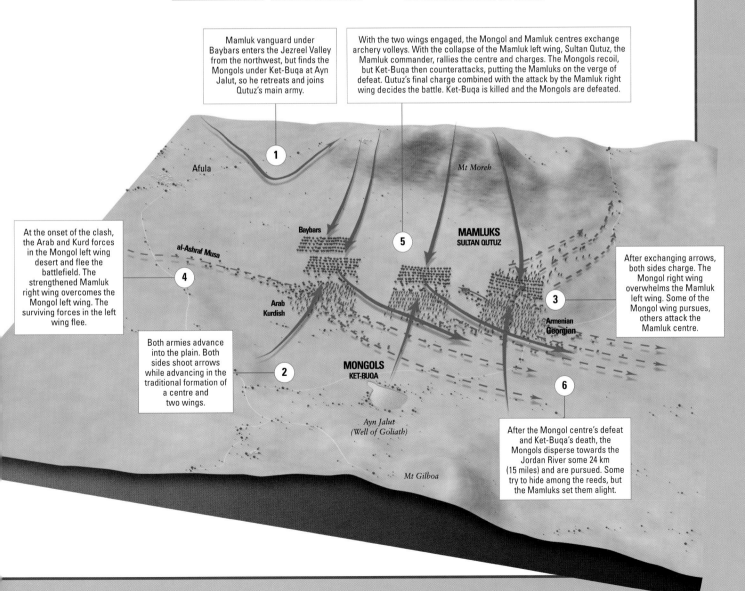

1 Mamluk vanguard under Baybars enters the Jezreel Valley from the northwest, but finds the Mongols under Ket-Buqa at Ayn Jalut, so he retreats and joins Qutuz's main army.

5 With the two wings engaged, the Mongol and Mamluk centres exchange archery volleys. With the collapse of the Mamluk left wing, Sultan Qutuz, the Mamluk commander, rallies the centre and charges. The Mongols recoil, but Ket-Buqa then counterattacks, putting the Mamluks on the verge of defeat. Qutuz's final charge combined with the attack by the Mamluk right wing decides the battle. Ket-Buqa is killed and the Mongols are defeated.

4 At the onset of the clash, the Arab and Kurd forces in the Mongol left wing desert and flee the battlefield. The strengthened Mamluk right wing overcomes the Mongol left wing. The surviving forces in the left wing flee.

3 After exchanging arrows, both sides charge. The Mongol right wing overwhelms the Mamluk left wing. Some of the Mongol wing pursues, others attack the Mamluk centre.

2 Both armies advance into the plain. Both sides shoot arrows while advancing in the traditional formation of a centre and two wings.

6 After the Mongol centre's defeat and Ket-Buqa's death, the Mongols disperse towards the Jordan River some 24 km (15 miles) and are pursued. Some try to hide among the reeds, but the Mamluks set them alight.

Afula

Mt Moreh

Baybars

MAMLUKS
SULTAN QUTUZ

al-Ashraf Musa

Arab
Kurdish

Armenian
Georgian

MONGOLS
KET-BUQA

Ayn Jalut
(Well of Goliath)

Mt Gilboa

Illustration of Mamluk *faris* or cavalry from the 14th-century Mamluk manual, *Treatise on the Art of War*. The 13th-century Mamluks developed a strict training regimen for new recruits in four areas: archery, fencing, lancing and equestrian training. Hippodromes were created specifically for the equestrian training.

alliances and treaties with the crusader states. Baybars, however, was clearly seeking to destroy any threat to his power. The Latin states along the Palestinian littoral occupied the best farmland, and their fortresses and ports threatened land and sea communications between Egypt and Syria. Most importantly, their continued existence meant there was a beachhead for any subsequent European invasion. Despite his victory over King Louis IX in 1250, Baybars was well aware of how close he had come to defeat.

A procession of dignitaries as depicted on the so-called 'Baptistry of St Louis'. Despite its Middle Eastern origins, the bowl focuses on the life of a European ruler: King Louis IX's invasion of Egypt played a pivotal role in creating the Mamluk sultanate.

Baybars successfully transformed his kingdom into a stable and defensible state with an army of approximately 40,000 men, and wielded more military power than the great Saladin. Nonetheless, he owed much of his success to diplomacy, as he entered into an alliance with the Golden Horde, the arch-rivals of the il-khans. This protected him for the most part from the wrath of the Mongols in Persia. When they attacked, Baybars held a strong defensive hand, and denied them allies and pasture.

Mamluk arms and armour. The 15th-century helmet is constructed of steel and gold. The battle-axe was typically a secondary weapon for the Mamluks and attached to their saddles for easy access in hand-to-hand combat. Although the armour of chain and plate is of 14th-century origin, the 13th-century Mamluks usually wore chain-mail armour and could engage in close combat with similarly armoured crusading knights.

THE LATER CRUSADES

Despite the recent civil wars, the Mongols still viewed themselves as the legitimate rulers of the world. However, after the battle of Ayn Jalut the diplomatic policy of the il-khan Mongols shifted from demanding submission to requesting alliances.

'Whenever the Mongols wish to make war on the Saracens they send Christians to fight against them, and on the other hand employ Saracens in any war against Christians.'

Jean de Joinville, vassal of
King Louis IX of France

In a letter dated 1262, Hülegü wrote to King Louis IX of France informing him of his plans to retake Syria, but also promising to return Jerusalem to Christian hands. This letter, however, was only an opening effort. In 1263 a rumour circulated in Rome of the baptism of Hülegü – perhaps prompted by Hülegü, as a piece of propaganda. These continuing diplomatic exchanges between the papacy and the il-khan Mongols raised fears of a Mongol–Frankish alliance in Baybars. However, serious religious barriers – such as the papal insistence on the Mongols converting to Christianity coupled with disapproval of the Mongol policy of toleration of non-Christian religions – hampered these efforts. Nonetheless, more practical military concerns triumphed. Although Hülegü refused to become a Christian, he did promise Pope Urban IV (r. 1261–64) that he would subjugate all of the Muslim powers. Naturally, the pope was overjoyed.

Despite the optimism of alliances, a decade of negotiations accomplished very little. King Louis IX died in 1270 at Tunis on the ill-fated Eighth Crusade, depriving the Franks in Palestine of not only reinforcements, but also much-needed leadership. Although Prince Edward of England (later Edward I) eventually reached Palestine, he lacked sufficient troops to oust the Mamluks. Consequently, when the Mongols invaded Syria in 1272 with a small army of 10,000 men, Baybars once again ousted them.

During this period, Baybars won one of his greatest victories. On 8 April 1270, the great Hospitaller castle of Crac des Chevaliers surrendered, which led to a series of peace treaties between the Franks and the Mamluks. With the Latin states under control and the Mongols still licking their wounds from the 1272 expedition, Baybars returned to Cilicia and sacked it once again in 1275, neutralizing any threat to his power. It proved to be a bad year for the il-khan Mongols; their other stalwart vassal Bohemund VI of Antioch died, leaving the fourteen-year-old Bohemund VII (1261–87) on the throne. Due to continual frontier wars with the Golden Horde (also known as the Jochid khanate) and the Chaghatayid khanate in Central Asia, the il-khan Mongols had few opportunities to focus their attention on Syria. When they did have the occasion to invade Syria, such as in 1281, they found only a small contingent of Hospitallers willing to join them.

Unfortunately for the Mongols, the new Mamluk sultan Qalawun (1222–90) defeated them at the second battle of Homs on 29 October 1281. Following Abaqa's death in 1282, succession matters dominated the il-khan Mongols, allowing the Mamluks to turn their attention to the crusader states once more. Tripoli fell in 1289 and then the Mamluks moved against Acre, which fell after a two-and-a-half month siege on 18 May 1291. Even after this event, the il-khan Mongols continued to cast about for allies. The fall of Acre, however, changed the mindset of Europe.

Christendom had little interest in another crusade in the Middle East, especially one founded on an alliance with Mongols, whom most Europeans distrusted.

The Mongols, however, did not end their hostilities with the Mamluks. Indeed, in late 1299 Ghazan Khan (1271–1304) successfully invaded and conquered Syria. The Mamluks fled to Egypt, as the Mongol forces reached as far as Gaza. During this invasion, a few knights from the military orders crossed over from Cyprus and joined the Mongols. Ghazan left behind a garrison, but this withdrew in 1300, as it could not hold Syria against the Mamluks without substantial reinforcements. Afterwards, Ghazan made numerous raids, at times even in conjunction with naval raids from Cyprus, but a significant joint military alliance never came to fruition. The il-khan Mongols and Mamluks finally came to terms in 1322, after sixty years of active hostilities, when the last il-khan ruler, Abu Said (r. 1316–35), and the Mamluks signed a peace treaty.

TIMUR (1336–1405)

Born near Samarkand in 1336, Timur began his career as a minor leader and sometimes bandit amid the disorder that existed in Central Asia after the dissolution of the Mongol empire. During this time, he suffered arrow wounds to his right arm and leg, paralyzing both limbs. This led his detractors to call him Timur-i Leng, Persian for 'Timur the Lame', which became 'Tamerlane'. Timur prospered in such opportunistic times, serving as the lieutenant of his brother-in-law Emir Husain. They gained control of Mawarannahr (Transoxiana), before falling out in 1370.

Backed by an army that used tactics similar to those of the Mongols, Timur spent the next decade consolidating his control on the region and defending it from raids by the remnants of the Chaghatayid khanate across the Syr Darya River. However, Timur became embroiled in external events in 1380 when he lent support to Tokhtamysh, a prince in the Golden Horde, during a civil war. Timur viewed this as an opportunity to secure his border and gain influence in the Golden Horde. Also in the 1380s, Timur decided to expand his state and crossed the Amu Darya River into Iran and Afghanistan. By 1394, he ruled much of modern Iran, Iraq, Azerbaijan, Armenia and Georgia.

As Timur expanded, his protégé Tokhtamysh challenged his authority. As a descendent of Chingiz Khan, Tokhtamysh viewed himself as the rightful leader of the post-Mongol empire world and considered Timur an upstart. Tokhtamysh invaded Timur's empire in 1385 and 1388, defeating Timur's generals twice. In retaliation, Timur invaded the Golden Horde in 1391 and defeated Tokhtamysh. However, the latter quickly regained power and invaded Timur's empire again in 1395. This forced Timur to pursue Tokhtamysh into the steppe. The nomadic

Opposite A Mughal-period miniature depicting the capture of Bayezid at the battle of Ankara in 1402.

Below A bust of Timur based on his skull, made by the Soviet scholar M. M. Gerasimov, who pioneered the science of facial reconstruction. An inscription in Timur's tomb stated that whoever disturbed his tomb would suffer an invasion worse than his wrath. The day his bones were recovered the Nazis invaded the Soviet Union.

'[T]he enemy sees them run, and imagines that he has gained the battle – but he has in reality lost it, for the Tatars wheel round in a moment when they judge the right time has come. And after this fashion they have won many a fight.'

Marco Polo on the tactics
employed by Timur's forces

armies of these two leaders clashed at the Kur River, with Timur emerging victorious. Timur then broke the power of the Golden Horde by supporting various contenders for the throne and destroying the cities of Sarai and New Sarai, although he ensured that none of the contenders could threaten his power. Timur did not incorporate the Golden Horde into his empire, though, perhaps realizing that the Mongol princes would always consider him an outsider, and would never accept him as ruler.

Timur's next target was the Sultanate of Delhi, India, which he attacked in 1398. He spread panic and confusion among his enemies on one occasion by releasing water buffalo with burning bundles on their backs into the enemy's lines. His troops sacked and burned Delhi in a wanton display of destruction, filling the coffers in Samarkand with plunder. Delhi never fully recovered. In 1399 Timur marched west against the Mamluk sultanate in Egypt and Syria and the Ottoman empire in Anatolia (modern Turkey); both had supported rebellions against him. In 1401 Timur invaded Syria and defeated the Mamluks, sacking Aleppo and Damascus in the process. He then invaded the Ottoman empire of Sultan Bayezid I 'the Thunderbolt' (1354–1403). As he crossed the frontier, Timur began talks with Turkic nomads who owed allegiance to the Ottomans. His diplomatic efforts succeeded, as the nomads deserted Bayezid at a critical moment in the battle of Ankara in 1402. As a result, Timur's forces crushed what remained of Bayezid's army, and took him prisoner. Timur then left western Asia and returned to Samarkand, leaving a further two empires unconquered but in turmoil.

Despite being confined to a litter for most of his later campaigns, Timur did not rest on his laurels. Instead, he planned an invasion of China, which was ruled by the Ming dynasty. The invasion ended prematurely following Timur's death on 19 January 1405 at the city of Otrar. Although he had designated a successor, his empire, which had been held together primarily through the force of his will, quickly disintegrated into smaller states ruled by his sons and grandsons.

Hülegü's siege of Baghdad, as depicted in Rashid al-Din's *Compendium of Chronicles*. The painting shows a pontoon bridge linking Baghdad to its outer defences. In addition, the Mongols are shown using trebuchets.

BATTLE TACTICS

The Mongols fought primarily as light horse-archers and perfected the timeless tactics of the steppe. These maximized their archery skills and mobility, allowing them to stay out of range of their opponents' weapons. They combined hit and run tactics in waves with concentrated firepower. Often they retreated before the enemy, utilizing the famous 'Parthian shot' (turning to shoot at a pursuing enemy while riding at full speed). At the right moment, normally when the enemy forces were drawn out, the nomads wheeled around and annihilated them. As with other steppe-based armies, the Mongols initiated combat when the enemy was within arrow shot range, closing for combat at the decisive moment when the enemy's formation broke or weakened. Their tactics ensured that they did not require superior numbers, relying on mobility, firepower and subterfuge, as opposed to numerical superiority, to gain victory.

A common tactic was the arrow storm or shower, in which they enveloped their enemy and then unleashed a hail of arrows. At longer ranges of 180–280 m (200–300 yd) their shooting was less accurate, but it could still disrupt an enemy formation. Once it was broken, the Mongols would charge. In the course of the arrow storm archers did not aim at a specific target. Rather, they loosed their arrows on a high trajectory into a predetermined 'killing zone' or target area. The arrow storm and other tactics also emphasized concentrated firepower. While the latter was not a new idea, the Mongols used it to its maximum effect in all aspects of war, including siege warfare.

The Mongols also combined the arrow storm with hit and run tactics, sending waves of men against enemy formations. As each wave charged, they shot several arrows and then circled back to the Mongol lines before they had made contact with the enemy. They loosed their final shot roughly 40–50 m/yd from the enemy lines before wheeling around. This distance was close enough to pierce armour, but distant enough from the enemy to evade a counter-charge. They changed horses to keep their mounts fresh. This tactic was often used in combination with other manoeuvres.

The practice of double envelopment or even encirclement was a traditional Mongol hunting method employed on the steppe, in which a great line of men gradually formed an ever-tightening circle that brought all of their prey into the middle, forming a dense mass from which it was difficult to escape. The Mongols did not always require large numbers of troops to achieve this; their archery skills and mobility allowed them to encircle an enemy force even when they were outnumbered. Whenever possible, the Mongols preferred to surround their enemies in this manner. At times, the Mongols extended their lines for tens of kilometres/miles in order to be able to encircle the enemy, using scouts to constantly relay intelligence to the Mongol commanders. This

A Mongol or Turkic archer. The Mongols, like most steppe nomads, kept their bows in a case and always strung. The composite bow, unlike self-bows such as the English longbow, did not lose any of its tension or power from being strung when not in use. Indeed, it was rarely unstrung.

Early 14th-century miniature from Rashid al-Din's *Compendium of Chronicles*, illustrating a Mongol siege. By the trebuchet are Mongol observers and a man in a turban, a Muslim engineer (possibly a captive) in the service of the Mongols. Also depicted is a black *tuq*, or standard, made from horse hair. The black *tuq* signalled a state of war, whereas a white *tuq* was used in peace. In the upper left-hand corner are two Mongol generals sitting on a chair and observing the siege.

tactic was also used when they attacked the Rus' lands. After the capture of the city of Vladimir in 1237, Mongol troops were sent out to reduce every town and fortress they encountered by encircling them and then gradually closing in so that any avenues of escape were narrowed. At times, they deliberately left gaps in their lines of encirclement, allowing the enemy an apparent means of escape. In reality, any gaps served as traps. In their panic and desire to get away, the enemy often discarded their weapons to flee faster and rarely maintained their discipline. This was the tactic that destroyed the Hungarians at Mohi in 1241.

Siege warfare was once a weak point for the Mongols, but they quickly learned and soon incorporated engineers into their armies. These were either conscripted or came to the Mongols voluntarily. Nonetheless, for the entire existence of the Mongol empire, they were dependent on Muslim and Chinese engineers who manned and manufactured artillery and other siege equipment. On occasion, such as in the Russian campaign and in Europe, the catapults appeared in field battles.

In addition to direct warfare, the Mongols employed numerous forms of subterfuge and psychological tactics. The Mongols realized it was more efficient to convince a city or fortress to surrender without resistance than to be drawn into a siege. As a consequence, the Mongols gained a notorious reputation for massacres. In general, these were not carried out in wanton blood lust – they served several purposes. The first was to discourage revolts by hostile populations behind the Mongol armies. Second, as news of the massacres spread, particularly in cases where the defenders had put up a determined resistance, other cities and peoples were intimidated and chose to surrender to the Mongols. Thirdly, as a massacre was the punishment for rebellion, it served as a powerful deterrent. In addition the Mongols spread propaganda and misinformation about the size of their armies, using rumours of their ferocity to maximal effect.

The Mongols resorted to subterfuge to confuse and intimidate their enemies. To mask their numbers, they lit numerous camp fires and sent troops to stir up dust behind their own lines by means of branches tied to the tails of their horses, thus creating the illusion of approaching reinforcements. In addition, they mounted dummies on their spare horses, and rode in single file to disguise their numbers. On other occasions they herded oxen and horses into the enemy lines to disrupt them and create confusion. This tactic was especially useful if the enemy appeared to be well organized or strong. Whenever they could, the Mongols weakened their opponents by promoting rebellion or discord among rivals and by courting the support of oppressed minorities (or majorities). While the Mongols made good use of their reputation for extreme brutality they took pains to portray themselves as liberators when circumstances warranted.

THE MONGOL CONCEPT OF WAR AND ITS LIMITATIONS

The Mongol method of waging war was based on a simple component: the horse-archer. This lightly armoured warrior was primarily armed with a double recurve composite bow, which could penetrate chain mail armour. Its range was well over 300 m (330 yd), but in battle it was typically used at shorter ranges. Although their lamellar armour, made from overlapping plates of leather, gave better protection against arrows than chain mail, it was less effective in hand-to-hand combat. The horse-warrior had been present since the ancient period, but the Mongols were perhaps the most proficient exponents, achieving both excellent mobility and impressive firepower under the umbrella of capable leadership and sound strategy. The well-disciplined Mongol soldiers easily outmanoeuvred their opponents while unleashing a hail of death.

'If anyone is found in the act of plundering or stealing in the territory under their power, he is put to death without any mercy. Again, if anyone reveals their plans, especially when they intend going to war, he is given a hundred stripes on his back, as heavy as a peasant can give with a big stick.'

John de Plano Carpini, Franciscan monk

The Mongols practised strategies of high mobility. While the mounts used by the Mongols, or their auxiliaries, were surpassed in terms of strength and speed by those of many of their enemies, they had better endurance and were deployed in larger numbers (see box on p. 138). The fact that the average trooper in the Mongol army possessed three to five mounts allowed him to remain mobile, even if a horse was lost or grew tired. Before invading a territory, the Mongols made extensive preparations in formal meetings. It was decided not only how the upcoming war would be conducted, but also which generals would participate in it. The Mongols, meanwhile, accumulated intelligence on their opponent, often by using merchants who benefited from Mongol protection of the trade routes. Only after intelligence had been gathered would there be a declaration of hostilities. Mobilization of the army then began, and a rendezvous and time schedule were both agreed upon. Although the planning of the campaign was a major component, the Mongol generals still maintained a high degree of independence. Thus they were able to complete their objectives on their terms, while still abiding by the timetable. This

A 15th- or 16th-century Chinese ink and watercolour painting of a convoy of Mongols. Although the illustration comes from the Ming dynasty, the illustration remains a good representation of 13th-century Mongols when travelling.

allowed the Mongols to coordinate their movements and concentrate their forces at prearranged sites.

The invasion began by attacking in several columns and in a set pattern. First, a screen of scouts, who constantly relayed information back to their main column, covered the invading forces. The Mongol order of march saw them divided into smaller concentrations, which meant they were not hindered by unwieldy, large columns stretching for miles; however, they were still able to fight united. They used their mobility to spread terror, appearing on many fronts at the same time, which in turn discouraged their opponents from concentrating their forces as the Mongols approached. The Mongols preferred to deal with all the field armies that faced them before moving deep into enemy territory. This was very practical. Reaching this goal was rarely difficult, as the enemy usually sought to meet the Mongols before they destroyed an entire province. Furthermore, the use of columns with their screens of scouts enabled the gathering of intelligence, so that the Mongols could locate enemy armies much more rapidly than a single army could. In addition, the Mongols could usually reunite their forces before the enemy was aware of all the different invasion forces, thus better concealing their troop strengths. This also meant that an embattled force could receive reinforcements or, in the event of defeat, they could be avenged.

By concentrating on the dispersion and movement of enemy field armies, the assault on strongholds was delayed. Of course, smaller fortresses or ones that could be easily surprised were taken as they came along, as shown during the Khwarezmian campaign. The smaller cities and fortresses were taken before the Mongols eventually captured Samarkand. This had two results. First, it prevented the principal city from communicating with other cities, from whence they might expect aid. Secondly, refugees from these smaller cities fled to the principal city, undermining the morale of the inhabitants and garrison forces there as well as straining its food and water reserves. The Mongols were then free to lay siege to the principal city without the interference of a field army, which had already been destroyed. Finally, the capture

of the outer strongholds and towns provided the Mongols with more siege experience, as well as raw materials in the form of labour, to either man the siege machines or to serve as human shields.

The Mongols also always tried to destroy the enemy's command structure. This was carried out by harrying the enemy leaders until they dropped. Chingiz Khan first carried out this policy in the wars of unification in Mongolia. In his first few encounters he failed to do this, and defeated enemies regrouped and began conflict anew. After that, it became a familiar tale, as shown in Khwarezm, where Muhammad was pursued to the Caspian Sea by the generals Jebe and Sübedei, and in Europe, where King Bela IV of Hungary was hounded after the disaster at Mohi. Being constantly on the move, the enemy leader was unable to serve as a rallying point for his armies. In addition, his armies also had to keep moving to find him. In many reports, perhaps exaggerated, the enemy leaders were often only a few steps ahead of the Mongols, who often also acquired new intelligence on other lands as their enemies fled further afield. Any such Mongol pursuit would be assigned to a force led by a capable general or generals. In addition, other forces were also sent to the outlying regions. In some cases, these regions were areas independent of the kingdom invaded by the Mongols, yet it did not exclude them and other provinces from receiving unwanted Mongol attention.

In the invasion of Khwarezm by Chingiz Khan between 1219 and 1223, it appears that Mawarannahr was the core territory. However, an army led by Jebe and Sübedei was sent beyond the core after Sultan Muhammad II. Meanwhile, Tolui (a son of Chingiz Khan) invaded and utterly devastated Khorasan (roughly eastern Iran), and Mazandaran (northern Iran) was also destroyed. Afterwards, despite the complete domination of the Mongols throughout the former empire of Khwarezm, the Mongols withdrew to Mawarannahr from the peripheral areas and only a small force remained there. This was another trend. Although the Mongol theatre of operations tended to be vast, when conquering they only kept a relatively small portion of the territory, which prevented them from overextending their armies. If one examines

The Mongol Horse

A major reason for Mongol military success was their horses. Though small in stature (about the size of a pony), the Mongol horse was strong and surpassed all others in endurance. On average, each soldier had five horses while on campaign. The spares were strung together and followed behind the rider. During battle, a few troopers watched the spare horses, but kept them close enough to the front for the Mongols to switch mounts. Part of the tactic of feigned retreat included riding to the fresh horses, switching and then turning to fight. When a horse tired, the rider would rest the horse for several days. By doing so, the Mongols maintained a high rate of travel, around 160 km (100 miles) a day, compared to the 15–30 km (10–20 miles) achieved by most armies of the era. In order to carry out such an action, however, the Mongols had to train their horses to increase their endurance. Through this process, the Mongols produced a horse that was easily managed by its rider. Unlike the stallions used in Europe, the Mongols preferred more docile geldings and mares. One advantage of this choice was that they used mare's milk as an essential part of their rations.

Unlike sedentary armies, the Mongols did not worry about bringing fodder to feed their mounts. Grazing comprised the entire diet of their horses, even in winter – the horses knew how to dig through snow to find grass. Of course, this meant that a constant source of pasture had to be found, which limited the areas in which Mongol armies could campaign successfully and for long periods of time. This, more than anything else, might have inhibited Mongol advances into India and southeast Asia and certainly into Syria-Palestine.

A 15th- or 16th-century Chinese depiction of a Mongol archer on horseback. Chinese art tends to illustrate the Mongol horse better than does that of the Persians, owing to trends in equine painting.

Early 14th-century Persian miniature of a battle between Mongol tribes, from Rashid al-Din's *Compendium of Chronicles.* The warriors, dressed in lamellar armour, are modelled after contemporary Mongol warriors in the il-khanate. The early 14th century also marked a transition in Mongol military practices towards increased use of heavy cavalry, although the bow cases and quivers of arrows, as depicted in this illustration, remained an essential part of the Mongols' military kit.

the borders of the empire in comparison with territories actually occupied and garrisoned by the Mongols, it seems probable that a definite policy was in force. First, by devastating Khorasan, Khwarezm and Mazandaran the new Mongol territory of Mawarannahr was protected by a broad belt of destruction. The inhabitants of this belt were either dead or dispersed, the rulers were in flight and there was simply no organized military to threaten Mongol control. Furthermore, the land that was cultivated could be occupied by nomads, and could thus serve as a staging area for further expansion. In the steppes of Russia, the east had already been secured. With the reduction of the Russian cities, the now subdued steppes were protected to the west and to the north. The Russians were now Mongol vassals, providing not only wealth through taxes, but also military service. Secondly, the Russians were not a military threat to the Mongols, although they could serve as a buffer to possible invasions from the west.

As a result of the Mongol invasions, Eurasia became united under one ruler and one military system dominated. Those defeated by the Mongols increasingly adopted Mongol tactics and abandoned their own. Although the Mamluks of Syria and Egypt demonstrated that the Mongols could be defeated, this was due to the fact that they waged a defensive war, in which they denied the Mongols pasture and ensured that the battles took place in favourable conditions. Not until the advent of portable cannon, which could break the cavalry formations and put fear into both men and horse, did the nomads find their methods of war failing.

6 The Teutonic Knights and the Northern Crusades, 1200–1450

Opposite Re-enactment of the battle of Tannenberg.
Right Chain mail and an iron hat were indispensable parts of every infantryman's equipment.

The native peoples of the Baltic territories in the 12th century were divided into tribes, each living in villages and on scattered farmsteads surrounded by forests and swamps. Tribes that shared common languages often assisted one another in warfare and trade, allowing scholars to lump them together as Estonians, Livs, Letts, Semgallians, Kurs, Prussians and Lithuanians. It would be incorrect to see these as nations, but it would be equally wrong to assume that they were unsophisticated about politics or their own self-interests. All of the tribes were pagans, except for a handful of noble converts to the Russian Orthodox church, conversion being a step towards political prominence. Political authority was exercised by tribal elders, and the heads of clans supported the shamans. Paganism incorporated concepts that lent themselves to a warrior society. The principal deity was a war god, to whom some captured goods and the occasional prisoners were offered in a fiery ritual. Raiding neighbours was important for tribal prestige and for young warriors to gather the resources necessary for marriage and starting a family. Mutual raids led to tribal hatreds, making revenge an important aspect of regional warfare.

Lithuanians were perhaps the most numerous group of Balts, as these peoples are sometimes called. Their language came from the same ancient family as those of the Prussians and the Latvians, which later formed from an amalgam of the smaller tribes south of the Estonians. Since their lands abutted Russian and Polish states, they felt pressure from expansionist princes, but it was not until the middle of the century that they came together as a state. This occurred largely because they were under attack from a new group of Christians – crusaders.

THE ARRIVAL OF THE WESTERN CHRISTIANS

The first westerners to visit the Baltic shores were merchants and missionaries. Originally most of these came from Denmark and Sweden, but over time ever more of them arrived from Germany. By the middle of the 12th century they had gathered on the island of Gotland, a central trading point visited by Balts and Russians too. These westerners then set off east together, for protection against pirates, for mutual aid in case of storms, and to guarantee one another fair treatment from their customers.

Missionaries attached themselves to these nautical caravans, then rented lodgings and bought food from the natives until, in time, they could raise crops for themselves. Efforts to establish churches in Estonia in 1143 and in Prussia in 1206 failed miserably, but a German mission to the Livs along the Daugava River (also known as the Dvina) in 1184 succeeded in winning a number of converts. This mission, led by a German monk named Meinhard, made a bargain with the natives: the Germans would build a castle for protection against Lithuanian attack if the natives became Christians and paid tithes and taxes to cover the costs of construction and the hiring of mercenaries. It was a first step, and the Pope named Meinhard the first bishop of the region. Unfortunately for the natives, the next bishop brought an army to enforce the contract, resulting in open conflict. The bishop died when his horse ran away with him, carrying him into the pagans' formation, but his crusaders made such a quick end to resistance that the third bishop, Albert, was able to establish himself as the de facto ruler of the region. Relatively quickly, his Liv subjects realized that they were now the dominant tribe of the region.

The core of the episcopal army comprised western, mostly German, knights. Some were landed volunteers, but many more were warriors of common ancestry, while others still were merchants accustomed to bearing arms. Since they could not be guaranteed in sufficient numbers every year, Bishop Albert created a small landed nobility, usually his relatives or close associates – but he soon realized that there were too few of them for his needs. In 1202 he founded a military order, the Swordbrothers, who were all at once skilled fighters willing to remain in Livonia through the winter, pious monks and inexpensive. He did not foresee that his promise to share the conquests with these monks would undermine his own position as the leader of the crusade and as the dominant political figure in Livonia.

The crusaders had numerous military advantages over the tribes. First of all, a feudal society provided unquestioned leadership. In contrast, native traditions worked against any leader gaining more than temporary power, and memory of past resentments held against potential allies was usually stronger than the desire to work together against the foreign invaders. Secondly, the westerners had superior technology – including the ability to build stone castles (see box on p. 145) and superior siege techniques – and better equipment, horses and weapons (chiefly the crossbow). Thirdly, the westerners could fight effectively in wintertime. Frozen lakes and rivers supported even the heaviest of horses, and they could bring supplies by ship and deliver them to isolated castles and to troops besieging native strongholds. Fourthly, the military order had men it could station deep in the interior of hostile lands, in castles which could be supplied and reinforced by boat, and from whence raids could be launched until the natives gave up the struggle, accepted baptism, agreed to pay tithes and taxes and offered support to the crusaders in their next war. Given that these wars were usually against a traditional enemy, the newly baptized

'We acknowledge your God to be greater than our gods.'

Baltic pagans surrendering to the crusaders in 1211

Christians often fought enthusiastically. Finally, the crusaders could call on help from Germany and Scandinavia.

The Swordbrothers, weakened by a well-coordinated revolt in Estonia and their reputation soiled by conflict with the Bishop of Riga and a papal legate, unwisely allowed visiting crusaders to pressure them into a raid into fiercely pagan Samogitia, a swampy, forested land lying north of the Nemanus River between Livonia and Prussia. The battle of Saule in September 1236 cost the order its field army. The Pope, recognizing the likelihood that Livonia would be overrun, thus leading to a resurgence in paganism, incorporated the surviving members of the order into the Teutonic Knights. This was not popular with all the members, however, since the Teutonic Knights wanted to return Estonia to the king of Denmark. These knights, together with German-speaking knights from Estonia and Swedes, invaded Novgorod in 1240. In early April 1242 this army met Alexander Nevsky (1220–63) in the famous battle on the ice of Lake Peipus, and was defeated. The events were immortalized in Sergei Eisenstein's 1938 film.

The Teutonic Knights employed their semi-autonomous northern branch – the Livonian Order – to put pressure on the pagans in low-lying Samogitia and the interior highlands of Lithuania. By 1250 the crusaders had persuaded the dominant Lithuanian noble of the highlands, Mindaugas, to accept Christianity and a crown. With the help of the crusaders and the Church, Mindaugas expected to make his kingdom powerful and respected.

> *'whoever...takes the cross for the aid of the faithful against the savageness of Prussia shall receive the same indulgence and the same privilege as those who go to Jerusalem.'*
>
> Pope Innocent IV, in 1245

Scene from Sergei Eisenstein's *Alexander Nevsky* (1938). The film tells us more about Stalin's Russia facing imperial Japan and Nazi Germany than about Alexander Nevsky, but is still a gripping drama. Here Prince Alexander of Novgorod overcomes and captures the Grand Master of the Teutonic Order, though in fact the Grand Master was not at this battle.

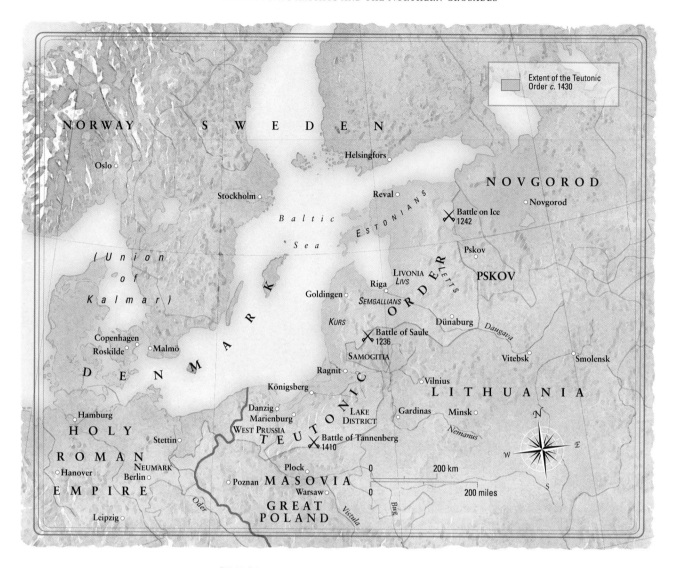

The territories of the Teutonic Order and the northern duchies of the kingdom of Poland, the grand duchy of Lithuania, and important Russian city-states.

CRUSADERS IN PRUSSIA

The first invasions of Prussia were made by Poles in the 12th century. The reasons are obscure, but one of these may have been the desire to subject the entire coastline to royal authority. The neighbouring regions of Pomerania and Pomerellia (in northern Poland) had just made themselves effectively autonomous, and royal control over powerful relatives who held the northern duchies was notoriously weak. The Piast dynasty had long passed the Polish crown to its eldest living member, thereby reducing the likelihood of civil war, but also weakening the power of the king. The latter would be of advanced years on ascending the throne, and his favoured nobles and clergy would have little connection with those of his predecessor, thereby affecting his leadership and interrupting political continuity. When the Prussians rebelled and then attacked the nearest duchies – Masovia, Great Poland and Pomerellia – the Duke of Masovia sought to bring in foreign military orders to assist him, and he founded a short-lived military order of his own.

Missionary activity in Prussia had been a failure as well, although a monk named Christian had established himself among one of the interior tribes. He had been

The Castles of the Teutonic Order

The local materials available for construction and labour skills in the 13th century made it impossible to recreate in Livonia and Prussia the castles found in Germany. Instead, log frameworks filled with earth were erected on hills or at the confluence of streams. Most often these forts served as bases for scouts, who could warn burghers and villagers of the approach of raiders, and where militias could gather to pursue the booty-laden intruders on their way home. Sometimes forts were constructed in enemy country, as a base for raiders intent on destroying the region's economic base and forcing the natives to surrender.

Brick castles became common in the 14th and 15th centuries, and were often built on the sites of disintegrating wooden forts. These were usually simple in design, the motte and bailey castle having a strong tower, a courtyard with housing for the garrison and storehouses, and a more lightly fortified outer perimeter for animals, servants and merchants. Some developed into powerful fortifications; Marienburg (*below*) impressed some of the most sophisticated nobles from the Holy Roman empire, France and Britain. Large, square brick or stone castles with a small interior courtyard were very practical on the frontier, since the dwellings and storehouses were an integral part of the fortification. Some had elevated external latrines. The castles were surprisingly comfortable. Most had covered ramparts to keep the guards dry, many had saunas for use of the garrison and guests, and some had central heating. The dormitories were clean, and officers enjoyed certain luxuries unheard of for cloistered monks. Everyone attended the daily religious services, observed the cycle of fasts and feasts, and divided up the many supervisory duties.

This depiction of Tannhäuser in the costume of a 13th-century Teutonic Knight, suggesting that he participated in the Fifth Crusade, is from an illustrated manuscript, the Manesse Codex, a collection of popular poems (1304–40). The helmet often appears in films, but would be awkward to wear on a battlefield; the shield would protect a mounted knight's vital organs without hindering mobility.

held prisoner for a while, presumably for ransom, which had the advantage of improving his language skills. Ambitious churchmen were eager to proselytize there, and the Duke of Masovia was keen to assist them – once he had stopped the attacks on his own subjects. In 1226 the duke invited the Teutonic Knights to help him, offering them a share of the conquests. Subsequently, the tide of battle shifted to the Christians' advantage. In ways similar to those in Livonia, the Teutonic Knights moved down the Vistula River to the Baltic Sea, then up the coastline. The duke attempted to move up the Narew River towards Lithuania, thus paralleling the German advance. However, the Mongol invasion of 1241 overran most of Red Russia (Podolia and Galicia) and stormed through southern Poland; after that, Poland was incapacitated as a military power for half a century. The Teutonic Knights, who were not affected, continued their march east until they clashed with the Lithuanians. After hard fighting, they established defensible borders across the Masurian Lake district in eastern Prussia.

The Teutonic Knights, like the Swordbrothers, were a military order; that is, they took all the vows of other religious orders, but their specialities were maintaining hospitals and waging warfare on behalf of the Church. The members were organized in three groups: first, knights who entered the order as adults; second, priests; third, serving brothers, some of whom were men-at-arms, while others performed important tasks in the administrative bureaucracy. The membership elected the Grand Master and the regional masters. A council assisted these officers, and exercised other duties, including command of convents in the most important castles. Each castle had an officer in command and subordinates with specific responsibilities; those who were most capable usually advanced to higher offices, though it helped greatly to be nobly born. Most knights were, strictly speaking, not nobles, but came from the *ministeriale* class; in this military order they could rise much higher than at home. They could command armies, defend communities against pagan attacks, win respect and advance the careers of their relatives.

A central crusader goal was the conquest of Samogitia, to facilitate communication during the winter months when sea travel to Livonia was impossible and to open the way to the Lithuanian highlands. Critics of the crusade employed a dual standard: kings could expand their lands by war, but not monks. The knights of the orders believed that, within the limits established by the Pope and Holy Roman emperor, they were entitled to all the privileges granted to them. Fortunately for the Teutonic Knights, the popes were strong supporters of crusading in all its forms, and they saw no alternative to military orders leading these wars. Nevertheless, the critics were a notable nuisance, and the pagan rulers of Lithuania understood well how to play Roman Catholic practices to their own advantage.

POLAND BECOMES AN ADVERSARY

For Livonia the Baltic Sea was the lifeline; therefore, a close relationship with the increasingly powerful Hanseatic League was important. This loosely organized alliance of German merchant communities provided vessels to transport and supply crusaders. Prussia's lifeline was the overland route from the Holy Roman Empire, parts of which were in the hands of unfriendly princes. This meant a strained relationship with the Polish king Władysław I 'the Short' (1261–1333) over Pomerellia. Between 1308 and 1309 the Prussians broke the deadlock by intervening in a conflict there, before annexing the territory. In the long term this was a mistake, since it turned Poland from a sometime ally to a habitual foe.

The seriousness of the situation was not immediately apparent, because crusaders from Germany and Bohemia made increasingly deeper invasions of Lithuania possible. Crusaders moved up the Nemanus River by land and on boats into Samogitia and toward Vilnius, and across the

Grand Master of the Teutonic Order Dietrich von Altenburg kneeling before Holy Roman Emperor Louis IV of Bavaria in 1337, being endowed with lands captured from Lithuania. In reality, the emperor sent the document to the aged Grand Master with his nephew, who had led crusaders to fight the Lithuanian pagans along the Nemanus River. The German Master was then in Avignon representing the emperor at the papal court.

lake district to Gardinas (Grodno), building castles as bases for storing supplies and making raids into the interior.

Polish attacks on Prussia disrupted campaigns and forced the Teutonic Knights to station knights and mercenaries all along the border. The Teutonic Knights, not surprisingly, struck back at the nearest Polish duchies. In 1343 a peace treaty was signed with Casimir III 'the Great' (1310–70) of Poland, which brought a temporary end to hostilities, allowing him to move southeast into Galicia and Podolia and make those regions part of his kingdom. The Germans were free to drive deep into central Lithuania.

The Grand Master and Livonian master were responsible for military strategy, assisted by skilled marshals and experienced officers. Since they faced powerful enemies – Novgorod, Pskov, Lithuania and Poland – it was of the highest importance to protect the overland route from Germany to Prussia. West Prussia was the vital link to the west, but it also provided the services of many skilled knights. Poles were encouraged to join Germans in settling vacant Prussian lands, thereby increasing the tax base and number of available warriors. Later an additional link in the overland route was acquired in the Neumark, which bordered on friendly Brandenburg. There were usually two major expeditions each year. One was in the winter when the rivers and lakes froze sufficiently for armies to use them as highways into Samogitia and Lithuania. The other was after the harvest had been gathered, so that native Prussians could accompany the army. The Prussians were valued for their courage, their delight in ravaging the property of hereditary enemies and their skill, but every commander understood that when faced by defeat, they, like all Baltic natives, would flee into the woods. Lithuanian exiles served gladly as scouts and guides for the crusaders, and were rewarded with grants of land in Prussia similar to those of the native nobility.

The crusaders gathered at frontier castles – at Königsberg or Ragnit in Prussia, in Dünaburg or Goldingen in Livonia. This permitted militia, secular knights, 'pilgrims' from Bohemia, Germany, France, England and Scotland, and even a few lords from Poland to come in at their own pace, the primitive roads and inns not being suitable for handling all the troops at once. When the king of Bohemia came, the pressure of numbers was even greater. Supplies awaited at frontier castles or, if the advance was up the Nemanus River, on ships. If the attack went in overland, through the dense frontier wilderness, supplies would be hidden for use on the way back to safety. During the campaign the armies lived off the land as much as was possible. Usually the expeditions were intended solely to burn villages, round up cattle and people and destroy crops, so as to deprive the garrisons of nearby castles of food, making it easier to capture them later by siege – a common European

A crossbow of the Teutonic Order that uses gears to pull the bowstring back into firing position. Crossbows used from horseback, fired at short range, were much simpler.

Artillery of the Teutonic Order

The Teutonic Knights possessed convents across the Holy Roman Empire, and as a result few developments in the military arts escaped their attention. Also, crusaders from France and England discussed the latest developments in warfare at the many banquets that were central to the 14th-century chivalric crusades. Thus, when gunpowder weapons appeared in Europe their importance was quickly recognized by knights of the order. Cost was no obstacle, since the Grand Master was wealthy, and, because warfare on the wilderness frontiers had long required adaptation to local conditions, there was no class resistance to change.

The first use of cannon seems to have been in 1362, in the siege of the Samogitian stronghold at Kaunas, but it is only in 1374 that records confirm their presence in armouries. All early weapons were very primitive. Siege cannon could be easily transported up the Nemanus River, and their stone shot was very effective against wood and earth fortifications. Smaller-calibre firearms appeared, too, with very long barrels and firing a small lead bullet. These were more mobile than siege cannon, but their weight and size made them easier to use in defending castles than in the chaotic conditions of battle in the wilderness.

Above The Powder Tower in Riga, Latvia, still has cannonballs from siege guns embedded in the wall. Riga was the most important city in Livonia, but was more independent than the Prussian cities.

Left Early artillery was primitive, but 'bombards' such as this one were effective in attacking fortifications.

practice. The crusaders possessed all the latest items of military technology, especially in siegecraft and weaponry (see box on p. 149). However, whatever they introduced was soon copied; when they demonstrated the value of cannon, the Lithuanians obtained their own artillery from Poland.

The Lithuanians were handicapped by the lack of transport and taxes to support garrisons, but they could draw strong reinforcements from their Russian domains. Since they could not easily feed a large army waiting for an invasion, they customarily summoned their forces only when they were certain of the route the raiders would take on the way out, and prepared an ambush. The Teutonic Knights' most famous commander, Winrich von Kniprode (1310–82), faced such a situation in the winter of 1348. Trapped on his retreat by superior Lithuanian and Russian forces, he put his international army into battle formation and maintained discipline until the moment came for his heavy cavalry to charge the more lightly armed enemy. This victory allowed the kings of Hungary and Poland to advance deep into Lithuanian possessions in Galicia and Volhynia. All crusader advances were stopped by the plague after 1348; the momentum resumed in the north after Winrich was elected Grand Master in 1352.

Roman Catholic incursions increased in number, while pagan Lithuanians raided Livonia, Prussia and Poland, destroying villages and carrying away prisoners to become serfs or be sold on the international slave market. In practice there was little difference between the contestants, and in time they came to value one another's skills, valour and honour.

Chivalry was one of the great attractions for visiting crusaders, because the Teutonic Knights knew how to stage impressive pageants and ceremonies. For this reason, and because the Grand Masters were skilled practitioners of realpolitik, some historians have questioned whether these were crusades at all. Contemporaries rarely raised the issue, although the Poles were disturbed that crusaders were used against them, and some Franciscans argued that war was not a practical or permissible method for converting pagans. The popes sought to avoid this dispute, preferring to concentrate on more important matters such as the Hundred Years War between England and France, the political chaos in Italy, and the awkward fact that through much of this period there were two men claiming to be the rightful Pope – one in Rome, one in Avignon – contemporaries being divided as to which one had the better claim. Each would have liked to claim credit for the conversion of the Lithuanians, a fact that the Lithuanian rulers exploited easily. Papal legates did condemn the Teutonic Knights' actions, but the verdicts were always reversed by the popes.

The Lithuanian situation was extremely complicated. At its height two Lithuanian brothers, Kestutis (1297–1382) and Algirdas (c. 1296–1377), worked together effectively. The former watched the western front, the latter the eastern, and other brothers ruled in the south and north. Their successors, Vytautas (c. 1350–1430) and Jogaila (c. 1348–1434), were often enemies, and each became an ally of the Teutonic Knights

Time has caused the handle of this 14th- to 15th-century iron sword to disintegrate, but one can still easily imagine its cutting power.

Below A 15th-century parchment document from the reign of King Władysław II Jagiełło, a grant by royal council. Typical of important documents of this era, each witness had his seal affixed to it.

when it was to his advantage. Throughout this period all the Lithuanian rulers understood how to play on Christian gullibility, often saving themselves from dangerous situations by asking for truces to consider conversion to Roman Catholicism. Such ploys became so common that the Teutonic Knights became sceptical of any Lithuanian duke's apparent sincerity.

THE CONVERSION OF LITHUANIA

The situation in Lithunia lent itself to crusader exploitation. Vytautas and Jogaila mistrusted one another, and with good reason; Jogaila had murdered Vytautas's father, Kestutis. Lithuanian warriors preferred Vytautas over the Polish king or the many brothers of the two rivals. Vytautas would conspire with the crusaders, then betray them, then conspire again. Each time Lithuania became weaker.

For many years it had appeared that Lithuania would not abandon its pagan beliefs and practices, or, if it did so, that it would adopt Orthodoxy, as many members of the ruling family had already done. However, a conjunction of events drew Jogaila, the supreme prince, to marry the heiress of Poland in 1387, a match that required him to promise the conversion of his entire state. In this way he could undermine the crusaders' claim to be defending Christianity, he could make a major element of the enemy coalition into a close ally and he

> '*There was a great meeting with Vytautas and his brother to end the war between Prussia and Livonia and the Lithuanians; the land that God's knights had won and held for many years, and developed, should remain theirs, while the wilderness should be divided with the Lithuanians.*'
>
> Detmar's Chronicle, 1399

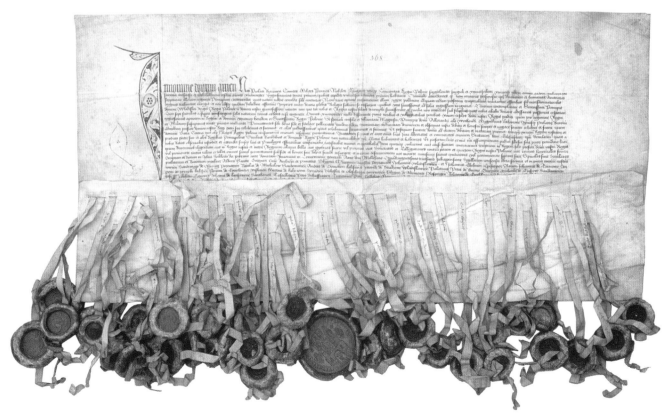

Fresco of King Władysław II Jagiełło, king of Poland, in the Holy Trinity Chapel in Lublin castle, Lublin, Poland. The paintings, in Russian style, were completed in 1418 by a team led by Master Andriej. Whitewashed in the 19th century, their restoration was completed only in 1997.

could end the civil war with his cousin Vytautas. (Henceforth, Jogaila is known by the Polish form of his name, Jagiełło.)

The Teutonic Knights proclaimed this conversion another pagan trick, then sought to attract yet more crusaders to capture the Lithuanian capital, which was now defended not only by Lithuanians and Russians, but by Polish knights. In 1394 a great army of Teutonic Knights, with crusaders from England, France and Germany, besieged Vilnius. The assaults failed, but peace talks followed, and the war ended in 1398, after which Vytautas and Jagiełło helped suppress the last Lithuanian pagans in Samogitia, then made a military alliance with the Teutonic Knights for war against the Tatars and grand duke of Moscow. Lithuanian troops even helped suppress piracy in the Teutonic Order's only nautical campaign – against the island of Gotland.

When the queen of Poland died in 1400, Jagiełło had to choose between Poland and Lithuania. He decided on the former, making his popular cousin Vytautas grand duke of Lithuania. It took Jagiełło time to win the trust of the Polish nobility and clergy, and it was not clear that Vytautas trusted him fully either. This may partly explain why in 1409 Grand Master Ulrich von Jungingen escalated a dispute over Samogitia into war; he did not believe that a Polish–Lithuanian coalition against him would be possible. An alternative explanation is that he was rash and foolish, and that he turned his back on his late brother's programme of friendship in favour of military glory. After a decade of seeking reasons for the military order to continue to exist, he decided to cut through the indecision with a sword.

THE SITUATION IN 1410

The government of the Baltic lands in this era is often summarized as the strict rule of an aggressive military order, the Teutonic Knights, and its semi-autonomous branch, the Livonian Order. The reality was more complex. Finland was Swedish, Estonia was Danish until the peasant revolt of 1343; Livonia had independent bishops, abbots and cities, and Prussia also had bishops and cities, though they were more subservient and cooperative. In addition, Livonia and Prussia would later feature important corporations of secular knights and gentry. These were feudal states, except that the knights of the order were recruited in Germany and the high offices were elective.

For a decade the crusaders, Poles and Lithuanians had campaigned together against Tatars, Russians and Baltic pirates. It was not a completely harmonious relationship, but it should have lasted longer than it did. Ulrich von Jungingen

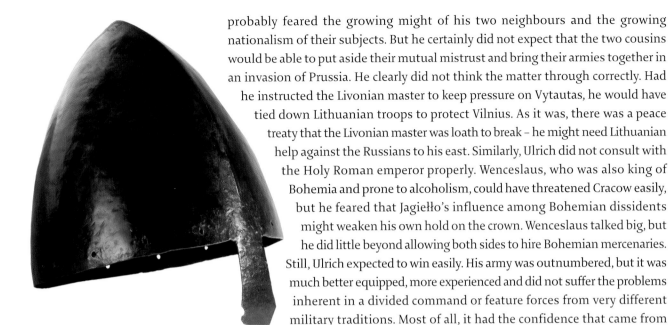

Reconstruction of an early helmet with nose guard. The holes would be used to attach light chain mail to cover the neck and throat.

probably feared the growing might of his two neighbours and the growing nationalism of their subjects. But he certainly did not expect that the two cousins would be able to put aside their mutual mistrust and bring their armies together in an invasion of Prussia. He clearly did not think the matter through correctly. Had he instructed the Livonian master to keep pressure on Vytautas, he would have tied down Lithuanian troops to protect Vilnius. As it was, there was a peace treaty that the Livonian master was loath to break – he might need Lithuanian help against the Russians to his east. Similarly, Ulrich did not consult with the Holy Roman emperor properly. Wenceslaus, who was also king of Bohemia and prone to alcoholism, could have threatened Cracow easily, but he feared that Jagiełło's influence among Bohemian dissidents might weaken his own hold on the crown. Wenceslaus talked big, but he did little beyond allowing both sides to hire Bohemian mercenaries. Still, Ulrich expected to win easily. His army was outnumbered, but it was much better equipped, more experienced and did not suffer the problems inherent in a divided command or feature forces from very different military traditions. Most of all, it had the confidence that came from continual victory.

THE ROAD TO TANNENBERG

Time being short, the Grand Master was not able to recruit volunteers. Instead, he hired a large force of mercenaries and called them crusaders. He summoned the heavily armed knights from the convents, some reinforcements from Germany, and the local levies of German and Polish secular knights. His troops possessed a number of cannons, though they were more accustomed to using them for sieges than on battlefields. He had about 27,000 men, mostly cavalry. Against him were perhaps 39,000 (possibly more) Poles, Lithuanians, Russians, Moldavians and Tatars.

Some of the Polish knights were equipped with heavy armour, but those who had military experience on the eastern steppe had found lighter equipment more effective. These forces were useful in mobile warfare, but less so in pitched combat, though this did not matter much, the Poles reckoned, as pitched battles were so rare. Nor did it appear that such a confrontation would occur in 1410. Jagiełło was too cautious to fight at a disadvantage, and emissaries from the Holy Roman emperor and the Pope were present to negotiate an end to the conflict. Wenceslaus expected the Teutonic Knights to obey his commands because he could easily confiscate their rich possessions in Bohemia; he expected Jagiełło to go along with him, rather than face his displeasure; and he was providing the Poles with fine Lithuanian mercenaries, among whom was one of the great generals of the future, Jan Žižka (c. 1360–1424). The Lithuanians were a diverse group. Vytautas left the Samogitians at home, to protect the frontier from attack out of Königsberg, but the cavalry from the highlands were skilled and experienced warriors. They could move quickly over any terrain, strike suddenly and follow in pursuit. They had absolute trust in Vytautas, who would command during any battlefield clash - even though Jagiełło would determine the general strategy and the movement of the armies to the field of battle.

Reinforcing the Lithuanians were large numbers of Russians brought from their eastern provinces, warriors fighting both on horse and foot, and very skilled archers.

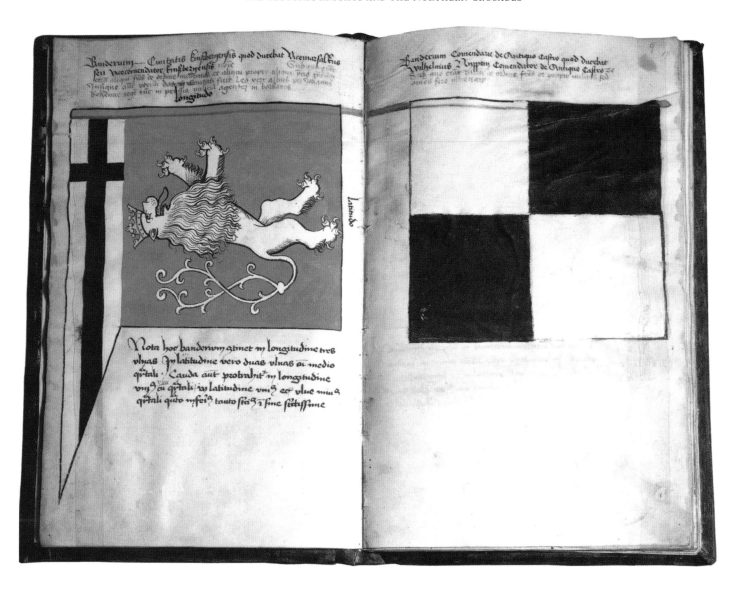

In 1448 Stanislaus Durink prepared a book illustrating the captured battle flags that King Władysław Jagiełło hung in the chapel of Wawel castle in Cracow. The pages depict, on the left, the battle flag of the Teutonic Order's vice-marshal, whose seat was in Königsberg, and on the right the banner of Eberhard von Ippenberg, commander of Althaus.

And then there were the Tatars, some of whom were fugitives from internal wars at home, some of whom were allies. These horsemen were excellent scouts and raiders, and could be counted on to throw every German and Prussian villager into panic, complicating Ulrich's plans by requiring him to deal with the refugees and their wagons on the roads.

Ulrich expected a Polish attack on West Prussia, which could be most easily reached by the Polish feudal array. He concentrated his forces west of the Vistula and at the Neumark; the region in between was sheltered behind rivers and marshes. He anticipated Lithuanian raids on the most eastern regions of East Prussia, raids that could be warded off relatively easily. He had sufficient forces to deal with any Polish army that threatened West Prussia. Ulrich must have been startled to learn that Jagiełło's men had stealthily built a bridge across the Vistula and transferred his army to the east bank – and then even more startled to learn that Vytautas had marched from Gardinas to the Narew River valley and downstream to join Jagiełło near Plock.

A list of Polish and Bohemian mercenaries taken prisoner at Tannenberg, dating from November 1410. Such mercenaries served in both armies, in this case in Grand Master Ulrich von Jungingen's army.

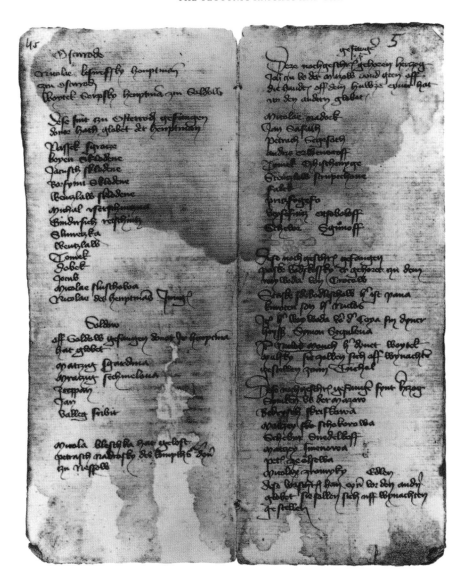

Still, the Grand Master was not worried. He had the shorter route to reach the Drweca River, where he easily blocked the Polish and Lithuanian forces marching north. When Jagiełło moved to the east, he moved to intercept them again. It would be only a matter of limited time, he thought, before the gigantic enemy forces would begin to suffer from lack of food and fodder, and the paths through the immense forests would make the rapid movement of armies impossible, if, indeed, scouts could find any paths at all. These woods were well-known hunting grounds, containing the giant European bison and even larger aurochs. Germans and Poles alike hunted here during the long periods of peace, carefully observing rules about bearing military weapons; in time of war it formed a combat zone of watchers and raiders, small units contesting vast stretches of wilderness and swamp. It was one matter to have a few hunters camping out, but something quite different for tens of thousands of men to seek places to pitch tents, trampling the meadows and polluting the water.

Had Ulrich remained on the defensive, keeping his army behind fortifications at fords and blocking small roads, he would probably have forced the Polish king

The battle began with desperate fighting, followed eventually by the Lithuanians falling back. Some, led by Vytautas, retreated to the Polish position, by which time the fighting had spread all along the line. Others, perhaps even most, fled the field, closely pursued by many German knights. This was the most controversial part of the battle. Lithuanians tend to see it as a tactical retreat, a trap often used by Tatars; Poles note that few of these troops featured later in the fighting. What certainly did happen was a disaster for Ulrich's line; when the 'crusaders' rode off into the distance it left a gap in the German formation, one that Vytautas instantly exploited, rolling up the line and causing some units to bolt for the rear. Since some of the units that fled the field were Polish-speaking knights, Germans later accused them of treason; in fact, they were probably more concerned about being killed or losing their valuable warhorses and not being adequately compensated.

The Grand Master, knowing that a swamp to his rear made an orderly retreat impossible, decided to gamble everything on one great charge, straight at the royal tent. The Teutonic Knights almost reached the Polish king, but were stopped short. When Ulrich fell, general panic set in. From that moment on, the battle was a massacre. Even the victorious mercenaries returning from collecting booty found they could not escape. Poles and Lithuanians slaughtered thousands pushing along the narrow forest roads, taking even more prisoner. Surrender was a poor option, it turned out. Vytautas took revenge on a few personal enemies, and ordinary knights and mercenaries were murdered, while prominent officers and nobles were spared for ransom. The corpses of the two armies – approximately equal in number, indicating that the Teutonic Knights had fought well – were buried in mass graves.

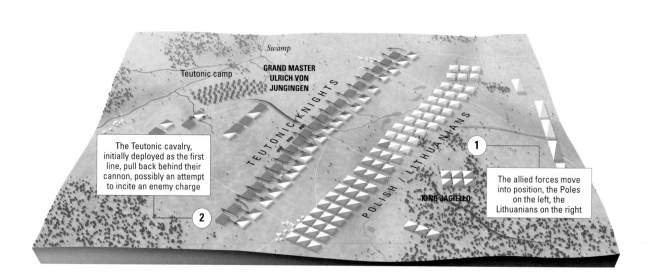

Swamp

Teutonic camp

GRAND MASTER ULRICH VON JUNGINGEN

TEUTONIC KNIGHTS

POLISH / LITHUANIANS

KING JAGIELLO

The Teutonic cavalry, initially deployed as the first line, pull back behind their cannon, possibly an attempt to incite an enemy charge

2

1

The allied forces move into position, the Poles on the left, the Lithuanians on the right

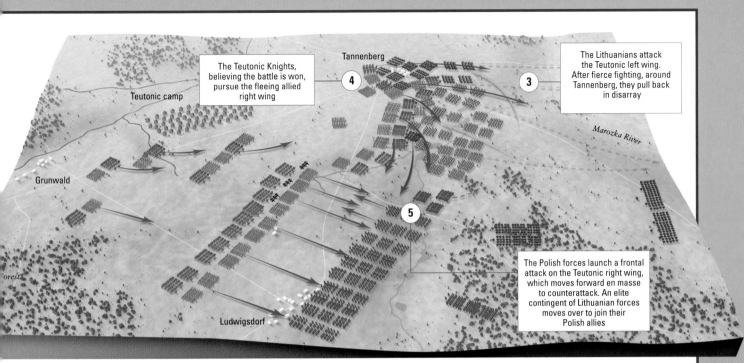

4 The Teutonic Knights, believing the battle is won, pursue the fleeing allied right wing

3 The Lithuanians attack the Teutonic left wing. After fierce fighting, around Tannenberg, they pull back in disarray

5 The Polish forces launch a frontal attack on the Teutonic right wing, which moves forward en masse to counterattack. An elite contingent of Lithuanian forces moves over to join their Polish allies

Tannenberg

Teutonic camp

Grunwald

Forest

Ludwigsdorf

Marozka River

	POLISH, LITHUANIANS AND ALLIES	TEUTONIC KNIGHTS
COMMANDERS	Jagiełło, Vytautas	Jungingen
STRENGTH	39,000	27,000
CASUALTIES	c. 8,000 killed	8,000 killed, 14,000 captured

Above, below and opposite below The defeat of the Teutonic Knights by Polish and Lithuanian forces at Tannenberg marked the beginning of the decline of the order and led to its eventual dissolution.

Opposite above Contemporary shield of Teutonic Knights infantry, decorated with the order's black cross on a white field. Sufficiently wide and heavy to provide protection from missile fire, such shields could be used by infantrymen to form a solid wall that could not be easily breached.

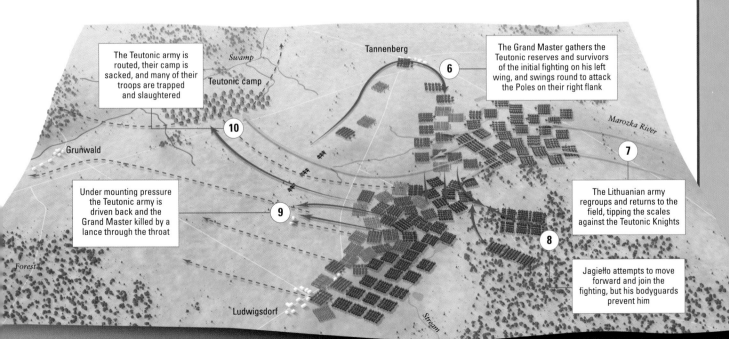

6 The Grand Master gathers the Teutonic reserves and survivors of the initial fighting on his left wing, and swings round to attack the Poles on their right flank

10 The Teutonic army is routed, their camp is sacked, and many of their troops are trapped and slaughtered

9 Under mounting pressure the Teutonic army is driven back and the Grand Master killed by a lance through the throat

7 The Lithuanian army regroups and returns to the field, tipping the scales against the Teutonic Knights

8 Jagiełło attempts to move forward and join the fighting, but his bodyguards prevent him

Swamp

Tannenberg

Teutonic camp

Grunwald

Forest

Ludwigsdorf

Marozka River

Stream

to make an ignominious retreat. However, he found this to be impossible, firstly because Tatars were raiding further into Prussia, burning villages and terrorizing the inhabitants – something Ulrich took as an affront to his order's pride in having kept enemy forces at a distance for decades. Secondly, the Poles and Lithuanians had found a way around the water obstacles and were moving north. Ulrich decided on a dramatic confrontation with the intruders; he ordered a night march, which would be followed by a dawn assault on the enemy camp.

THE BATTLE OF TANNENBERG

Ullrich's march ended in failure. The roads were too narrow and his forces lacked competent guides, and as a result the Teutonic Knights did not reach the Polish and Lithuanian camp. Moreover, it left Ulrich's army exhausted, hungry and thirsty, facing a rested and fit enemy. To make matters worse, Ulrich could not easily retreat. If his rear guard was attacked, there was no way to rescue it. Given his limited options, Ulrich drew up a defensive position on a field between the villages of Tannenberg and Grunwald – each name indicative of the fir forests surrounding the field. He ordered his men to dig pits and cannon emplacements, then had them pull back to new positions so that the enemy could come onto the field. Now his cannon were essentially useless and his men even more exhausted. However, if the battle began soon, it would be worth the risk.

Jagiełło was in no hurry. He formed his men up for battle, then awaited an attack. Both sides understood that standing on the defensive, then delivering a strong counterattack against retreating troops, was the best tactic. Perhaps to calm himself, perhaps to ward off persistent rumours that he was still a pagan at heart, and perhaps to delay the onset of battle, Jagiełło attended mass after mass in his centrally located and easily visible tent. With each passing hour the German army became weaker.

The disposition of forces had the units of the Teutonic Knights on the right, facing the Polish troops. Ulrich probably felt this was to his advantage, since the Poles had great respect for the military skills of their adversary. Ulrich stationed his mercenaries on the left, facing the Lithuanians and Tatars. And so the two armies waited, watching each other.

At last Ulrich sent a herald to Jagiełło, presenting him with two swords and demanding that he fight. It was a studied insult, and word of the gesture must have been passed down the ranks of both armies. Soon thereafter Vytautas launched a powerful attack, striking directly at the mercenaries. Furious fighting followed, and at one stage the Lithuanians controversially fell back, leaving a gap in the German formation (see box on pp. 156–57). Vytautas instantly seized his opportunity, and began to roll up the line. Unable to retreat further, the Teutonic Knights made one last charge, but were stopped short. Ulrich was killed, and the Teutonic forces were routed.

Jagiełło and Vytautas invaded Prussia as soon as they had cared for the wounded, buried the dead, and rested their troops and mounts. Though they spread terror widely, they failed to capture the great castle at Marienburg, thanks to the swift actions of Heinrich von Plauen, a Teutonic Knight (and future Grand Master) who had been left to defend West Prussia. He had hurriedly ridden to Marienburg, summoned all available men to join him, hired mercenaries, and transformed the city and castle from a quiet peacetime administrative centre to a formidable military post. Jagiełło lacked the *matériel* for a proper siege. Even though he possessed cannons taken from other captured castles, he could not transport them to Marienburg quickly enough, and his men began to complain that they had fulfilled their feudal obligations. Meanwhile, Vytautas had gone home, saying that his men were ill from the rigours of the campaign and from gorging on rich food. In any case, relief armies were approaching from both east and west.

After the Polish retreat, the Teutonic Knights recovered all their territories, but nothing was the same thereafter. Every summer Jagiełło would summon his knights to perform their military service, whereupon the Grand Master faced the choice of doing nothing and perhaps suffering an invasion that would destroy his country economically, or hiring an expensive mercenary army that would bankrupt him. In this way the Polish king wore the Grand Masters down, forcing them to exhaust their resources and overtax their subjects. This led to a revolt against the Teutonic Knights in West Prussia, the secular knights and burghers there appealing to the Polish king for help. The resulting Thirteen Years War (1454–66) exhausted the order, and by its end the Grand Master had been forced to swear allegiance to the Polish king, and even to serve in his armies. In 1525 the last Grand Master in Prussia became a Lutheran, dissolved his convents, and became a Polish vassal.

7 The Challenge to Chivalry: Longbow and Pike, 1275–1475

Opposite The battle of Crécy in 1346 was the first major English victory in the Hundred Years War.
Right Longbowmen in the margin of a 15th-century manuscript.

On 26 August 1346 an English army lined up at the top of a slope outside the little village of Crécy in northern France. All were on foot. The archers, in triangular formations, were carefully stationed to the fore. Small pits that they had dug earlier dotted the ground in front of them. The knights and men-at-arms, in three divisions, stood in line ready for the French onslaught. As they charged, the flower of French chivalry was cut down by the English longbowmen. The horses were maddened as the arrows struck home, bucking uncontrollably. Successive waves of French attacks broke on the steady lines of the English. As they tried to push forward in the mêlée, some in the French army clambered over the bodies of their dead and dying compatriots. Casualties literally piled up. Crécy was a spectacular example of the way in which warfare changed in the 14th century. The balance had shifted from the heavily armed cavalryman to the infantryman. In the case of the English the latter was the archer armed with the longbow; for the Scots, it was the pikeman.

WAR IN BRITAIN: WALES AND SCOTLAND

This was an age of war on a quite new scale. The armies of Edward I of England (r. 1272–1307) conquered Wales in a massive display of strength. Two campaigns, in 1277 and between 1282 and 1283, destroyed the power of the princes of Gwynedd. The conquest was cemented by the building of a chain of great castles in north Wales, unprecedented in their might. That at Caernarfon echoed the splendour of imperial Rome. A Welsh rebellion in 1294 was successfully put down, and it was not until the early 15th century, with the rising under Owain Glyndŵr, that the Welsh again threatened English authority.

Above Caernarfon was the greatest of the castles built by Edward I to cement his conquest of Wales. The angular form of the towers was not seen in his other castles. It echoed Roman architecture, and made allusion to the legend that Magnus Maximus, father of Constantine, was buried here.

Opposite It was in Italy that Sir John Hawkwood became famous. He had a notable career as a mercenary there, above all in the service of Florence. His life was celebrated in this fresco in the cathedral there.

Opposite right A typical late-medieval longsword, a standard part of a knight's equipment.

Scotland presented much more formidable problems. Here, Edward I's attempt at conquest began in 1296. Initial success was followed by defeat at the battle of Stirling Bridge in 1297. Edward's victory at Falkirk in the next year was not conclusive. Though resistance came to an end briefly in 1304, the war reopened with Robert Bruce's seizure of the Scottish throne in 1306. The dismal years of Edward II's reign (1307–27) saw Scottish resistance triumph at Bannockburn in 1314, and in a series of punishing raids into the north, the Scots took the war to the English. Under Edward III, however, the English won a major battle at Halidon Hill in 1333, and in 1346 the Scottish king David II was captured outside Durham, at the battle of Neville's Cross. Although punctuated by periods of truce, Anglo-Scottish conflict had become endemic. In 1388 the Scots defeated an English force at Otterburn, but by now this was a war of few battles. The 15th century was a period of border skirmishing rather than full-scale warfare, though the siege of Roxburgh in 1460 saw the death of James II of Scotland, killed when one of his own guns exploded.

'*Twice our archers and soldiers retreated, but our men-at-arms stood firm and fought stubbornly until the archers and foot soldiers reassembled. And God, by his grace and virtue, gave us victory.*'

Thomas Sampson on the battle of Neville's Cross, 1346

IOANNES·ACVTVS·EQVES·BRITANNICVS·DVX·AETATIS·S
VAE·CAVTISSIMVS·ET·REI·MILITARIS·PERITISSIMVS·HABITVS·EST

·PAVLI·VCIELLI·OPVS·

Within England, civil war was not a serious problem until the end of this period. Rebellion led by Thomas of Lancaster against his cousin Edward II ended with little more than a skirmish at Boroughbridge in 1322. Henry Percy, known as Hotspur, rebelled against Henry IV (r. 1399–1413), and was killed at the battle of Shrewsbury in 1403. The long minority of Henry VI saw the crown faced by many challenges, but it was with the king's personal rule that the situation deteriorated into civil war, with the battles of the Wars of the Roses (1455–87). The first encounter between Lancastrian and Yorkist forces took place at St Albans in 1455; by far the most savage battle was at Towton in 1461.

THE HUNDRED YEARS WAR (1337–1453)

The war between England and France dominated the period discussed in this chapter. The king of England held the duchy of Aquitaine, also known as Gascony, in southwestern France as a vassal of the French king. This was a certain recipe for conflict. The claim of Edward III (r. 1327–77) to the French throne through his mother, Isabella, made matters yet more difficult. French support for the Scots, and English backing for Flanders, exacerbated the situation. War between Edward I and Philip IV from 1294 to 1297 provided an hors d'oeuvre, but the long series of conflicts known as the Hundred Years War is generally considered to have begun in 1337. Initial campaigns achieved little, but then the English victory at Crécy in 1346 was followed by the triumph of Poitiers ten years later. However, Edward III's ambition to gain the French throne foundered in an inconclusive campaign in 1359, and peace of a sort was reached in the next year with the treaty of Brétigny. When the war restarted in 1369, the English found that fighting from an increasingly defensive position was both costly and unrewarding. For ambitious soldiers, there were better opportunities in serving as mercenaries in independent companies. One of the most notable of these was Sir John Hawkwood (1320–94), who took his skills in war to Italy,

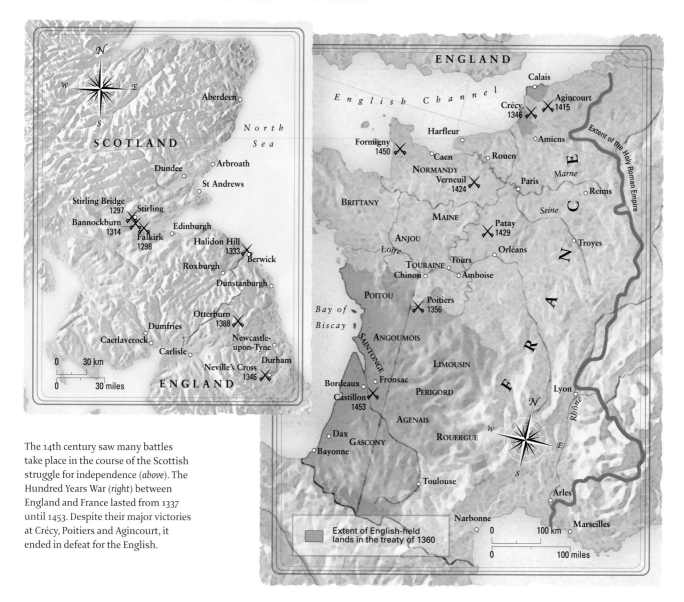

The 14th century saw many battles take place in the course of the Scottish struggle for independence (*above*). The Hundred Years War (*right*) between England and France lasted from 1337 until 1453. Despite their major victories at Crécy, Poitiers and Agincourt, it ended in defeat for the English.

where he served Florence with distinction. Another was Hugh Calveley (d. 1393), who served for a time in Spain as a captain under the French commander Bertrand du Guesclin.

Under Henry V (r. 1413–22), a brilliant and charismatic leader, the English position in the war with France was transformed by the unexpected English victory at Agincourt in 1415. This was followed by the steady wholesale conquest, castle by castle, town by town, of Normandy. This was a type of campaign the English had not attempted previously. The momentum could not be maintained after Henry's death, nor could Agincourt be repeated; success was achieved at Verneuil in 1424, but the English could not keep the war effort going on the scale that was needed. The relief of the siege of Orléans in 1429 by Joan of Arc (c. 1412–31) was followed by further French success at Patay. There, cavalry succeeded in cutting down unprepared English archers. The final defeat came at Castillon in the southwest in 1453. All of the English territories, which had once stretched from the Channel to the Pyrenees, were lost, with the sole exception of the port of Calais.

The revival of the French cause in the Hundred Years War under the charismatic Joan of Arc was dramatic. In this illustration from a late 15th-century manuscript of the Vigils of Charles VII, she is seen in 1429, directing an assault on Paris, then in Burgundian hands.

ARMIES, THEIR SIZE AND ORGANIZATION

English armies were at their largest at the start of the period under discussion. Edward I mobilized some 30,000 troops (though not all in one force) in 1294 to deal with the Welsh rebellion. At the battle of Falkirk in 1298, he had about 24,000 infantry under his command, and up to 4,000 cavalry. In contrast, Edward III probably took some 14,000 troops to France in 1346, while most of the forces that fought in France were much smaller. The army of Edward's son, the Black Prince (1330–76), for his raid across southern France in 1355 probably numbered some 6,000 men, and his force at Poitiers the following year was probably not very much larger. Henry V's army in 1415 may have totalled about 9,000, but some estimates put it at no more than 6,000. It is less easy to work out the size of French armies; they were undoubtedly much larger than the English. In 1340 Philip IV had 28,000 men-at-arms and 16,700 foot soldiers in his pay, not all in one army, and in the 1380s Charles V had some 16,000 men-at-arms enrolled. The French probably outnumbered the English at Agincourt by about three to one.

The king's household provided the core to royal armies under Edward I and his son, as it did under Edward III when the king campaigned in person. The king's knights provided a force that Henry V could rely on, while he could also call on all those who were in receipt of annuities from the crown. In the field, knights and men-at-arms served in retinues. These might vary greatly in size; there was no standard unit. For the Agincourt campaign in 1415, the Duke of Clarence contracted

Under Edward III the English achieved many successes against French forces. The reverse side of his seal shows the king in traditional pose, mounted in full armour, holding his sword.

to provide 240 men-at-arms, 222 esquires and 720 mounted archers, while Thomas Tunstall agreed to campaign with 5 men-at-arms and 18 archers. The very large retinues would be made up of a number of smaller ones. In contrast, infantry in the late 13th and early 14th centuries was organized in what seems a far more logical system, in units of twenties and hundreds. A major change in Edward III's reign was that archers were increasingly integrated into the retinue system. A magnate would take on campaign, therefore, a force consisting of some knights, other mounted men-at-arms, and archers, many or all of whom would have horses. The proportion of knights changed over time. In Edward III's reign about a quarter of the men-at-arms would be knights, but by the 15th century knightly numbers had declined dramatically. At Agincourt less than one in ten of the men-at-arms were of knightly status. Men were not always enthusiastic about serving. In 1420 one Yorkshire knight excused himself on the grounds that he would become ill if he went abroad, and another complained that he could not afford a horse or arms.

Under Edward I and Edward II, cavalry service was part paid and part voluntary. The earls in particular were reluctant to accept royal wages. Traditional feudal service was on occasion demanded. This was an increasingly outdated system, which required the king's tenants-in-chief to provided fixed quotas of men for 40 days of unpaid service. Up to 500 men might be recruited in this way. They did not serve as a separate unit, but were integrated into the various retinues. By Edward III's reign pay was universal. It was normal for the crown to enter into an indenture with a magnate or knight, so that he would be contracted to serve for a given period with a specified number of men. This was far simpler in administrative terms than paying men wages on a regular basis. Thus in 1347 Thomas Ughtred contracted to provide 20 men-at-arms, of whom six would be knights, and 20 mounted archers, for a year's service. He was promised a fee of £200, as well as wages. After Edward III's reign, there was little change in the essential methods of recruitment and organization. The English continued to rely on the magnate retinue as the core element of the army.

French armies in the early 14th century were formed on a very similar basis to the English. The traditional feudal summons was becoming a general request to the nobility to serve, rather than a specific requirement that the nobles produce their formal quotas. Contracts for paid service were increasingly common. By means of the general summons, known as the *arrière-ban*, common soldiers were recruited in large numbers. One element in French armies not paralleled in English forces was the use of mercenaries. At Crécy significant numbers of Genoese crossbowmen fought for the French, though they were of little use as in the haste of preparation they had not unloaded their great shields. Furthermore, a heavy shower of rain slackened their bowstrings. Whereas the organization of English armies changed relatively little after Edward III's reign, under Charles V in the late 14th century the French began to reform their military institutions, notably with a major ordinance in 1374. Regular pay, the use of contracts, with some companies permanently employed, and the abandonment of the *arrière-ban* characterized a determined set of reforms. The mid-15th century was another period of major reform and change in French armies, with the recruitment of carefully selected *ordonnnance* companies between 1445 and 1456, and the establishment of a new militia, that of the *franc-archers*, in 1448.

STRATEGY

Different wars demanded different strategies. For Edward I, the conquest of Wales involved marching large armies along the coast of north Wales to threaten the heartland of Gwynedd in Snowdonia. Engagement with the Welsh in battle was not a necessary element in Edward's plans. In Scotland it was a matter of marching large armies north every summer, and using castles to hold territory through the rest of the year. This strategy of wholesale conquest appeared to have succeeded by 1304, but Edward's achievement began to look increasingly flimsy after Robert Bruce seized the Scottish throne in 1306. The strategy adopted by Robert I (as Bruce became) and his supporters was one of guerrilla warfare. English-held castles succumbed to surprise attacks, and were demolished. The land was emptied before English armies advanced, depriving them of food. The Scots took the war to the English in a series of raids that devastated the countryside in the north. Robert I had no intention of engaging Edward II on the field of battle, but at Bannockburn he was faced with no choice; agreement had been reached that Stirling castle would surrender if no relieving army appeared before midsummer, and when Edward's army duly appeared, it had to be fought, with devastating results for the English.

Ambitious strategies were a feature of the wars between England and France. Edward I's intention in the 1290s was to meet the French threat with the help of a grand coalition of allies, built up in the Low Countries, Germany and Burgundy. It proved impossible, despite the lubrication provided by English silver, to swing the whole coalition into action, but the strategy was one re-adopted by Edward III in the initial stages of the Hundred Years War. The failure of the siege of Tournai in

Stirling castle is built on an exceptionally powerful site, and was capable of holding out for long periods. Edward I took it after a long siege in 1304. Under his son Edward II, the Scots besieged the castle. Negotiations with the garrison led to the agreement that resulted in the Scottish victory at the battle of Bannockburn in 1314.

1340 showed how hard it was for a multi-national coalition to succeed. Throughout the long conflict, however, both English and French monarchies conducted the war on the diplomatic front as well as on the battlefield, manoeuvring to gain allies. In the early 15th century the divisions in France between the Burgundians and the Armagnacs gave ample opportunity to the English, until they were isolated in the negotiations at Arras in 1435, which saw the divisions between Charles VII of France and Duke Philip the Good of Burgundy resolved.

At an operational level, under Edward III the strategy of employing swift savage mounted raids (*chevauchées*) brought havoc and destruction to the French countryside. The Scots had shown how mounted forces could do immense damage, burning villages and destroying crops over huge swathes of countryside. It became impossible in Edward II's reign for the crown to levy taxes in the north; surveys and rent rolls reveal massive falls in income for landlords. This was even the case where there were castles nearby; rents were well down in the little port of Warenmouth, close to Bamburgh castle, 'because of the frequent arrival of the Scots in those parts'. The Scots even killed all the rabbits in the castle's warrens. The English in turn took the technique of devastation to France. Raids, such as that conducted in 1355 by the Black Prince, when he and his men rode from Bordeaux to Narbonne and back, were marked by the smoke of burning villages and towns. 'Hardly a day passed without our men taking towns, fortresses and castles by assault, plundering them and setting them on fire.' The prince's officials gleefully calculated the loss to the French treasury. The French countryside was mercilessly exploited by the English, and by unattached free companies, levying what amounted to protection money on a huge scale.

This 14th-century manuscript illustration shows soldiers setting fire to a village. Burning and plundering were normal practice in warfare of this period, and devastation was widespread.

The hope of gaining booty was one of the reasons that led men to fight; there was much to be gained from the sack of a city. In this late 14th-century illustration, soldiers are seen ransacking a house during the Hundred Years War.

Where, however, the Scots had used raids to gain booty and revenue, and to put pressure on the English government, Edward III's strategy was, he consistently claimed, intended to force the French to fight him in battle. In 1339 neither side would engage when the armies faced each other at Buirenfosse; but in 1346 and 1356 the French attacked at Crécy and Poitiers when they thought they had the advantage. In 1373, however, when John of Gaunt led a remarkable march all the way from Calais, through Burgundy, and on to Gascony, he failed to provoke the French to fight. Charles V was not prepared to take the risk.

In the later 14th century the English developed a much more defensive strategy, that of the so-called barbicans, with major French ports, notably Brest and Cherbourg, serving as bases for English forces and, it was claimed, providing protection for England and the seas. This proved too expensive. With Henry V, a different approach was taken to the war. Agincourt was the product of a desperate gamble, a march through northern France in emulation of Edward III. Thereafter, however, Henry's strategy was to conquer and hold Normandy in a war of sieges and steady advances. The increasing difficulties that the English faced after his death did not mark an end to strategic thinking; one of the great English captains of the last stages of the war, John Fastolf, produced an elaborate memorandum in 1435, advising on the ways in which 'war, cruel and sharp' might be conducted. Two forces should be sent to France, to burn and destroy all they could, not to force the French into battle, but to reduce the economic resources available to them. Further, argued Fastolf, 'better is a country to be wasted for a time than lost'.

BATTLE TACTICS

It was above all tactical skill, rather than strategic awareness, which led to the English successes of the Hundred Years War. Edward I had relied on the massive deployment of military resources to achieve success in Wales; under Edward III the English had

Qibabis nos pane lacrimarum: et potum dabis nobis in lacrimis in

English archers are shown here training with their longbows. They were remarkably effective in battle in the 14th century, particularly against cavalry. The English tactic, developed in the Scottish wars, was to use archers in combination with dismounted knights and men-at-arms.

to develop methods of fighting that would enable their smaller forces to deal with the heavy cavalry and larger numbers deployed by the French. The key was the use of archers and dismounted men-at-arms, deployed in defensive positions.

An indication of the vulnerability of the mounted knight came in Wales in 1282, when a force that crossed the new pontoon bridge, built by Edward I's engineers, from Anglesey to the mainland was caught in a Welsh ambush, and some sixteen knights died. Stirling Bridge in 1297 was a much more serious defeat; again, the English, under Earl Warenne, were caught unawares when crossing a bridge. The Scots, on foot, rushed down from nearby heights, and routed their enemy. The real wake-up call for the English came with the battle of Bannockburn in 1314. The Scottish tactic was to use tight-packed formations, known as schiltroms. These were first employed at Falkirk in 1298, and, bristling with spears, were very hard for cavalry to attack. After two days of fighting at Bannockburn on ground unsuitable for cavalry charges, the schiltroms emerged triumphant. Infantry had worsted horsemen, much as had happened in the Low Countries at Courtrai in 1302.

Bannockburn was a devastating shock, which compelled the English to rethink their tactics completely. The use of archers, with troops drawn up in schiltroms in Scottish fashion, by the royalist commander Andrew Harclay in the English civil war of 1322 marked a stage in the evolution of new methods of fighting. It was not, however, a simple matter of copying the schiltrom and making use of spearmen. For the English, the solution was to dismount the cavalry, and to make full use of archers. Troops summoned to the campaign against the Scots in 1327 were asked not to bring their great warhorses; they were to ride on lighter mounts, and fight on foot. The army drew up near Stanhope in the Wear Valley, with knights and men-at-arms dismounted, ready to meet the Scots. In fact, the Scots would not fight, and departed from their encampment by night, to the frustration of the young Edward III. The new tactics, however, were used to superb effect by a small English army at Dupplin Moor in Scotland in 1332, and in the following year by Edward III at Halidon Hill. There, even the king himself was dismounted. When Edward III drew up his men in the same way at Buirenfosse in 1339, his allies were amazed to see knights ready to fight on foot. No battle took place on that occasion, and the French took little note of the disposition of the English forces. It was at Crécy in 1346 that they encountered the new tactics for the first time in action on a large scale. The cavalry onslaught was softened up by the English archers, and the line of men-at-arms fighting on foot proved formidable. In the mêlée the English triumphed, though there were some worrying moments in the course of

This illustration from the mid-14th-century Holkham Picture Bible shows, in the top panel, cavalry warfare in the first half of the century; the lower portion shows common people at war. The arms and equipment are typical of the period.

'Sir James, I and all the rest of us deem you the bravest knight on our side in this battle; and to increase your renown, and furnish you withal to pursue your career of glory in war, I retain you henceforth, for ever, as my knight, with 500 marks of yearly revenue.'

The Black Prince addressing Sir James Audley after the battle of Poitiers, 1356

the fighting, notably when the Black Prince appeared to be surrounded. At Poitiers, the French tried to respond to the English tactics by advancing on foot themselves. This must have exhausted them (the English tactic was to wait for the enemy to advance), and they were still vulnerable to English archery. The battle was hard-fought; Sir James Audley, one of the founder knights of the Order of the Garter, in particular displayed great heroism when seriously wounded. In the concluding stages of the battle, it was a cavalry charge by the Gascons fighting for the English that routed the French.

French cavalry, shown in this 14th-century illustration led by King Jean, charge English archers at the battle of Poitiers in 1356. In fact, the French advanced on foot. Their king was captured during the battle.

The French, particularly under their great commander Bertrand du Guesclin in the later 14th century, found ways of combating the English tactics. Tight formations of men-at-arms, shields held above their heads, proved not to be vulnerable to English arrows, as was shown in such minor engagements as Cocherel and Auray in 1364. However, in 1367 at Najera in Spain, English forces were once again triumphant over a Franco-Castilian army. English archery did its usual work, and the cavalry of the English rearguard routed the enemy, who included du Guesclin among their number. Another demonstration of the continued effectiveness of the longbow was given at the battle of Aljubarrota in 1385, when English troops aided the Portuguese in defeating a Castilian army. The Portuguese tactics followed the English model very closely, with dismounted men-at-arms flanked by archers drawn up in a strong defensive position. Excavations have revealed the hundreds of pits dug by the archers as a defence against cavalry.

At the battle of Aljubarrota in 1385 an Anglo-Portuguese force defeated the Castilian army. English archers, seen on the right of this illustration from Jean de Wavrin's *Chroniques de l'Angleterre* (c. 1470–78), played an important role in the victory.

It was surprising that the French suffered a further major defeat at English hands at Agincourt in 1415 (see box on pp. 176–77). They had worked out a battle plan in advance, and this time did not make the mistake of attacking headlong. When, however, they did advance, English archers once again did a great deal of damage before the French reached the English lines. Again, the dismounted knights and men-at-arms triumphed in the mêlée, as horrific mounds of dead and dying men were built up. At Verneuil in 1424 the French, with many Scots in their army, employed a force of Italian mercenaries. These men and their mounts were splendidly armoured in the latest Milanese style. Archery was ineffective against them, and they were able to punch their way right through the English lines. The battle, however, went the English way, in part thanks to the morale-boosting example of a Norman knight, who succeeded in rescuing the English standard after it had fallen. In this battle, it was the English men-at-arms fighting in the mêlée, not the archers, who proved decisive. The final battle of the Hundred Years War, at Castillon, was an unusual engagement. The English under John Talbot attacked a well-defended encampment that the French had constructed for the siege of Castillon. Guns, backed up by crossbowmen, proved devastating to the English force. Talbot was killed, and the English (or rather Anglo-Gascon) force was routed. The dominance of the longbow on the battlefield was coming to an end.

The battles of the Wars of the Roses did not witness significant changes in tactics. At Towton in 1461 the Yorkists had some success with archery volleys at the start, but the battle was characterized by a long, hard fight between the opposing men-at-arms, which led to an exceptionally high level of casualties. Analysis of the skeletal remains from grave pits there has yielded remarkable evidence about the savagery of medieval battle and its aftermath. There was less indication of arrow wounds than might have been expected, but a great many cases of brutal cuts to faces and skulls from a variety of weapons.

Above The battle of Towton in 1461 was the most savage encounter in the Wars of the Roses. Excavation of grave pits has revealed skeletons displaying dreadful wounds. This man was killed by a brutal blow to the face.

THE LONGBOW

One weapon dominated in English hands, and made the new tactics possible. The longbow, 1.8 m (6 ft) long and carved from yew or elm, was simple and astonishingly effective. Volleys of arrows, hissing as they fell, were terrifying; the effect on horses might be particularly dramatic. An experienced archer, pulling the bowstring to his ear, could shoot a dozen arrows in a minute, and could kill at 180 m (200 yd).

The bow was not new in this period, but the scale of its deployment was novel. In Edward I's time men, or their local communities, were expected to provide their own equipment; records of musters suggest that this was of poor quality. At Falkirk in 1298 the English infantry had to resort to throwing stones at the Scots, as they soon ran out of arrows. By the mid-14th century, however, the English government was making great efforts to collect and distribute bows and arrows, ensuring that armies were properly equipped. Supplies were stockpiled centrally in the Tower of London; in the late 1350s there were over 500,000 arrows stored there. Between 1418 and 1422 the Crown bought some 1,350,000 arrows for use in the French war. Even finding sufficient feathers for the flights was a problem; on one occasion Henry V sent out orders that six feathers should be taken from every goose in the entire country for this purpose.

Below This sketch from the *Pageants of the Birth, Life and Death of Richard Beauchamp, Earl of Warwick,* shows a group of crossbowmen in battle. It was not possible to shoot a crossbow at the rate of a longbow; the latter was therefore more effective in battle.

'Most of these archers were without armour, dressed in their doublets, their hose loose round their knees, having axes or swords hanging from their belts.'
The French chronicler Monstrelet on the English archers at Agincourt, 1415

Above This 14th-century manuscript illustration shows a trebuchet being prepared for action in a siege. One man places a stone in the sling, while another holds down the swinging beam. The figures are grossly over-sized, but the principal elements of beam, sling and counterweight are clearly shown.

SIEGE WARFARE

There was far more to warfare than battles. Sieges, of castles and towns, dominated many campaigns. The three-month-long siege of Stirling castle was the major event of Edward I's campaign of 1304, rather than a battle. The failure of Edward III's siege of Tournai in 1340 was a serious blow to his plans, while Henry V's long blockade of Rouen in 1418 was a vital stage in his conquest of Normandy.

Sieges took many forms. At Stirling Edward I employed a dozen great siege engines, trebuchets that could hurl a 110 kg (250 lb) stone a few hundred metres with ease. When the greatest of his engines, the Warwolf, was eventually prepared for action, the Scots immediately offered surrender. At one castle in France in 1359 miners proved highly effective. After they had dug a tunnel, Bartholomew Burghersh invited the constable to surrender. Initially disbelieving, he was shown the mine, and promptly handed the castle over. Henry V's siege of Harfleur in 1415 saw the English use the full panoply of siege weaponry. The place was blockaded, and pounded with guns and stone-throwing trebuchets. A mine was met with a countermine. The ditches were filled up, and movable siege-towers prepared for hauling up the walls. Once the town's barbican was taken, surrender followed. Sieges might not always be so elaborate. In the early 14th century the Scots had shown that they were past masters at taking castles by surprise attack and trickery. Simple equipment, notably rope ladders, proved sufficient to deal with formidable defences. At Roxburgh they came up to the castle at night. Going on all fours, they deceived the sentries into thinking that they were a herd of cattle. Local knowledge, such as how to climb the rock on which Edinburgh castle stands, proved invaluable.

The advent of gunpowder did not immediately transform siege warfare. Edward I used gunpowder, packed into clay pots, as an explosive incendiary at the siege of

Right A modern reconstruction of a trebuchet. The two wheels are treadmills, used to haul in the ropes that pull down the throwing beam. The counterweight on the left provides the motive power.

The Battle of Agincourt, 1415

At Agincourt Henry V drew up his troops to meet the French in battle; they were tired, and many were suffering from dysentery. The English chose their ground well; thick woods to either side created a narrow front, which nullified the French advantage in numbers. The armies faced each other at a distance, neither moving until Henry ordered his archers to advance. An initial French charge met with disaster; their horses, terrified by arrows, turned and crashed though the lines of men-at-arms. The main advance by the dismounted French men-at-arms met stubborn resistance. The battle was hard-fought, particularly on the English right, where the Duke of York was killed. As the French tried to drive forward, bodies began to pile up. Many died of suffocation, others drowned in the thick mud. The English archers joined in the mêlée with swords and axes. At one stage, thinking that the French were about to rally, Henry V ordered the killing of those who had been captured, fearing that they might join in the fight. A final rally by the French rearguard failed. French casualties in the battle were very high; they included three dukes, eight counts, one viscount and one archbishop.

Above A fanciful 15th-century depiction of the battle of Agincourt, showing English cavalry, supported by archers, charging the French. In reality, archers played a decisive role in the early stages of the battle, and most of the fighting was between dismounted knights and men-at-arms; cavalry played a very small part.

Opposite At the battle of Agincourt the English advanced at a short distance and then repulsed successive French attacks on their lines. English archers and dismounted men-at-arms won the day.

	ENGLISH	FRENCH
COMMANDERS	Henry V	Charles d'Albret
STRENGTH	5,000 archers c. 900 knights and men-at-arms	13,000 knights and men-at-arms c. 12,000 crossbowmen and archers
CASUALTIES	c. 700 killed	c. 7,000 killed

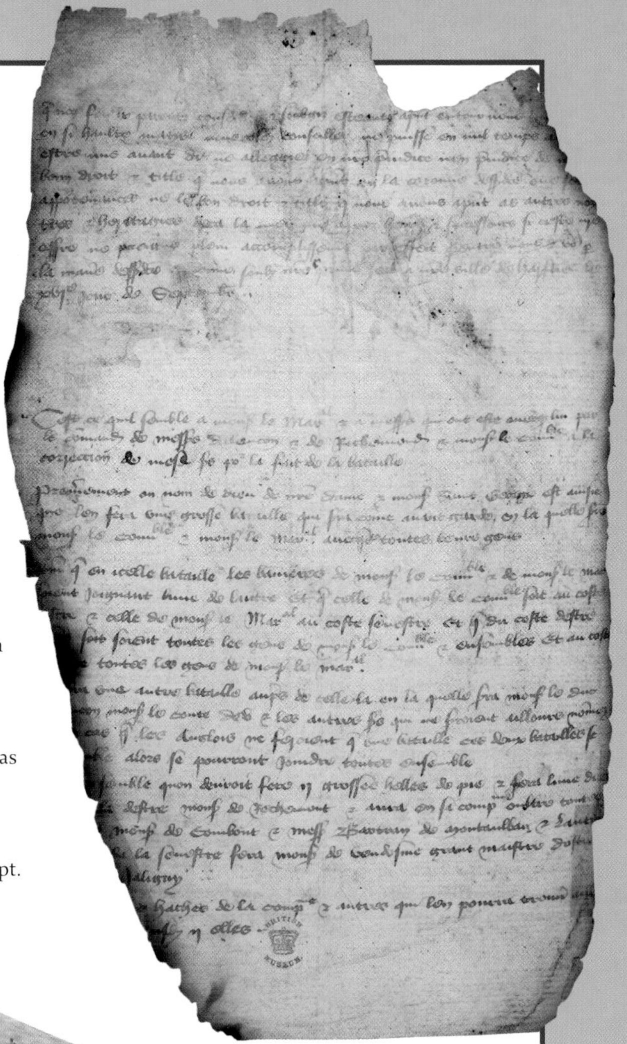

A English archers

B English men-at-arms

C French men-at-arms (dismounted)

D French men-at-arms (mounted)

E French lightly armed combatants (mostly mounted)

F French crossbowmen

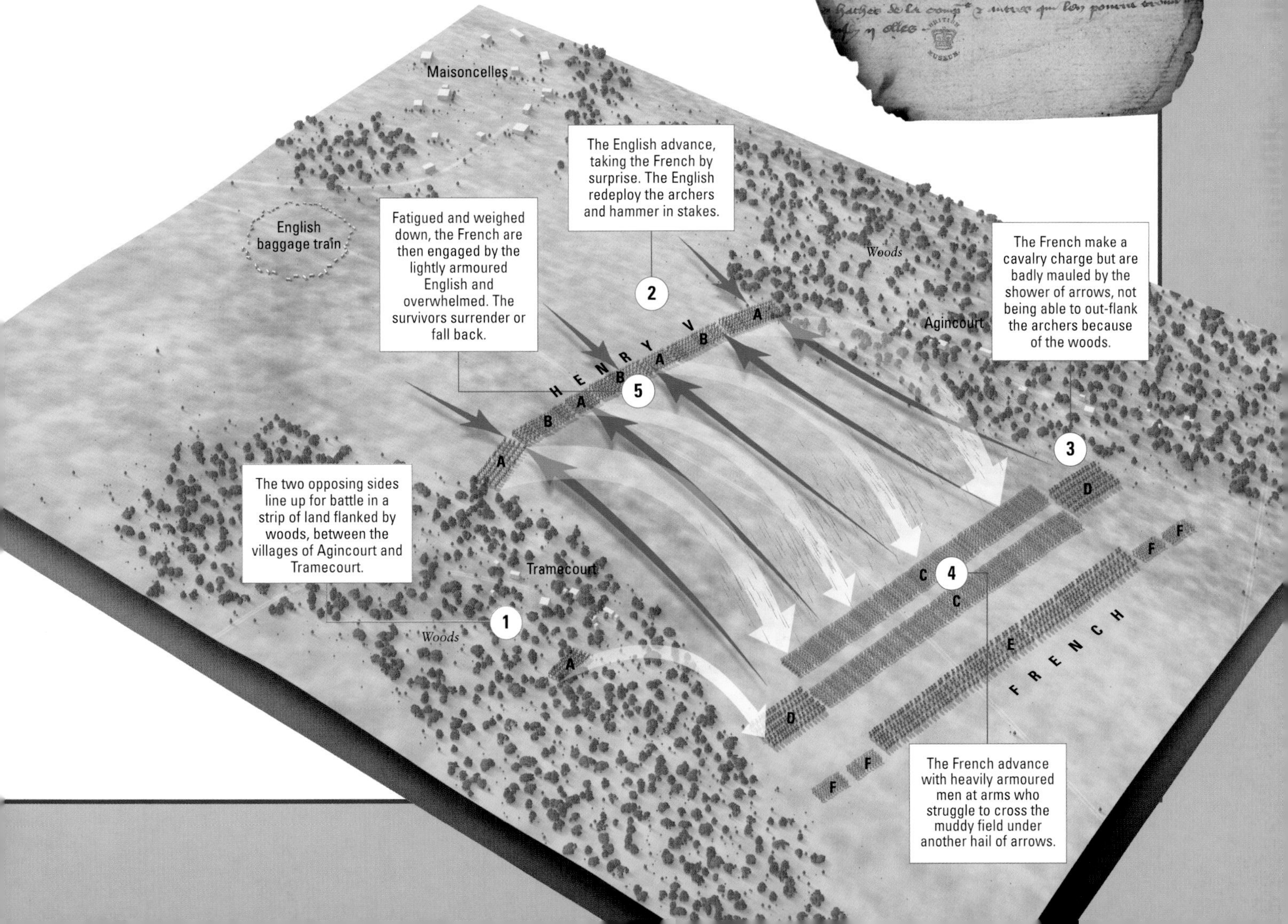

Right This manuscript, the French battle plan, drawn up before the battle of Agincourt by Marshal Boucicaut, is a remarkable rare survival. Events did not work out as Boucicaut had envisaged, but the plan shows that medieval commanders thought carefully about the tactics they should adopt.

Maisoncelles

English baggage train

The English advance, taking the French by surprise. The English redeploy the archers and hammer in stakes.

Fatigued and weighed down, the French are then engaged by the lightly armoured English and overwhelmed. The survivors surrender or fall back.

The French make a cavalry charge but are badly mauled by the shower of arrows, not being able to out-flank the archers because of the woods.

Agincourt

Woods

HENRY

The two opposing sides line up for battle in a strip of land flanked by woods, between the villages of Agincourt and Tramecourt.

Tramecourt

Woods

FRENCH

The French advance with heavily armoured men at arms who struggle to cross the muddy field under another hail of arrows.

Stirling in 1304, though guns did not appear in English records until early in the reign of Edward III. However, by the mid-15th century huge siege guns were highly effective. In 1464 the mere sight of Edward IV's great guns terrified the garrisons of Alnwick and Dunstanburgh into surrender, while a brief bombardment soon dealt with Bamburgh.

CHIVALRY AND THE CONVENTIONS OF WAR

The impact of chivalry on warfare was complex. It provided an ideology that helped both to justify war, and to persuade people to fight. Arguably, it provided a means of making the unacceptable acceptable. On occasion it led to noble acts of heroism, but its dictates might also be conveniently sidestepped when it came to the tough decisions required in war.

Chivalry led men to perform deeds of valour. William Marmion charged a Scottish besieging force at Norham castle single-handedly in Edward II's reign, because he had sworn to his lady love that he would make famous the crest she had given him. In the early stages of the Hundred Years War a number of young men wore black eye-patches, which they would remove only when they had performed some gallant feat of arms. On one occasion Walter Mauny swore that he would never kiss his mistress again unless he routed a French cavalry troop. On the 1346 campaign Sir Robert Colville accepted the challenge issued by a French knight, and engaged him in single combat. At Crécy the blind King John of Bohemia, driven by a sense of honour, insisted on being taken into the fight by his knights; the next day he was found dead on the field, surrounded by his slain companions. Chivalric attitudes could lead to organized combats. In 1350 a conflict was arranged between thirty men on each side, meeting on absolutely equal terms. In 1390 the French set up camp at St Inglevert, outside Calais, and their champions met all comers in a series of jousts.

At the same time, there were many acts of atrocity that appear far removed from the romantic world of honour and glorious feats of arms, and far from the advice provided by treatises such as *The Book of Chivalry* written by the French knight Geoffroi de Charny in the mid-14th century. The English collected heads of their Welsh and Scottish opponents, sometimes placing them on pikes at the Tower of London. After Robert I's brother Edward Bruce was killed in 1318 at the battle of Faughart in Ireland, his head was salted, put in a box and sent to Edward II in England (though the Scots came to believe that it was in fact the head of Gib Harper, Bruce's minstrel, that suffered this fate). Edward I did not merely imprison the Countess of Buchan and Mary, Robert I's sister, but did so by putting them on public display in cages hung from the walls of Roxburgh and Berwick. Slaughter might take place on a horrendous scale; the sack of Berwick in 1296 was one particularly notorious incident, and that of Limoges by the Black Prince in 1370 another. At the siege of Rouen in 1418,

In 1390 at St Inglevert, near Calais, three notable French knights challenged all comers to joust against them (as recorded in Froissart's Chronicle). The event lasted a month, and it is likely that about five hundred individual bouts took place. There were no serious casualties, but two of the three French knights were said to have had to take nine days off to recover from their bruises.

Armour

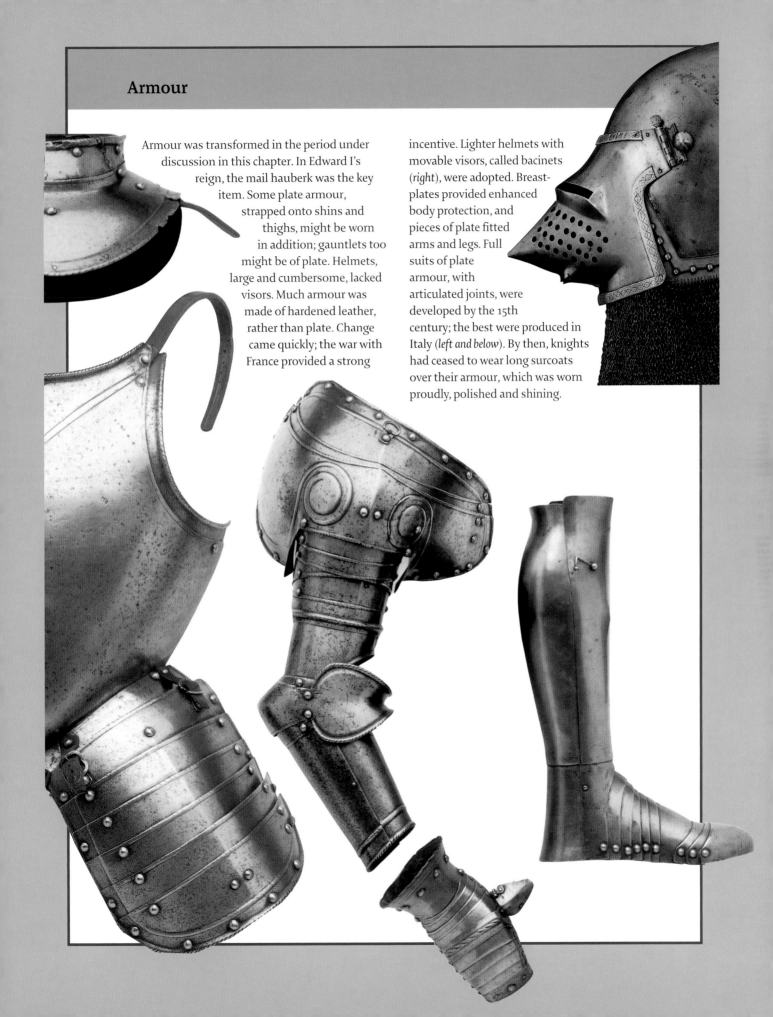

Armour was transformed in the period under discussion in this chapter. In Edward I's reign, the mail hauberk was the key item. Some plate armour, strapped onto shins and thighs, might be worn in addition; gauntlets too might be of plate. Helmets, large and cumbersome, lacked visors. Much armour was made of hardened leather, rather than plate. Change came quickly; the war with France provided a strong incentive. Lighter helmets with movable visors, called bacinets (*right*), were adopted. Breast-plates provided enhanced body protection, and pieces of plate fitted arms and legs. Full suits of plate armour, with articulated joints, were developed by the 15th century; the best were produced in Italy (*left and below*). By then, knights had ceased to wear long surcoats over their armour, which was worn proudly, polished and shining.

Most ships were single-masted, with a square sail. Designed to carry cargo, rather than to fight, they were broad in the beam. The type shown in this early 15th-century illustration was known as the cog. Fleets could be very large; in 1346–47 the English probably used at least 750 ships to take their forces across the Channel.

desperate refugees, old and sick, were left between the walls of the town and the English siege lines with no food. One explanation for such events is that the chivalric code, and the law of arms, applied to the knightly classes, and were of little relevance outside that exclusive sector of society. It is also the case that some of these incidents could be justified according to the laws of war.

The taking and ransoming of prisoners raised many questions and issues; war was a business in which there was much money to be made. The English victory at Poitiers in 1356 transformed the fortunes of many individuals, while the ransom of the French king Jean had a dramatic effect on Edward III's finances. There could be problems over who actually captured a prisoner; at Poitiers three men claimed to have taken the Count of Dammartin. Litigation over ransoms could prove astonishingly lengthy; arguments over the ransom of the Count of Denia, taken at Najera in 1367, lasted for over a century. The importance of ransoms was such that in the 1370s it was expected that English forces could finance themselves from this source, after an initial six months at the king's wages.

WAR AT SEA

War in this period was fought at sea as well as on land. There were no permanent navies. Edward I built a few galleys in the 1290s, but they do not appear to have lasted. Edward II and Edward III both owned ships, up to forty in number, and a fleet of similar size was again built up by Henry V. In addition, the English crown could demand naval service from the Cinque Ports in the southeast, and might requisition shipping on a large scale. Between 1346 and 1347, no fewer than 738 ships were needed

Tournaments provided men with opportunities to display their skill at arms. In about 1460 René of Anjou, king of Naples, wrote a treatise about them. This illustration, probably by Barthélemy d'Eyck, shows the king at arms about to start a tournament. Two men with axes wait to cut the ropes which separate the combatants; ladies watch from elevated stands, with judges in the centre.

'*Our galleys are light, and their large ships and large barges are heavy and fully loaded. And they will not be able to move when the water is low, and we will attack them with fire and projectiles.*'

Spanish admiral before the battle of La Rochelle, 1372

to transport Edward III's forces across the Channel. The French not only made use of their own ships, but also hired galleys from Italy.

Battle at sea was rare, for single-masted ships were slow and difficult to manoeuvre. It was not until Henry V's reign that ships were built with two or even three masts. It would have required great skill to bring two fleets into contact on the open sea, and so battles took place in coastal waters. The most notable was Sluys, fought in the complex waterways of the Zwin Estuary in 1340 – the great English naval victory of the Hundred Years War. The French fleet were chained together in their anchorage; the English, with wind behind them, crashed into their lines, and the battle was won in hand-to-hand encounters. In 1350 Edward III defeated a Castilian fleet in the battle of Les Espagnols sur Mer (also known as the battle of Winchelsea). Here again, it was a matter of boarding and fighting hand-to-hand, once the ships had crashed together. English dominance of the seas was not maintained; the pressures of war on English seaports took their toll on shipping. The battle of La Rochelle in 1372 showed that English fleets were far from invincible. Henry V's reign saw naval successes achieved by the earls of Bedford and Huntingdon in 1416 and 1417, but the king's work on building up his navy did not bring him any major triumphs at sea. The real importance of ships in this period, however, did not lie in occasional naval battles, but in the transport of supplies to Wales and Scotland, and of armies from English ports to the Continent.

24

Clusa iubet qp̄ sic m̄ equo rex stem m̄o sessor
Militis armati signi sum naq̄ professor
Druiensis referens suam sic stando figuram
Indulge fidei subiecte respice puram
Mentem deflexam tibi semper ubiq̄ paratam
Nam d̄no micchi te d̄m q̄ re f̄oc̄ gratam
Esse meum nostas m̄ preaīnctis quia cerno
Rex qua uirtutes sequeris niuq̄ tua sperno
Iussa pretor dignare preces audire precantis
Sponte tibi uero fidei celo famulantis
Preces mea tibi matre preces cū suplia mete
Porrigo pro Roma genitrice mea m̄o fl̄ente
Nūc eget ipa parens tutela nuncq̄ senatus
Sensato senio rex cuius tu trabeatus
Quondam consil amor quia scaris urbe Senator
Te rogat ut culpe ne crescat sto medicator
Indiget ipa tui p̄senti conditione ✠

Suplico puate qui regia carmina audit
Re tua que trudit in unida pro breuitate
Exaudire uelis que possit nomine prati
Ut tibi sint gn̄ti uiuentes rex pie celis
Gloria laus q̄, deo tibi rex decus inde paritur
Uetantiq̄, datur exunc spes magna tropheo
Res faciendi scu uerbor̄ scito labore
Iusta salus fore qua poscitur ut mala scui
Nūc patrare putent si formido uideatur
Ipsi necis dantur sic prelia dum fore mitet
Uel quasi re mim contingere qp̄ meditant
Unde retardantur ne figant uulnera dira
Pesca complent sedabit bella uetusta
Uumq̄ uia iusta reddet comota quieta
Non fiunt facile que no in pace petuntur
Donaq̄ planguntur senio q̄ iam iuuenile
Tempus ndebāt rex dapsilis ~ pius esto
Ut facias presto tuus ut pater ipe solebat

✠ Cum manet an capit mentis luctantis agone
Si uirtute tua quam sperat pace fruetur
Confidas felix qp̄ te fortuna sequetur
Scilicet ipa dei que gr̄a p̄spera reges
Sublimat fuat letatur condere leges
Sic ego spero quidem timor hinc orietur in orbe
Uqp̄ discedes longe tu pessime morde
Plene doli qtium te falso putasse pudebit
Et qp̄ qui sequitur tua pessima uota dolebit ❧

8 The Gunpowder Revolution, 1300–1500

War and plague dominated Europe in the later Middle Ages. The pressures were many as nations, towns and companies of soldiers competed for resources. Success came to unlikely groups, as infantry forces showed that they were capable of overcoming heavily armed cavalry. The cities of Flanders demonstrated how townsmen might challenge the might of French aristocratic armies. The farmers of the Swiss mountain valleys proved to be soldiers of rare courage and ability. In Bohemia, the Hussites, inspired by religious zeal, showed how effective new tactics and weapons could be. Italy was the honeypot that drew soldiers from all over Europe to fight both for themselves, and as mercenaries for the wealthy cities of Tuscany and the Po Valley. War was endemic in the peninsula. In the 14th and 15th centuries armies became more professional, and technological change began to transform many aspects of warfare. All this took place against a backdrop of economic change as Europe faced the problems caused by a dramatic fall in population.

THE LOW COUNTRIES AND BURGUNDY

In 1302, the men of the Flemish towns achieved a startling triumph over the French at the battle of Courtrai. Townsmen routed traditional powerful cavalry in what appeared to be a social, as well as a military, revolution. The Low Countries were prosperous largely because of the thriving cloth industry; towns such as Bruges,

Opposite A 14th-century Italian knight, with lance, sword and shield.
Right The battle of Courtrai.

Right War was endemic in Europe in the later Middle Ages. This map shows the location of battles that took place during the wars in the Low Countries, Bohemia, Switzerland and northern Italy.

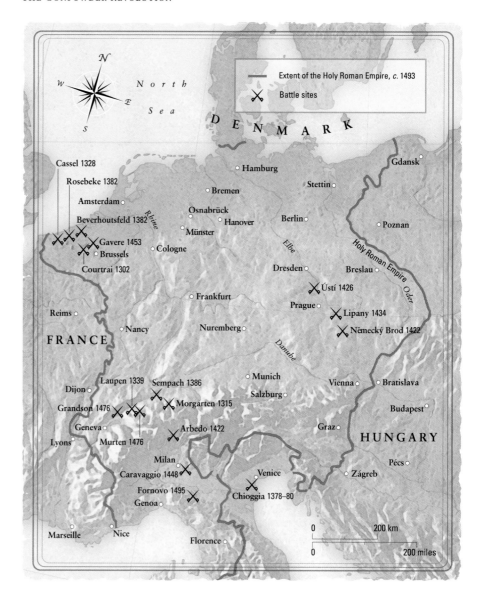

Opposite below Burgundian troops lined up for battle. This late-15th century woodcut shows archers protected by a line of stakes, with armoured infantrymen ranged behind. The Burgundian army was divided into companies of 100, subdivided into squadrons of 25. Regulations prescribed the proper equipment for troops in one of Europe's first standing armies.

Ghent and Antwerp were spectacularly successful. They were not, however, able to achieve political independence in the long term. In addition to competition between the towns, rivalries and conflict between the various duchies and counties of the region in the 14th century meant that political authority was fragmented.

In 1363 Philip the Bold, younger son of King Jean of France, was invested with the duchy of Burgundy. He held Artois by inheritance, and in 1384 took over the county of Flanders on the death of his father-in-law. Within the next twenty years the house of Burgundy had established its dominance in the Low Countries. It was there that the economic powerhouse lay. Though the state, stretching as it did from Burgundy proper to the North Sea, lacked obvious geographical cohesion, it lasted until the death of Charles the Bold in 1477. The Burgundian court was ostentatious, extravagant and brilliant.

The military record of the Low Countries and of Burgundy in the 14th and 15th centuries was chequered. The triumph of Courtrai was exceptional. In 1328 at Cassel Flemish infantry faced French cavalry again. After three days of waiting, Flemish

Above Charles the Bold, Duke of Burgundy (r. 1467–77) by Rogier van der Weyden (1460). A keen military reformer, Charles had few successes in war, and his armies suffered disastrous defeat at the hands of the Swiss.

patience snapped. Rather than fighting from a defensive position, they launched a surprise attack on the French encampment, and were routed. An early effective use of guns in battle took place in 1382, at Beverhoutsfeld, when the citizens of Ghent under Philip van Artevelde defeated the count of Flanders and the men of Bruges. Van Artevelde had a large number of guns with him, ready to besiege Bruges. However, the Bruges army came out of the town, to fight a field battle. A volley from the Ghent guns, said to have numbered 300, caused chaos. The approaching lines of men were halted and broken. Revenge came later that year, at Rosebeke, when a combined French and Burgundian force defeated the Ghent army. Fog made it impossible to use the guns, and heavy cavalry outflanked the dense infantry formations of the townspeople.

By the 15th century the urban levies of the Low Countries were proving to be of little value in war. They lacked the discipline that was increasingly needed, and could not face up to the more professional troops employed by the Burgundian dukes. The battle of Gavere in 1453 provided a clear demonstration of this, when the rebellious citizens of Ghent were resoundingly defeated. Their morale cracked when one of their gunners accidentally set off a gunpowder explosion, while ducal gunfire also demoralized them.

Charles the Bold, who became duke of Burgundy in 1467, was a military enthusiast, eager not only to fight, but also to reform his forces; he created one of the first standing armies in Europe. Yet this was of little benefit to him when it came to the realities of warfare. His forces proved surprisingly inept when faced with the determined foot soldiers of the Swiss cantons in 1476, and he died in battle at Nancy in 1477 at the hands of a Swiss mercenary army. He left no male heir, and the disintegration of the Burgundian state followed.

SWITZERLAND

The Swiss were the most consistently effective and successful fighting men of the later Middle Ages. This is surprising, for they did not have financial resources to match those of the Italian cities, nor the manpower that the French or Burgundians could amass. Nor did they have a powerful aristocracy; theirs were triumphs of free peasantry and townspeople. Switzerland owes its origin to an alliance of local self-governing communities, the forest cantons (*Waldstätten*), at the end of the 13th century; later the confederation gained in strength as towns such as Lucerne, Bern and Zurich joined it. In 1315 the foot-soldiers from two of the forest cantons, Schwyz and Uri, ambushed and routed a Habsburg army at Morgarten. The battle of Laupen took place in 1339. The men of the forest cantons, with their allies from Bern, were stationed on the heights of the Bramberg, outside the town of Laupen, which was under siege from Habsburg coalition forces. The attack on them came in the late afternoon, and their tight infantry formation triumphed over the heavy cavalry of their opponents. The halberd, with its cutting blade and vicious spike, was proving to be a potent weapon. In 1386 at the battle of Sempach the Swiss again routed an Austrian army, killing Duke Leopold III. His expedient of dismounting his cavalry and getting them to use their lances as pikes had failed.

The battle of Arbedo in 1422 saw a small Swiss force outnumbered and defeated by an army from Milan. However, they succeeded in withdrawing without too many losses. Subsequent debate led to a change of weaponry and tactics. While the halberd was still used, the much longer pike was adopted as a main weapon. This was deployed by tight formations of infantry, each rank holding their pikes at different levels, presenting their opponents with a bristling mass of close-packed sharp points. This was not just a defensive formation: an advancing phalanx of pike-men was extremely hard to resist.

Swiss success was in considerable measure due to skilful choice of battlefields. This was demonstrated at Morgarten, and repeatedly thereafter. At Ragaz in 1446 a small Swiss army defeated an Austrian force that outnumbered it four to one. In 1476 a Burgundian army captured the Swiss castle of Grandson. Two days later a Swiss army faced their enemies; when the Swiss advanced downhill towards them, the Burgundians fled. This was followed by a further victory at Murten. The Burgundians were besieging the town; a Swiss force came to relieve it. Burgundian artillery failed to halt the Swiss advance. A flank attack proved decisive,

At the battle of Sempach in 1386, depicted a century later in the Spiez Chronicle, the troops of the Swiss confederation, seen on the right, triumphed over an Austrian army. A flank attack by Swiss pikemen proved decisive. Duke Leopold III of Austria was killed, and his forces routed.

and the Burgundian army was routed. The pike-men had once again shown how effective they were. Morale was important; when the Swiss confederation was in danger, it was possible to mobilize whole communities. There were some inspiring leaders, notably Hans Waldmann, who headed the troops from Zurich during the Burgundian war, but the Swiss triumphs were not the work of single commanders. They were truly collective achievements.

The success of the Swiss was remarkable. War became a way of life for many in the confederation, and by the later 15th century, hardly surprisingly, Swiss soldiers were in much demand as mercenaries throughout Europe. Though the Swiss had some handguns, these were not a significant element in their triumphs. Their tactics were unique, with the use of deep columns of men armed with pikes. These were extremely effective against cavalry and powerful against other infantry forces.

The Swiss suffered a rare defeat at Arbedo in 1422, shown here in a 15th-century German manuscript. A Milanese army under the celebrated *condottiere* Carmagnola showed that dismounted men-at-arms supported by crossbowmen were more than a match for the Swiss with their halberds. The defeat prompted the Swiss to adopt the pike as their chief weapon.

BOHEMIA

The Bohemian Hussites, like the Swiss, showed how non-noble peoples could challenge more traditional armies. Jan Hus himself was no soldier. A follower of the radical ideas of the Englishman John Wycliffe, he was a religious reformer and rector of Prague university, and was burned to death for heresy in 1415. However, his followers proved to be formidable warriors when they rebelled against the authority of the king, Sigismund. They were regarded as heretics, and successive crusades were launched against them. The Hussite leader, the one-eyed Jan Žižka (who was to lose his remaining eye soldiering), was astonishingly successful in battle from 1420 to 1422. One of his great triumphs over Sigismund's forces took place at Německý Brod in 1422. On Žižka's death from plague in 1424 a priest, Prokop the Great, took up the leadership; the Hussites went on the offensive, conducting raids that reached far into Silesia, and even to the shores of the Baltic. Prokop, however, was killed in battle in 1434 at Lipany. Two years later the Hussite wars ended in compromise.

The Hussites lacked heavy cavalry, and developed wholly distinctive and highly successful battle tactics. Weapons were developed, from simple battle flails that were effective even in the hands of untrained men, to war wagons, which were chained together to form heavily fortified enclosures (*wagenburg*). Each wagon would be manned by about twenty soldiers: crossbowmen, handgunners, pike-men, flail-men and drivers. Large guns, known as *houfnice*, were mounted on the wagons. The Hussite guns would pound the enemy as they approached the formation of wagons. When they came close, the flail- and pike-men would emerge from the wagons, and attack. Light cavalry would then lead the rout.

'*Then one Czech stood up from the ranks of the knights, a man most brave, one-eyed, named Žižka, by the grace of God, and he stood up grimly and took the field to fight against those who did not take the Body and Blood of Christ in both kinds. These he took for his enemies, and he also held them to be heretics.*'

From *The Very Pretty Chronicle of Jan Žižka, the Servant of King Wenceslaus*

Jan Žižka, commemorated in this 16th-century portrait by an unknown German artist, was the greatest military leader of the Hussites. Blind in one eye, he led the Hussite faction of the Taborites. He showed immense skill both as a tactician and strategist, winning a series of remarkable victories.

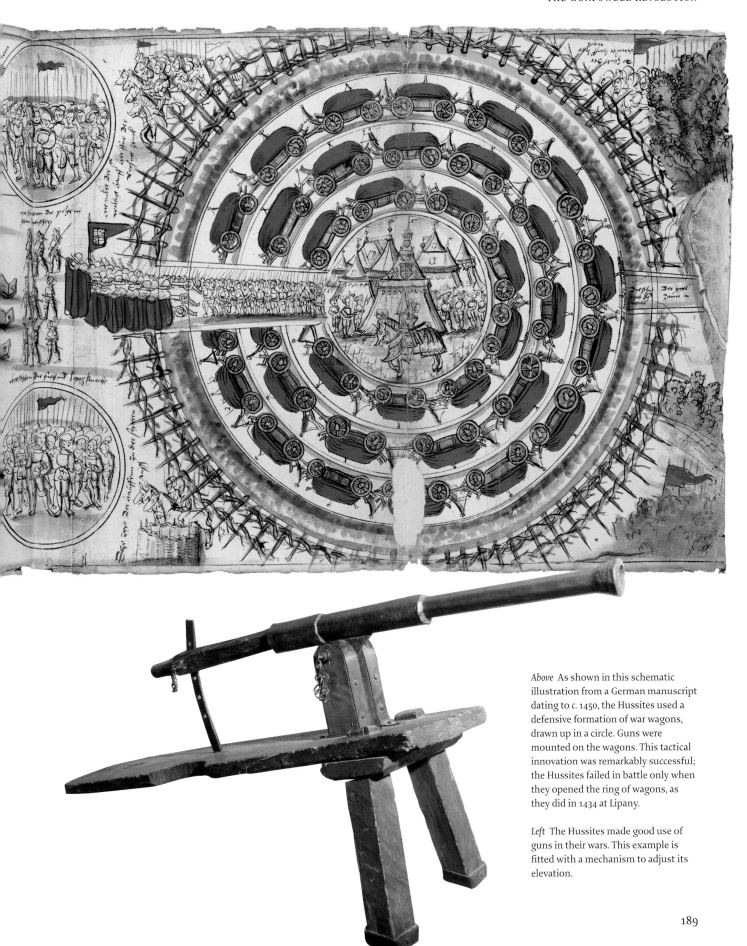

Above As shown in this schematic illustration from a German manuscript dating to *c.* 1450, the Hussites used a defensive formation of war wagons, drawn up in a circle. Guns were mounted on the wagons. This tactical innovation was remarkably successful; the Hussites failed in battle only when they opened the ring of wagons, as they did in 1434 at Lipany.

Left The Hussites made good use of guns in their wars. This example is fitted with a mechanism to adjust its elevation.

189

A 15th-century German woodcut showing Jan Žižka and his troops attacking a town. Some are shown armed with small handguns. They were the first soldiers to use such weapons.

'Žižka's army was like a many-armed monster which unexpectedly and quickly seizes its prey, squeezes it to death, and swallows up its pieces. If individuals succeeded in escaping from the wagon maze, they fell into the hands of the horsemen drawn up outside and were killed there.'

Enea Silvio Piccolomini, the future Pope Pius II (r. 1458–64)

The battle of Ústí in 1426 provides an example of classic Hussite tactics. The Hussites awaited the German army on the top of a gentle hill. They sent messengers to their opponents, asking to put off the battle by a day so as to avoid fighting on a Sunday, and requested that no one who surrendered should be killed. These demands were rejected. The Germans advanced and as they neared the wagons, the Hussites fired. Wind blew smoke from the black powder in the face of the German troops, who fled from the hand-to-hand fighting that followed the initial bombardment. When the firing ceased, Hussite cavalry moved in. Victory was total, and the town of Ústí surrendered.

There were problems with the tactics of the *wagenburg*. At Lipany in 1434 the formation of wagons became a huge disadvantage, for once the Hussites were persuaded by a feigned retreat to open the circle of wagons and leave it, their enemies were able to attack them both from behind and in front. The Hussites were surrounded, and many were killed.

The Hussites had other advantages besides their war wagons and guns. The leadership provided by Žižka, Prokop and others was impressive. Their morale was excellent, spurred as it was by a sense of religious mission. The hymns they sang were themselves a weapon, terrifying their enemies. At the same time, they did not face the most formidable of foes; the German emperor did not have the financial resources, or the manpower, available to him that the Burgundians, French or major Italian cities could deploy.

ITALY

The cities of northern Italy were wealthy, and competitive. Theirs was a world of frequent warfare, of manoeuvres, sieges and battles. The cities of Milan, Florence and Venice were the most powerful in a complex changing kaleidoscope. It made sense for the cities to hire mercenaries to fight on their behalf, rather than risking the lives of their own citizens. In the 14th century, foreigners were seen as less likely to become involved in the difficult world of Italian politics, and so were thought more trustworthy. They were drawn from a range of nationalities; initially Germans dominated, with Englishmen coming to play leading roles later. By the 15th century, Italians had come to the fore. The Great Company formed by Werner of Urslingen in 1339 took its name from an earlier Catalan company that had been active in Greece. Werner, 'enemy of God, pity and mercy', was followed by other leaders and other companies, such as the English White Company commanded by Sir John Hawkwood,

a man of relatively humble birth who became a major player, particularly in the service of Florence. Alberico da Barbiano, from the Romagna region, was a noted late-14th-century soldier of fortune. Braccio da Montone and Muzio Attendolo Sforza, noted *condottieri*, began their careers in his company. Bartolomeo Colleoni, who died in 1475, was highly successful. He served first under Braccio, but then fought against him. His main employer was Venice, but he also took pay from the Milanese. There were many arguments with his employers, and even periods of imprisonment, but he became Captain-General of Venice, and built up a huge fortune. Mercenaries were eager for rewards and plunder, not death and glory. Battle was best avoided.

The elite of the companies comprised heavy cavalry; light horse did not appear until the second half of the 15th century. Infantry consisted of men with lances, shield bearers, and crossbowmen, operating in combination. Braccio experimented with more lightly armed infantry, and by the mid-15th century substantial numbers of men armed with handguns were to be found. Colleoni was a firm advocate of the use of guns in warfare. At the battle of Caravaggio in 1448 the smoke from firearms was such that the men could not see each other.

The warfare of the *condottieri* in Italy involved few major battles, and, for the most part, relatively low casualties. Machiavelli wrote that 'Wars were commenced without fear, continued without danger, and concluded without loss.' He exaggerated, of course, claiming that only one man died at Anghiari in 1440, when in practice casualties probably amounted to 900. Nevertheless, Michelotto Attendolo's account books show that in his force of 512 men just 15 died between 1425 and 1449. There was much marauding

Above Muzio Attendolo Sforza, portrayed in this 15th-century miniature, was the son of a farmer and became one of the great Italian *condottieri*. He fought for many masters, and became Grand Constable of the Kingdom of Naples. He died in 1424. His son Francesco became Duke of Milan and began a dynasty.

Left Bartolomeo Colleoni asked in his will for this equestrian statue (by Verrocchio) to be erected in Venice. He had a highly successful career as one of the *condottieri*, largely in Venetian service. He became Captain-General of Venice in 1455, and died, having accumulated considerable wealth, in 1475.

The Battle of Fornovo, 1495

Fornovo was the first full-scale engagement between the Italians and the invading French army under Charles VIII. The French had been astonishingly successful in their invasion of the previous year, conquering Naples and entering Rome unopposed. In 1494 Charles marched north, to return to France. As his army, which included Italian, German and Swiss mercenaries, descended from the Apennines into the Po Valley, it found a large Italian army, mostly Venetian but with some Milanese troops and also a number of Greek-Albanian mercenaries (Stradiots) opposing them. They marched down the left bank of the River Taro. Francesco Gonzaga, Marquis of Mantua, was in overall command of the Venetian army; his uncle Ridolfo drew up the battle plan. There were nine Italian divisions in all. The scheme was to block the French advance, and then to launch the main attack across the river. A substantial reserve of three divisions was kept back.

The artillery duel that began the battle was ineffective; rain had dampened the powder. The Venetian plan to cross the river was partly thwarted by the unexpected height of the water, and the troops had to be moved further upstream than had been intended. The fighting lasted little more than an hour, but was fierce; Ridolfo Gonzaga was mortally wounded. Both sides found manoeuvring difficult given the terrain, but the French showed discipline as they rallied around their banners. The Venetian command structure was hampered by the enthusiasm of some of the leaders; Francesco Gonzaga acted 'more as soldier than general' as he fought his way into the enemy lines, only returning to his men to replace his horse. Many of the Stradiots were initially reluctant to join the fighting, but when they saw the opportunity to fall upon the French baggage train, they did so with enthusiasm. As darkness fell the armies pulled back, with no clear victor. The Venetians had failed to prevent the French march north; on the other hand, they took more prisoners than the French, and they captured the vast booty Charles had accumulated. The spoils even included a book illustrated with nude pictures of the king's mistresses.

	FRENCH	LEAGUE OF VENICE
COMMANDERS	Charles VIII	Francesco Gonzaga
STRENGTH	12,000	20,000
CASUALTIES	1,200	2,000

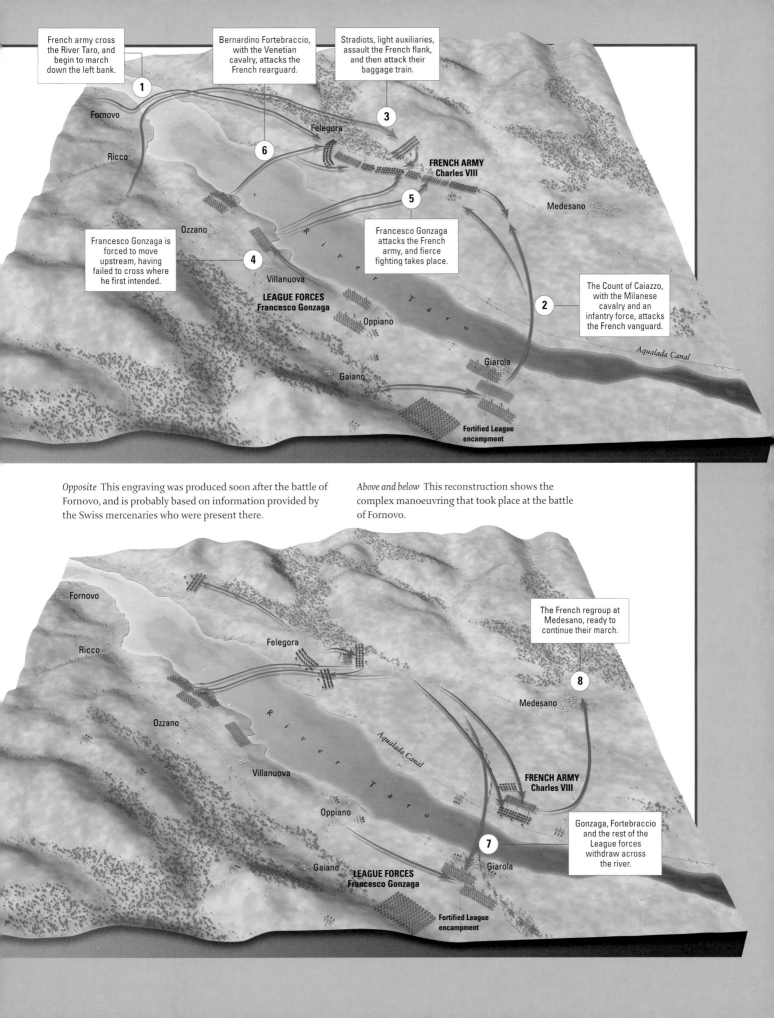

1 French army cross the River Taro, and begin to march down the left bank.

6 Bernardino Fortebraccio, with the Venetian cavalry, attacks the French rearguard.

3 Stradiots, light auxiliaries, assault the French flank, and then attack their baggage train.

FRENCH ARMY
Charles VIII

Medesano

4 Francesco Gonzaga is forced to move upstream, having failed to cross where he first intended.

5 Francesco Gonzaga attacks the French army, and fierce fighting takes place.

2 The Count of Caiazzo, with the Milanese cavalry and an infantry force, attacks the French vanguard.

Fornovo

Ricco

Felegora

Ozzano

Villanuova

LEAGUE FORCES
Francesco Gonzaga

Oppiano

Giarola

Gaiano

Aqualada Canal

River Taro

Fortified League encampment

Opposite This engraving was produced soon after the battle of Fornovo, and is probably based on information provided by the Swiss mercenaries who were present there.

Above and below This reconstruction shows the complex manoeuvring that took place at the battle of Fornovo.

Fornovo

Ricco

Felegora

Ozzano

Villanuova

Oppiano

Gaiano

River Taro

Aqualada Canal

Medesano

8 The French regroup at Medesano, ready to continue their march.

FRENCH ARMY
Charles VIII

7 Gonzaga, Fortebraccio and the rest of the League forces withdraw across the river.

LEAGUE FORCES
Francesco Gonzaga

Giarola

Fortified League encampment

'On every side the sky repeatedly flashed with fire and thundered with artillery and was filled with wails and cries. Iron, bronze and lead balls sped hissing aloft, and these threw the ranks of cavalry and infantry into turmoil even without slaughter.'

Alessandro Beneditti on the battle of Fornovo, 1495

and ravaging, intended to place opponents under economic pressure. If a company was not employed by a city, it might engage in raiding, kidnapping and extortion. Towns formed leagues, usually with little success, in order to try to deal with such problems. Spies and informants played a large part in Italian warfare. Decisions were not always taken on rational grounds; the use of astrologers to assist commanders was common. When battle was fought, sophisticated tactics were employed, with flanking movements, feigned retreats and the careful use of reserves.

Italian warfare was increasingly characterized by the use of fortifications. In the field, when armies encamped they dug simple but effective defences. More sophisticated engineering saw attempts to divert rivers; in 1429 the Florentines tried to flood Lucca this way, but their enemies managed to inundate their encampment instead. Much was done in the second half of the 15th century to improve and modernize existing castle and city defences, with the development of bastions both to resist artillery and to provide effective gun platforms.

TECHNOLOGY

There was keen interest in the later Middle Ages in the possibilities presented by new technologies. At the start of the 15th century a Bavarian, Konrad Kyeser, wrote his *Bellifortis*, an extensively illustrated work drawing on the classical past that included guns and trebuchets (counterweight siege engines), along with various imaginative machines. In Italy, Taccola produced two treatises in the second quarter of the century, with illustrations of trebuchets, rams and other siege engines. Roberto Valturio wrote his *De re militari* in the 1450s; it was printed in 1472. It included a wonderful and imaginative set of pictures and descriptions of siege engines. Guns featured, but so did trebuchets and other machines, along with ideas for paddle-wheeled ships, war chariots and other devices. It is hard to believe that works such Kyeser's or Valturio's had much practical impact; they did, however, demonstrate the keen interest that there was in warfare, and the belief that technology held important keys to achieving victory.

The foundation on which the military technology of the later Middle Ages lay was the production of iron. This was done in bloomeries, using lower temperatures than could be achieved in blast furnaces. As larger blooms of iron became available, it became possible to manufacture guns of considerable size, and to make much bigger pieces of plate armour.

The first clear evidence for the existence of guns dates from the mid-1320s. Knowledge of the new technology spread rapidly through Europe. Wrought iron was most commonly used for gunmaking, with barrels forged from strips or staves of iron, and bound round with hoops, not cast in one piece. Copper alloy was also used, with guns cast in a single piece using similar techniques to those used for bells. There is also some evidence from the 15th century for cast iron guns, though these were a

Right This drawing shows a cannon with an elaborate mount, constructed so as to enable the elevation to be altered easily. It is taken from Roberto Valturio's *De re militari*, first printed in 1472, which included many designs for military machines of all types.

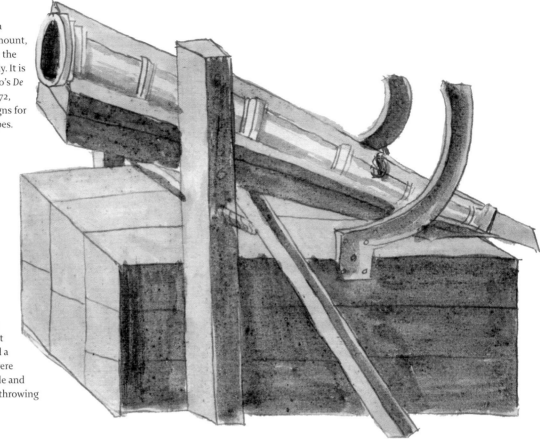

Below A huge wide-bore bombard can be seen at the bottom right of this depiction of a 15th-century siege of Troyes in northeast France. These weapons had a very slow rate of fire, but were more effective against castle and town defences than stone-throwing machines.

Right Daggers were used for fighting at close quarters, and were a normal part of the equipment of a knight or man-at-arms. The hilt in this example has been reconstructed.

rarity. Stone ammunition was used for the large guns; smaller ones might fire bolts similar to those used in crossbows, or lead bullets. Iron cannon balls did not come into widespread use until the later 15th century.

Effective siege guns were not deployed until the late 14th century. By the 15th century, huge bombards were being constructed. These were normally breech loading, with a separate barrel and chamber. Mons Meg, now in Edinburgh castle, is one surviving example, and Dulle Griet, in Ghent, another. These were long-barrelled, the latter with a bore of over 60 cm (24 in.). One exceptionally large bombard took two years to construct, and required 32,200 kg (71,000 lb) of iron. There were also short-barrelled mortars, which were lighter, but must have been less accurate with their high trajectory. These large weapons were wholly unsuitable for battle conditions, but were far more effective at breaching town or castle walls than stone-throwing machines such as trebuchets. The largest were capable of firing a stone projectile of 270 kg (600 lb) or more. Siege guns had their problems. Firing rates were very slow. In 1412 the Burgundian gun Griette fired twelve stones in a day. At the siege of Karlštejn castle in 1422 the main Hussite guns shot no more than seven stones a day, though one smaller gun was capable of firing thirty.

There were many types of smaller guns, and it is often difficult to know from the terms used for them what the distinctions were. The term 'cannon' was a generic one. Cannons came in different sizes, and were capable of firing both balls and bolts, though the latter fell out of use by the 15th century. *Veuglaires* came in different sizes, and appear to have been relatively short-barrelled with removable chambers. In the second quarter of the 15th century Burgundian records list large numbers of *crapaudeaux*, which appear to have been long guns of a relatively narrow calibre. One problem with all these weapons, until the late 15th century, was that they had no trunnions (pivots on the side of the barrel); this made the construction of carriages difficult, as it was not easy to restrain the weapon when it recoiled, nor was it a simple matter to create a mechanism to elevate it.

Slow loading made guns problematic for battlefield use. One solution to this problem was the *ribaudequin*, a carriage forming a multi-barrelled weapon; a single volley from four or more barrels could be devastating. More effective, however, were weapons such as *coulouvrines*. These were either handheld, or supported on a stake, and fired a lead ball. Firing mechanisms were unknown; gunners must have applied a lighted match to a touchhole. Some were fitted with a separate breech, making the loading process complex. Aiming a heavy weapon must have been difficult. Yet handguns were effective; the Hussites in Bohemia were pioneers in their use. In the second quarter of the 15th century the use of guns on the battlefield became increasingly common. By 1476 a fifth of the Milanese infantry were handgunners, or *schiopettieri*, and it was not long before

Below Mons Meg, now at Edinburgh castle, is a surviving example of a 15th-century bombard. It was probably made in Flanders in 1449, and was fabricated from many strips of iron. The barrel burst when it was last fired in 1680. The carriage is a modern reconstruction.

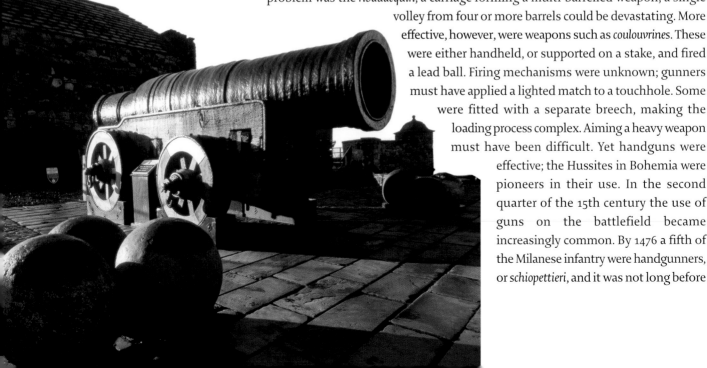

Karlštejn castle, built by Charles IV of Bohemia in the 14th century, was besieged by the Hussites in 1422. Their guns proved insufficient for the task, and the castle survived the siege.

the harquebus, which had a wooden stock and a serpentine lock mechanism, made its appearance. The reason why the handgun began to replace the crossbow may have as much to do with economics as with power, accuracy and speed of firing, for handguns and their ammunition became cheap to manufacture in large quantities.

Guns were used on ships in the 14th century. The first battle in which naval gunnery was significant took place in 1380 at Chioggia, when Venetian galleys destroyed the Genoese fleet. A Burgundian ship sent to the Mediterranean in 1445 to fight against the Turks was equipped with five *veuglaires,* two *coulouvrines* mounted on pivots, and twelve handguns. However, one major technical innovation that helped to transform the potential of ships – the use of gunports with hinged lids – did not take place until the early 16th century.

The efficacy of medieval gunnery should not be exaggerated. The siege of Neuss, on the Rhine, by Burgundian forces from 1474 to 1475 provides one example among many. The town came under a lengthy bombardment from a massive collection of artillery pieces, yet despite considerable damage to the walls and gates, the defences were not breached. Nor did the introduction of guns mean that the use of stone-throwing engines, such as trebuchets, was abandoned. The Sienese claimed to have used 300 trebuchets against Florence in 1390, while the Florentines paid more to the *maestro di trabocco* (trebuchet) than to the *maestro della bombarda.* Brunelleschi – architect of the famous dome of Florence's cathedral – designed siege engines for the city in 1429, and even by the end of the 15th century stone-throwing machines were not completely obsolete.

The later medieval period saw the art of manufacturing armour reach great heights. The best was that produced in Italy, notably in Milan. High-quality armour was also made in southern Germany, where the workshops of Nuremberg became famous. Much armour was also fashioned in the Low Countries; Tournai was one centre of production, and in 14th-century Brussels there were seventy-three armour makers. The mail of the early Middle Ages was replaced by plate, with elaborately jointed pieces giving the wearer remarkable mobility. One problem was that hard metal cracks easily,

while soft sheets would buckle and dent. The solution was a complex process of case-hardening and tempering, to give the steel a hard outer surface, and a softer core.

The finest armour was produced more for display than for war, serving as an indication of wealth and status. For military purposes, more important than a suit of the best Milanese armour for a great noble was the fact that an increasingly large proportion of soldiers were equipped with effective helmets, breastplates and protection for arms and legs. A Florentine law of 1387 specified full armour, sword, dagger and lance for the leader of a 'lance'; his squire would have iron helmet and breastplate, and iron gauntlets, but the page lacked any armour. Infantry from Flanders in the 1470s were described as having sallets (open helmets), jackets, swords and pikes.

Some of the most effective weapons of this period were hardly new. Crossbows became more sophisticated, with windlasses used to draw the bowstring of powerful versions. Large shields, or *pavises*, were employed to give crossbowmen protection on the battlefield. Pole weapons, such as halberds, gisarmes and billhooks, gave infantry forces considerable capabilities. The Swiss in particular demonstrated that close-packed footsoldiers armed with halberds and pikes were devastating on the battlefield.

RECRUITMENT

Money was the most important element in recruitment, though when communities such as the Flemish towns or the forest cantons of Switzerland were threatened, men were naturally ready to fight without pay. Traditional feudal obligation, under

Women at War

It was very rare for women to play an active role in warfare, though they might of necessity be involved in the defence of a town under siege. In the late 15th century Caterina Sforza (*right*) was a remarkable exception, commanding garrisons and armies with considerable verve; in 1491 she was responsible for constructing impressive purpose-built barracks at Forlì in Italy (*below*). Women made a contribution to the Hussite campaigns, helping to defend the ramparts of Prague. They also fought in the field; the Margrave of Meissen captured 156 Hussite women, who were armed and dressed as men. The normal role of women in armies was not, however, to fight, but to provide other services. In 1386 when the Paduans defeated an army from Verona, they captured 211 prostitutes. Charles the Bold of Burgundy forbad his soldiers from bringing their own women on campaign; instead, each company was to have the services of thirty prostitutes held in common. The Hussites, driven by religious fervour, were an exception; Žižka's army ordinance listed whores and adulteresses among those who were to be driven away from the army.

Opposite above This 16th-century painting, by an unknown artist, shows the Venetian fleet attacking the town of Chioggia, which was held by the Genoese. The town eventually surrendered in 1380, at the end of a two-year war.

Opposite below The best armour was made in Milan. This fine suit was constructed in about 1440, in the workshops of the Corio brothers. It is one of the earliest near-complete sets to survive, and was intended for use in war, rather than tournament.

which men held land in return for service, was of limited importance. A general obligation to serve was used by the Swiss in the mid-15th century to develop systems of conscription. In general, however, it was wages that mattered. In Italy the *condottieri* were named after the *condotte*, or contracts, under which they served. These would stipulate the length of service, and the type and number of troops to be provided. In addition to pay, it was common until the late 14th century for cavalrymen to be promised compensation for horses lost in war. A market operated, in which a notable *condottiere* could demand high pay. War was commercialized to a greater extent in Italy than elsewhere, but contracts or indentures were extensively used throughout Europe. Charles the Bold, Duke of Burgundy, attempted to revive feudal methods, but he had little success in this. Levies of ordinary foot-soldiers took place, with towns such as Antwerp and Malines providing useful contingents. However, it was the recruitment of mercenaries, largely from Italy and England, in permanent companies that transformed Charles's forces, and saw the emergence of a standing army.

ARMIES IN THE FIELD

Much was done in this period to ensure that armies were properly organized and disciplined. The mercenary companies operating in Italy were carefully structured. Their captains were elected, and below them was a hierarchy of marshals and corporals. Squadrons were composed of twenty to twenty-five men. The smallest fighting unit was the lance, consisting of a man-at-arms, a squire and a page. In the second half of the 15th century the lance became larger, with four and even five men. Columns made up of several squadrons, commanded by a colonel, appeared in the same period. A mercenary company needed more than fighting men; chancellors provided the expertise needed to draw up legal documents, and treasurers the necessary accounting skills. There would also be commissaries representing the employer; trouble was caused on one occasion when a Venetian commissary seduced the mistress of an army captain. Military ordinances were issued to regulate armies. In 1439 the *condottieri* Gattamelata and Sforza laid down the way their joint army was to operate. Billeting was carefully organized, foraging parties were to be protected by cavalry units, and troops were not to break ranks when on the march.

Similar ordinances were issued by commanders elsewhere. Jan Žižka, leader of the Hussites, issued a celebrated ordinance in 1423, which emphasized the need for obedience. Troops were to be formed up properly, each under its own banner. Passwords were used as a means of identification. The army was to 'march with proper care, having regard to protect the van, the rear and the flanks of their troops'. Booty was to be properly distributed; no one was to keep anything for himself.

Charles the Bold, Duke of Burgundy, was responsible for far-reaching military reforms, with a series of ordinances that set the pattern for armies of later periods. Described as having 'a mind like Caesar's', he involved himself in the minutiae of army affairs, even on one occasion pardoning a man from military service, as he was too fat. In his 1473 ordinance he structured his forces into companies, divided into four squadrons, each again subdivided into four units of five men-at-arms. Training was important; the men were to practise manoeuvring in the field, charging and withdrawing in good order. Pike-men were to practise advancing, and kneeling in front of the archers so they could shoot over them. There were regulations for the use of ensigns, so that units could be recognized in the field. Strict discipline was, of course, to be maintained.

The Swiss were well disciplined and organized. In the Covenant of Sempach (1393) a code was agreed for the behaviour of the troops, and in the field they displayed consistent cohesion, as their tactics demanded. It was highly exceptional that in 1444 at St Jacob-en-Birs they disobeyed orders to retreat, leading to disaster. By the 15th century their armies were normally divided into three columns, the *Vorhut* in the lead, followed by the *Gewalthut* in the centre and the *Nachhut* to the rear.

SIZE OF ARMIES

Philippe de Commines, writing in the late 15th century about Burgundian forces, was justifiably sceptical about some of the figures given by other chroniclers: 'Many people speak lightly of thousands and make armies much larger than they are.' Armies were not large in this period; it was less common than in the past to deploy large numbers of ill-trained and poorly equipped infantry. The evidence is strongest for Italy, and suggests that the largest 14th-century armies were some 15,000 strong; the Milanese put 7,000 cavalry and 8,000 infantry in the field in 1351. Most were much smaller. Milan's army of 1391 totalled 2,000 cavalry and 4,000 infantry. In the 15th century it was very rare for an army to number over 20,000, and though the Milanese drew up plans for a force of almost 43,000 in 1472, this was distinctly optimistic. However, Milan did have contracts with *condottieri* for over 10,000 cavalry, and in all possessed a paid army of more than 20,000. It is likely that at Fornovo in 1495 the French and their allies had some 12,000 troops, and the Venetians twice that number (see box on pp. 192–93).

In the Low Countries, evidence suggests that it was possible in the 14th century for the Duke of Brabant to raise an army of some 5,000 men, but most forces involved in the raids, skirmishes and sieges that characterized the warfare of the region were very much smaller. Burgundian armies of the 15th century were small, often no more than 5,000 strong. In 1471 Charles the Bold created a standing army of some 5,000 men, which was soon increased, at least in theory, to 8,400. In all, he was probably able to muster no more than about 15,000 men.

LOGISTICS

Where possible, in hostile territory, armies lived off the land; in Italy it was normal for special troops to be appointed to engage in foraging, rather than allowing every man to fend for himself. Merchants were encouraged with safe-conducts to come to army camps to sell their goods. In their contracts, *condottieri* might require the supply of food at market prices, or even for free. One method of dealing with an enemy was to try to deprive him of food supplies; in 1390 the Milanese, faced with Sir John Hawkwood's Florentine forces, burned the fields so that they could not forage. Hawkwood's army was reduced to eating its own horses.

A manufacturing industry developed in response to the demand for guns. Jean Cambier of Mons was a particularly noted gunmaker, responsible for Mons Meg and Dulle Griet. In Venice weapons both for naval and land warfare on a massive scale were produced at the Arsenal. In central Italy Spoleto was an important base for arms manufacture. Gunpowder was needed in quantity (see box on p. 203). Burgundian accounts for 1447 show purchases of 2,000 kg (4,500 lb) of saltpetre and a similar quantity of sulphur, as well as charcoal. The manufacture of armour took place on a large scale. Very considerable quantities could be produced at speed; between 1362 and 1363 the armourers of Nuremberg produced 1,816 sets of armour for the emperor Charles IV.

Although small cavalry forces could move as far as 80 km (50 miles) a day, the quantity of equipment required by large armies meant that they marched slowly. Great bombards in particular were difficult to transport; in one example from Burgundy in 1432, it took one large cart pulled by 34 horses to take the barrel of one weapon, and

'It was then the most honourable practice among the Burgundians that they should dismount with the archers, and always a great number of gentlemen did so in order that the common soldiers might be reassured and fight better. They had learnt this method from the English.'

Philippe de Commines on the dominance in the late 15th century of fighting on foot another with 32 horses was needed for the chamber. In 1475 it was calculated that to take a bombard with all its equipment and ammunition no fewer than 108 horses would be needed. The Milanese had 16 guns in 1472; it took 227 carts and 1,044 oxen to transport them along with the gunpowder, handguns and lances.

INFANTRY VERSUS CAVALRY

By the end of the 15th century, fighting on foot had become dominant. Courtrai, the Hussite victories and the triumphs of the Swiss all point to the difficulties that cavalry faced in the 14th and 15th centuries when opposed by determined infantry troops. There is no simple explanation for this. The English longbow may explain what happened at Crécy, Poitiers and Agincourt, but though some longbowmen fought with the *condottieri* in Italy, even as late as the 1430s, and in the armies of Charles the Bold, theirs was not a weapon adopted by other nations. At Arbedo in 1422 a cavalry charge met with disaster when faced by Swiss halberds and lances; the Milanese won the battle only when Carmagnola ordered his men-at-arms to dismount and fight with sword and lance. Part of the reason for infantry successes lay in the great improvements that took place to the troops; no longer were large numbers of untrained peasant levies recruited as in the past. Better-quality infantry meant improved tactics. There was, also, a shift in attitudes; no longer was it seen as unchivalrous to dismount to fight. It is important, however, not to exaggerate infantry successes. Cavalry forces did prove vulnerable, but they also achieved some notable triumphs, as at Cassel and Rosebeke. In Italy at Caravaggio, it was the flanking moves by Francesco Sforza's cavalry that won the battle for the Milanese.

A MILITARY REVOLUTION?

Warfare changed in many ways in the period under discussion. The advent of guns was the main technological change, though their impact was more gradual than revolutionary. Armies marched more slowly as gunpowder artillery was dragged along in their wake. Guns gave besieging forces new capabilities, but did not by any means render old-fashioned defences useless. The development in the 15th century of guns that could be used on the battlefield added smoke and noise to the confusion of the fight. An initial volley might be very effective, but the length of time it took to load, combined with the relative inaccuracy of early guns, meant that while these were a useful addition to any armoury, they did not totally transform fighting methods.

There were other important developments. In a series of battles infantry demonstrated that cavalry forces could be mastered. Halberds, pikes and even flails were highly effective against mounted armoured knights, and tight-packed infantry formations were hard to break. Ordinances from all over Europe show that increasing efforts were made to ensure armies were organized effectively and professionally. Mercenaries played a major role, above all in Italy. Popular movements, whether of townspeople in the Low Countries, or farmers in the Swiss valleys, or religious fanatics in Bohemia, showed that aristocratic armies could be effectively challenged. The organization and financing of war became more complex. A new armaments industry developed, and there were new costs to be met. As a result, war was a crucial element in the development of the states of this period, from the Italian republics such as Milan and Venice, to the brilliant yet vulnerable duchy of Burgundy.

Gunpowder

Gunpowder was known in China as early as the 11th century, if not before. Knowledge of it did not reach Western Europe until the middle of the 13th century, well before it was used in guns. It is made from sulphur, saltpetre and charcoal; the proportions that were advised varied in different recipes. One problem with early powder was the use of lime saltpetre, obtained by composting organic material in pits. This produced calcium nitrate, rather than potassium nitrate. Calcium nitrate takes up moisture very easily, and gunpowder made with it deteriorated rapidly. By the 15th century techniques for producing potassium saltpetre were being developed, and gunpowder was 'corned' into granules, which prevented its components from separating, and made for a far more effective propellant. From the early 15th century huge quantities of gunpowder became available, necessary since a large bombard took a charge of about 35 kg (80 lb). In 1477 the Duke of Burgundy paid one powder-maker for over 6,300 kg (14,000 lb) of gunpowder, produced in a six-month period. Gunpowder manufacture had become a major industry.

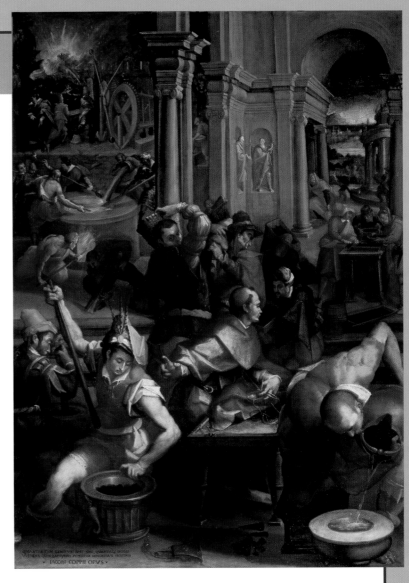

Above A 16th-century depiction, by Jacopo Coppi, of the invention of gunpowder.

Below Leonardo da Vinci was well aware of the potential of gunpowder, as his drawing of mortars shows.

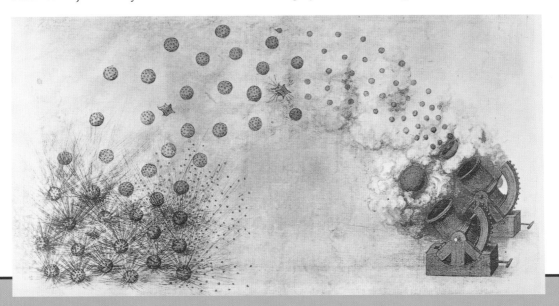

9 The Ottoman Challenge: The Conquest of Constantinople and Military Expansion in Europe, 1350–1550

Opposite Portrait of Mehmed II by the Venetian artist Gentile Bellini, 1480.

In 1453, Sultan Mehmed II (r. 1444–46, and 1451–81), ruler of the Ottoman Turks, conquered Constantinople, the capital of the thousand-year-old Byzantine empire. Mehmed II's empire thus replaced that of the Orthodox Christian Byzantines as the defining power in Asia Minor (Anatolia), the Balkans and the eastern Mediterranean. The ancestors of Mehmed had been driven out of their Central Asian homeland by the Chingizid Mongols in the 13th century. They settled in the former Byzantine province of Bithynia in northwestern Asia Minor shortly before 1300, and established their first bridgehead in Europe at Tzympe, southwest of Gallipoli on the European shore of the Dardanelles, in 1352. Within fifty years, through military conquest, diplomacy, dynastic marriages and the opportunistic exploitation of the Byzantine civil wars, Murad I (r. 1362–89) more than tripled the territories under his direct rule, reaching some 160,000 sq km, whereas Bayezid I 'the Thunderbolt' (r. 1389–1402), the first Ottoman ruler to use the title of sultan, extended his control over much of southeastern Europe and Asia Minor, up to the rivers Danube and Euphrates respectively.

European attempts to halt early Ottoman expansion failed repeatedly. The Serbian lords were defeated at the battles of Çirmen (1371, on the River Maritsa) and Kosovo Field (1389, near present-day Priştina). Alerted by Bayezid's conquests in his realms' vicinity, the Hungarian king Sigismund of Luxembourg (r. 1387–1437), who had been planning a crusade since 1392, amassed an international army to march against Bayezid. However, in 1396 the 35,000 strong crusader army from Hungary, Wallachia, France and Burgundy, led by Sigismund, suffered a humiliating defeat at the battle of Nicopolis on the River Danube by Bayezid's army of 45,000 men.

The first phase of Ottoman expansion was ended not by European crusaders but by Timur (see Chapter 5), a skilful and cruel military leader of Mongol descent from Transoxiana (modern Uzbekistan) and the founder of the Timurid empire in Central Asia and Iran. Ottoman defeat at the hands of Timur at the battle of Ankara (1402), near the present-day capital of Turkey, ended the former's early experiment in empire building (see box on pp. 208–09). Bayezid was captured, and many of his territories in Anatolia were restored to their former Turkoman lords by Timur. The Ottomans also lost most of their possessions in the Balkans, where their former vassals regained their independence. Bitter fighting began among Bayezid's sons over the remaining Ottoman territories. Fortunately for them, the basic institutions of the Ottoman state (standing and provincial troops, land tenure, the taxation system and central and provincial administration) had already taken root, and large segments of Ottoman society had vested interests in restoring the former system.

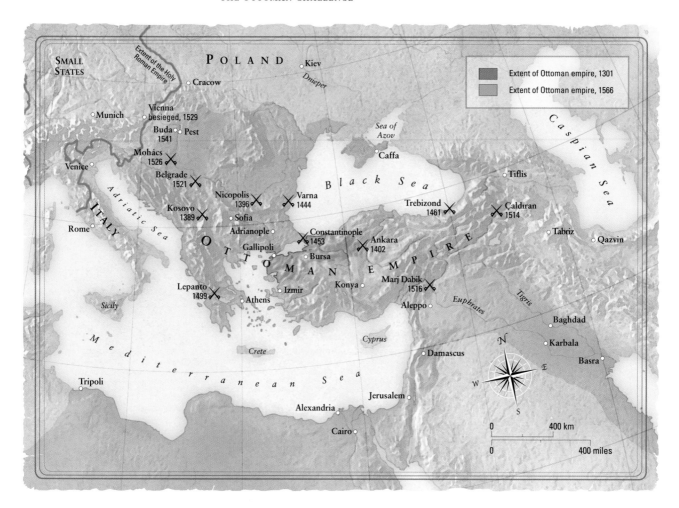

The expansion of the Ottoman empire. Note that Wallachia, Moldavia, Transylvania (present-day Romania) and the Crimea were only vassals, incorporated into the empire's administrative system.

FROM RAIDERS TO MEDIEVAL EUROPE'S FIRST STANDING ARMY

In the early years of the Ottoman state, the bulk of the Ottoman army consisted of the ruler's military entourage: the cavalry troops of Turkoman tribes who had joined forces with the Ottomans, and those peasants who had been called up as soldiers for military campaigns. These were the forerunners of the sultan's salaried troops that by the 15th century had become the pillars on which Ottoman military organization stood. The Turkoman cavalry received a share of any military spoils and were granted the right to settle on conquered lands. In return, they had to provide men-at-arms in proportion to the amount of benefice in their possession. Later they became the fief-based provincial cavalry, whose remuneration was secured through military fiefs (*timar*); both the Seljuqs and the Byzantines operated similar systems.

The main function of the Ottoman military fiefs was to pay the troops and bureaucrats, but they were also used by the Ottomans to incorporate conquered peoples into the military-bureaucratic system of the empire. Ottoman revenue surveys from the Balkans in the 15th century recorded large numbers of Christian fief-cavalry who, by performing military and bureaucratic services for the Ottomans, managed to preserve, at least partly, their former military fiefs and hereditary possessions, as well as their privileged status within society. From the 1370s or 1380s onwards, these men and their sons were sometimes called *voynuks* (Slavic for fighting men or soldiers). Such troops were to be found in significant numbers in Bulgaria,

The fall of the Byzantine imperial city of Constantinople to Mehmed II in 1453 was a recurring theme in European art and literature. Here the arrival of the sultan is depicted in a fresco dating to 1537 in the Moldovita Monastery in Moldova.

Serbia, Macedonia, Thessaly and Albania, and large numbers of Christian nomads in the Balkans were also incorporated into their ranks.

Since the salaried troops of slaves and the fief-cavalry proved insufficient in number to fulfil the needs of an expanding state, the Ottomans also recruited young, volunteer, peasant boys into their military. These youths were later formed into infantry and cavalry corps. Paid by the ruler during periods of mobilization, they returned to their villages at the conclusion of the campaigning season, where their military service exempted them from the payment of certain taxes.

By the latter part of the 14th century the Ottoman military had been transformed from the ruler's raiding forces into a disciplined army, paid from the central treasury and through the military fief system. Under Sultan Murad I the volunteer youth cavalry were gradually replaced with salaried palace horsemen, and the role of the youth infantry was taken up by the 'unmarried' infantrymen and by the Janissaries (whose name derived from the Turkish *yeni çeri*, 'new army'). Together, these two new formations were known as the 'slaves of the (Sublime) Porte', and to all intents were the sultan's standing army. The sultan could thus claim a monopoly on the deployment of armies, in sharp

'Then each was ordered to kill his own prisoners.... [T]hey took my companions and cut off their heads, and when it came to my turn, the king's son saw me and ordered that I should be left alive...because none under twenty years of age were killed, and I was scarcely sixteen.'

Johann Schiltberger on the aftermath of the battle of Nicopolis, 1396

The Battle of Ankara, 1402

The battle between the Ottomans under Bayezid I and Timur's army began in the morning of 28 July around 9 a.m., and lasted until late evening. Despite all their disadvantages (numerical inferiority, exhaustion and the lack of fresh water), the Ottomans fought successfully for a while. However, the critical moments came when Black Tatars on the Ottoman left wing, in treacherous agreement with Timur, attacked the Ottoman rear, and when the cavalrymen from the Anatolian Turkoman emirates, who had recently been subjugated by

'At Angora the Ottoman Turks were totally defeated by Timur's Tatars, and Bayezid...is said to have been carried with him eastward by his conqueror in an iron cage.'

Ruy Gonzales de Clavijo on the battle of Ankara, 1402

Bayezid, deserted. The fate of the Ottoman army was sealed. The sultan fought bravely with his elite Janissary infantry and Serbian vassals, until he was captured and his forces defeated. Ottoman domains in eastern and central Anatolia were restored by Timur to their former Turkoman lords. A bitter struggle broke out between Bayezid's sons over the remaining Ottoman possessions, and the ensuing interregnum decade of civil war almost led to the downfall of the Ottoman sultanate.

	TIMURIDS	OTTOMANS
COMMANDERS	Timur	Bayezid
STRENGTH	140,000	85,000
CASUALTIES	c. 15,000–20,000 killed or wounded	c. 15,000–40,000 killed or wounded

Opposite above Known as 'the Thunderbolt' for his valour as a fighter and his swift conquests, Bayezid I was 48 years of age when he suffered a crushing defeat at the hands of Timur in the battle of Ankara. Though later chroniclers claimed that Timur put Bayezid in an iron cage when he retreated from Anatolia to his empire, historians have questioned the veracity of this episode.

Opposite below According to Johann Schiltberger, an eyewitness who became Timur's captive, Timur had 32 war elephants at the battle of Ankara. He used them to launch incendiary devices at the Ottomans, causing much confusion and terror in the Ottoman army. The weapon used by Timur could have been similar to, but was probably different in its composition from, the famous 'Greek (or Byzantine) fire', which was made to a closely guarded secret formula.

Below The battle of Ankara led to a decade of internecine strife among the defeated sultan's sons, and a temporary reprieve from the Ottoman threat for the Byzantine empire.

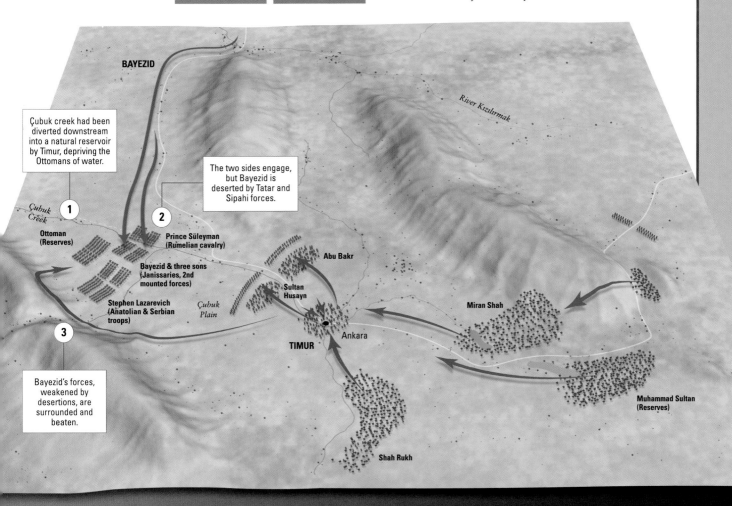

BAYEZID

River Kızılırmak

Çubuk creek had been diverted downstream into a natural reservoir by Timur, depriving the Ottomans of water.

1

Çubuk Creek

Ottoman (Reserves)

The two sides engage, but Bayezid is deserted by Tatar and Sipahi forces.

2

Prince Süleyman (Rumelian cavalry)

Bayezid & three sons (Janissaries, 2nd mounted forces)

Stephen Lazarevich (Anatolian & Serbian troops)

Çubuk Plain

Abu Bakr

Sultan Husayn

Miran Shah

Ankara

TIMUR

Muhammad Sultan (Reserves)

3

Bayezid's forces, weakened by desertions, are surrounded and beaten.

Shah Rukh

contrast to his European counterparts, who had to rely upon and negotiate with local power holders when they wished to deploy forces. Although the standing army was important, until the beginning of the 16th century the freelance light cavalry or 'raiders' within the sultan's forces remained numerically and militarily significant.

THE JANISSARIES AND THE CHILD LEVY

The sultans originally used prisoners of war to create their own independent military guard. However, in the 1380s a child levy system was introduced in order to recruit new soldiers for the Janissary corps. Under this system, Christian children between eight and twenty years old – but ideally between twelve and fourteen years of age – were periodically taken from their families, at varying rates. During the collection, for each group of 100–200 boys (designated 'the flock') a detailed register was compiled. This listed the boy's name, the name of his father, that of his Ottoman 'landlord' (*sipahi*) and his village. It also gave a physical description of the boy, so that if he escaped he could be found. The 'flock' then travelled on foot to the capital. Many perished during the long journey of hundreds of kilometres. Some ran away, while others escaped service because their families bribed the recruiting officers.

This drawing of a Janissary by Gentile Bellini shows the sultan's elite infantryman in his government-issued heavy woollen cloak and cap. Also shown is the Janissaries' famous recurved composite bow. This weapon had formidable armour-piercing capability, noted by many European military experts who fought against the Ottomans as late as the latter part of the 17th century.

Those who made it to the capital were, upon arrival, inspected, circumcised and converted to Islam. The most intelligent ones were singled out for education in the palace schools, and in due course might go on to achieve the highest offices in the empire. The rest were hired out to Turkish farmers for seven to eight years, during which they learned the rudiments of the Turkish language and Islamic customs. All the boys were delivered by name and listed in registers so that the sultan could call upon them when they were needed. Government officials inspected the boys every year, and also collected an inspection fee, equal to the price of three to four sheep, from the family on whose farm the young man was working. After seven or eight years of hard work in the fields, the boys were recalled to the capital. There they joined the ranks of Janissary novices and lived in their own barracks under strict military discipline. They also served as cheap labour for public works. Some worked in the sultan's gardens or in the imperial dockyards in Constantinople and Gallipoli, as blacksmiths, caulkers, carpenters and oar-makers. Others started their apprenticeship in the imperial cannon foundry or in the naval arsenal. Only after several years of such service did the novices become Janissaries or fill vacancies in the corps of gunners, gun carriage drivers, bombardiers and armourers.

With the broadening of the pool of recruitment, the sultan's initial guard was soon transformed into the ruler's elite household infantry. By the battle of Kosovo Field in 1389 the Janissaries numbered some 2,000. By the mid-15th century their number had increased to 5,000, and by the end of his reign (1481) Sultan Mehmed II had doubled the size of the corps.

CONQUEST AND EMPIRE

After eleven years of civil war, Mehmed I (r. 1413–21) emerged victorious. He set about reunifying the Ottoman territories, defeating rebellious vassals and suppressing popular uprisings in Anatolia and the Balkans. Although he is rightly considered the 'second founder of the Ottoman state', at the time of his death the territories of his realm were still smaller

'The Janissaries number about 12,000....
They are clothed once a year by the [sultan]
with coarse blue cloth.... They go on
foot, and part of them are musketeers,
and part halbardiers, and part use
the scimitar alone.'

Benedetto Ramberti on the Janissaries, 1534

Most Ottoman cavalrymen were protected by mail-and-plate armour. The plates were often engraved with various motifs and writings. Under the armour, cotton and linen undershirts were worn, inscribed with quotations from the Quran. This steel and silver mail shirt was made in the early 16th century.

than those held by his father before the catastrophic defeat at Ankara in 1402.

Further expansion of the Ottoman territories took place under Murad II (r. 1421–44; 1446–51), and Mehmed II (r. 1444–46; 1451–81). Also during this period the Ottomans faced their first major challenge in Europe since 1396. In 1440, the five-month-long Ottoman siege of Belgrade – the key fortress of the southern Hungarian border defence line – forced Hungary to take a more active stance against renewed Ottoman expansion. Despite their initial victories in 1443, however, the Hungarians and their crusader allies were defeated at Varna (1444) and at the second battle of Kosovo Field (1448).

Mehmed II's greatest achievement was the conquest of Constantinople in 1453 (see box on p. 213). To assume control over the Bosporus (the straits separating Europe from Asia) the sultan had a fortress built at its narrowest point. Rumeli Hisarı (the 'European castle') stood opposite the old, Anatolian castle that had been erected by Bayezid I during his long blockade of Constantinople (1392–1402). With their cannons deployed on the walls of the two castles, the Ottomans effectively sealed off Byzantium, depriving it of reinforcements and supplies.

During their military preparations the Ottomans constructed sixteen large and sixty light galleys and twenty horse-ships in Gallipoli. The Edirne foundry cast some sixty new guns of various calibres, the largest of which fired shots of 240, 300, 360 and 400 kg (530, 660, 790 and 880 lb, respectively). With 80,000 men, Mehmed's forces greatly outnumbered the defenders (8,000 Greeks, 2,000 foreigners and 30,000–40,000 civilians). On 29 May, after 54 days of constant bombardment and repeated attacks, Constantinople fell to Mehmed's forces.

The conquest of the Byzantine capital was of major historical significance for the peoples of the Balkans, Asia Minor, the Mediterranean and the Black Sea littoral, affecting their lives for centuries to come. To the Byzantines, it meant the end of their empire and civilization. To the Ottomans, it brought military, geopolitical and economic rewards, as well as political and psychological prestige in both the Muslim and Christian worlds. With the conquest of Constantinople – known in colloquial Turkish as Istanbul (a corruption of the colloquial Greek *is tin polin*, 'to the city') and on coins and in sultanic documents as Konstantiniyya (the Islamic form of the city's Greek name) – the expanding Ottoman state acquired a true capital city with a thousand-year-old imperial tradition. The conquest eliminated a hostile wedge that had separated the empire's European and Asian provinces. It gave the Ottomans an ideal logistical base for further campaigns and a commanding position over the trade routes between Asia and Europe, the Black Sea and the Mediterranean. The possession of the city enabled the Ottomans to

Built just before the siege of Constantinople in 1453, Rumeli Hisarı is located on the European shore of the Bosporus, at its narrowest point. It was used, along with the Anadolu Hisarı ('Anatolian castle') standing opposite across the Bosporus, to seal off the Byzantine capital from the straits and deny it any possible relief.

'Either I shall take this city, or the city will take me, dead or alive.... If you persist in denying me peaceful entry into the city, I shall force my way in and I shall slay you and all your nobles.... The city is all I want, even if it is empty.'

Mehmed II to Constantine XI,
on his desire for Constantinople, 1453

cement their rule in southeastern Europe and Asia Minor and to create the strongest contiguous empire in the area.

The sobriquet 'the Conqueror' and the Roman-Byzantine title of 'Caesar' that Mehmed II assumed signalled both his ambitions for universal sovereignty and the beginning of a new era of Ottoman expansion. The new policy was carried out with new statesmen of child-levy origin, who replaced the scions of ancient Turkish families that had dominated Ottoman politics prior to 1453.

Following his possession of Constantinople, Mehmed now had two initial objectives: to defend his new capital, and to consolidate his rule in the empire's core provinces (the Balkans and Anatolia) and the adjacent seas (the Adriatic and Black seas). The Conqueror's failure to capture Belgrade in 1456 halted the Ottoman advance beyond the River Danube until the early 1520s, but could not save Serbia from final subjugation (1459). It was followed by the conquests of the remaining Byzantine territories of the Despotate of the Morea (in the Peloponnese, 1460) and the 'empire' of Trebizond (northeast Turkey, 1461), and of Bosnia (1463) and Albania (1468). The Ottoman capture of Negroponte (Euboea, Greece, 1470) in the

The Last Ottoman Assault and the Conquest of Constantinople

On 28 May 1453 Mehmed II ordered his troops to rest before the final attack on Constantinople. In the city, Emperor Constantine XI assembled the defenders and delivered what the 18th-century English historian Edward Gibbon called 'the funeral oration of the Roman empire'. The emperor urged his soldiers to stand firm and promised them 'crowns of martyrdom and eternal fame'. The next day, shortly after midnight, the final Ottoman assault began. While the Ottoman shipboard artillery bombarded the walls along the Sea of Marmara and the Golden Horn, the army attacked the landward walls. Mehmed first sent his irregulars and volunteers against the walls, but the defenders drove them back. These were followed by more experienced and disciplined troops, but they, too, were forced to withdraw. At the break of dawn, Mehmed ordered his elite Janissaries against the walls. Several of them forced their way through the breaches that the constant bombardment had opened. Last seen near the Gate

of St Romanos, Constantine died as a common soldier, fighting the enemy. Riding on horseback, Mehmed entered the city through the very same gate, known to the Ottomans as Topkapı.

Above The famous map of Constantinople commissioned by Süleyman I as part of an illustrated campaign history.
Below A Romanian fresco presenting a wishful account of the siege, depicting the Christians routing the Ottomans.

Opposite The battle of Lepanto in 1499, depicted here by an unknown Venetian artist, was the first major Ottoman naval victory in the Ottoman–Venetian war of 1499–1503. During the war, the Ottomans captured most of the Venetian Republic's coastal cities on the Adriatic and its possessions on mainland Greece, thus attaining control over major sea lanes. At the same time, Ottoman land forces raided Venetian territories up to the doorstep of the republic. The war, in which the sultan's marines further honed their skills in naval battles and amphibious warfare, proved that under Bayezid II the Ottomans had become a naval power to be reckoned with.

Venetian–Ottoman war of 1463–79, and of the territories of the Venetian–Ottoman border in Albania and in the Morea in 1479, secured Ottoman possessions in the western Balkans and the Peloponnese. Having annexed the southern shores of the Black Sea in 1461, Mehmed now turned to the northern shores. He eradicated the Genoese trading colony of Caffa in the Crimea (1475) and made the Crimean Tatar Giray dynasty, the rulers of northern Crimea and the adjacent steppes, his vassal (1478), thus turning the Black Sea into an 'Ottoman lake' for the following three centuries.

In Anatolia, Mehmed eventually defeated the Karamans (1468), but only managed to re-annex their lands after he had overcome the Ak Koyunlu ('White Sheep') tribal federation in 1473. Under Uzun Hasan (r. 1453–78), this Turkoman confederation had been transformed into a major power that controlled eastern Anatolia, Azerbaijan, Iraq and western Iran from its capital Tabriz, challenging Ottoman legitimacy and authority in Asia Minor. Mehmed II's victory over Uzun Hasan at the battle of Tercan (or Otlukbeli) in 1473 proved the superiority of Ottoman standing forces over the traditional Turkoman tribal army organization and warfare. By the time of his death in 1481, Mehmed II had successfully reintegrated most of the Balkans and Anatolia into his realm, and could justly claim that he was 'Lord of Two Continents and of the Two Seas'.

NEW CHALLENGES, NEW STRATEGIES

Ottoman expansion slowed down during Bayezid II's long reign (1481–1512), for several reasons. The sultan spent the first half of his reign in the shadow of a possible crusade by his European rivals, who held his brother Cem (d. 1495), a defeated pretender to the Ottoman throne, in their custody in France and Italy, using him as a pawn to check Ottoman ambitions. Bayezid also had to consolidate Ottoman rule in parts of Anatolia and the Balkans. Anatolian territories southeast and east of the Taurus Mountains formed a buffer zone between the Ottomans and the Mamluks, who had ruled Egypt and Syria since 1258. Since the allegiance of the emirs of both the Ramazan and Dulkadır principalities remained questionable, the two empires fought an inconclusive six-year war between 1485 and 1491 over these frontier territories. The Ottomans were more successful in reasserting their suzerainty over Moldavia, a reluctant Ottoman vassal. In 1484 Bayezid captured Kilia and Cetatea Alba (in the Ukraine), two strategically important castles that guarded the Danube delta and the mouth of the River Dniester, and forced the Moldavians to accept their vassal status.

Following Cem's death, Bayezid's hands were freed against his western rivals. In the Ottoman–Venetian war of 1499–1503, the sultan captured Lepanto (modern Navpaktos in southern Greece), and Modon, Navarino and Koron on the southwest coast of the Peloponnese.

The last decades of the 15th century required major readjustments in Ottoman policy due to major changes in international politics, of which Portuguese expansion in the Indian Ocean and the emergence of Safavid Persia were the most important. In 1501 Ismail, the leader of a militant Shi'a religious group, routed the Ak Koyunlus, took Tabriz and declared himself Shah of Iran. Many saw in Ismail the reincarnation of Imam Ali, the cousin and son-in-law of the prophet Muhammad and the founder of the minority Shi'a branch of Islam. Others hoped that Ismail was the long-awaited

Right This gold inlaid dagger, with jewelled rock-crystal hilt, was made for Sultan Selim I.

hidden Imam. Shah Ismail's belligerent policy and persecution of Sunni Muslims, and his propagandists' proselytization in the eastern provinces of the Ottoman empire, undermined Ottoman authority among the Turkoman and Kurdish tribes. Bayezid II proved unable to deal effectively with the Safavids and their followers in eastern Asia Minor, who were known as 'red heads' after their twelve-tasselled red hats symbolizing the Twelver (or Ithna Ashar) Shi'a branch of Islam. Bayezid was deposed in 1512 by his son Selim I (r. 1512–20).

Selim I's reign introduced a major shift in Ottoman policy, for the new sultan devoted most of his energies to fighting the Shi'a Safavids. Although his victory over Shah Ismail at the battle of Çaldıran in 1514 did not end Safavid rule in Iran, he secured Ottoman rule over most of eastern and southeastern Asia Minor.

Historians disagree as to whether Selim had planned the conquest of Mamluk Syria and Egypt. Whatever the sultan's plans were, his annexation of Dulkadır territories (which lay between the Ottomans and the Mamluks) inevitably led to confrontation with the Mamluks, the Dulkadırs' nominal sovereign. Selim defeated the Mamluks north of Aleppo at Marj Dabik in August 1516, and at Raydaniyya, outside Cairo, in January 1517. The former Mamluk territories were incorporated into Selim's empire as the new provinces of Aleppo, Damascus and Egypt.

215

This rendition of the battle of Çaldıran is from the *Sharafnama* ('History of the Kurds'), written in Persian in 1597 by Sharaf al-Din Khan Bitlisi, himself of Kurdish extraction. The battle, in which Sultan Selim I's artillery and Janissaries routed the Safavids, had major consequences for the geopolitics of the region. Thanks to their victory, the Ottomans cemented their rule over eastern Anatolia and Azerbaijan, including the Kurdish regions.

The conquest had major strategic consequences. It expanded the Ottoman empire's territories from 883,000 sq km (341,000 sq miles) in 1512 to 1.5 million sq km (580,000 sq miles). More importantly, revenues from Syria and Egypt accounted for one-third of the empire's income. Protection of the maritime lanes of communications between Constantinople and Cairo thus became vital, and necessitated the further strengthening of the Ottoman navy. It also led to confrontation with the dominant Christian maritime powers of the Mediterranean: Venice, Spain and the Knights of St John, based on the island of Rhodes. Protecting the Hejaz (which contained Islam's holiest sites) on the Arabian Peninsula against Portuguese encroachment into the Red Sea, on the other hand, brought the

Right This 16th-century painting by a member of Titian's circle shows the young Sultan Süleyman I, known as 'the Magnificent' in Europe and as 'the Lawgiver' (or 'Law Abider') to his subjects. Several paintings of the young sultan, similar to this one, are known from European museums.

Below This lavishly decorated sword of Süleyman I is made of ivory, steel, mastic, gold, ruby and turquoise. Swords made for the sultans were often inscribed in gold calligraphy with quotations from the Quran and prayers for the sultans' victory.

Ottomans into conflict with the Portuguese. However, all these conflicts were left to Selim's successor, Süleyman I 'the Magnificent' (r. 1520–66).

Süleyman reoriented Ottoman strategy to focus on the empire's Christian enemies. By the time he ascended the throne, it had become clear that Selim I's policy vis-à-vis the Safavids could not be maintained. Warfare since 1511 had exhausted the eastern provinces and the imperial army had arrived at a point of strategic overstretch. Distance, an inhospitable climate (early winters and snow) and Shah Ismail's battle-avoidance tactic and scorched-earth policy, which destroyed crops and poisoned wells, caused serious problems for the otherwise well-organized Ottoman campaign logistics, rendering seasonal campaigning ineffective. The sultan's Asian troops fought reluctantly against the shah's Anatolian followers (mainly Turkoman and Kurdish nomads), and often deserted or allied with the enemy. They had had enough of the eastern wars and wanted instead to fight against the Hungarian 'infidels', whom they considered weaker warriors. The sultan's troops in the Balkans likewise lobbied for the renewal of

European campaigns, from which they hoped to profit economically through spoils of war and new military fiefs.

In 1521, Süleyman marched against Hungary and conquered Belgrade. The next year, his navy captured the island of Rhodes, evicting the Knights of St John to Malta. These swift conquests in his early years, especially in the light of previous Ottoman failures (at Belgrade in 1456, and Rhodes in 1480) under Mehmed II, established Süleyman's reputation in Europe as a redoubtable adversary. Altogether, the sultan led his armies on thirteen campaigns. These brought Hungary (1526 and 1541) and Iraq (1534–35) under Ottoman rule, and threatened the Habsburg capital Vienna twice (1529 and 1532), while his victories at Rhodes in the eastern Aegean (1522) and at Preveza in northwestern Greece (1538) made the Ottomans masters of the eastern Mediterranean, where only Malta and Cyprus remained unconquered for the time being.

Historians have found it difficult to agree on an assessment of Süleyman's strategy. Some have claimed that his policy suffered from 'a crisis of orientation'. Others have maintained that his conquests, especially that of Hungary, were in accordance with the old Ottoman strategy of step-by-step enlargement, first applied during the subjugation of the Balkans. A somewhat revisionist historiography portrays Süleyman's policy as defensive and reactive to Habsburg threats. While all these explanations contain some elements of truth, Süleyman's strategy is best described as pragmatic; it readjusted itself to the changes in geopolitics, notably to the emergence of the Safavids and the Habsburgs as the Ottomans' major rivals. While ideology and propaganda played an important role in strengthening the legitimacy of the shah and sultan, in their military confrontation realpolitik won the day. Thus, it is hardly surprising that Süleyman undertook his eastern campaigns between 1534 and 1535, and 1548 and 1549, after he had concluded an armistice (1533) and a peace treaty (1547) with the Habsburgs.

THE OTTOMAN NAVY

Ottoman conquests would have been unthinkable without the support of the Ottoman navy. Under Mehmed II and Bayezid II the Ottomans acquired the common naval technology of the Mediterranean, adopting the galley as their principal vessel. The size of the Ottoman navy was already impressive under Mehmed II. He employed some 280 and 380 galleys and other ships in his naval expeditions

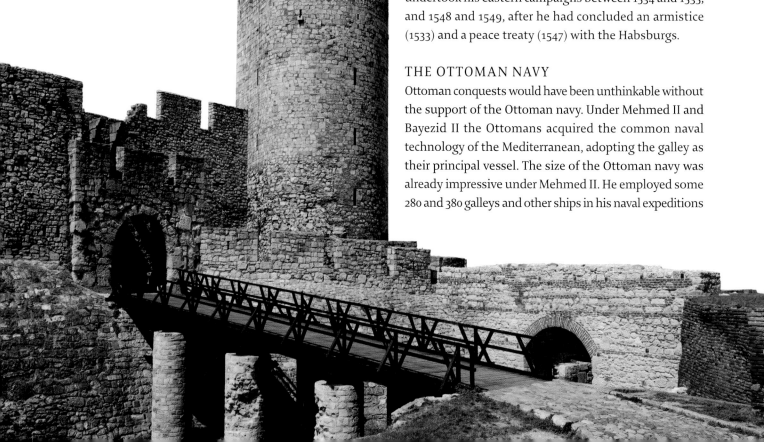

Opposite The fort at Belgrade (*below*) was the key position in the Hungarian line of defence from 1427. Mehmed II besieged it in 1456, three years after his conquest of Constantinople, but the fort was successfully defended by János Hunyadi. In 1521 Sultan Süleyman I captured Belgrade (*above*), which meant the beginning of the end for the Kingdom of Hungary, whose armies were annihilated by the sultan just five years later at Mohács.

Below This Turkish miniature from the 16th century shows the port of Genoa, with the Ottoman fleet commanded by Hayreddin 'Barbarossa' blockading the fort. Barbarossa successfully extended Ottoman control over the eastern Mediterranean at the expense of Venice, Genoa and Spain.

against the Greek island of Euboea in the Aegean in 1470, and against the Genoese-administered Crimean port town of Caffa in 1475, respectively. By this time the Ottomans could operate two large armadas independently. In May 1480, an Ottoman fleet of 104 vessels arrived at Rhodes. At around the same time, another Ottoman armada of 28 galleys and 104 light galleys and transport vessels left Constantinople for Otranto in southern Italy. During the 1499–1503 Ottoman–Venetian war, Bayezid considerably strengthened Ottoman naval power: in the winter of 1500/01 alone, he ordered the construction of no fewer than 250 galleys. Starting in the autumn of 1502, Bayezid initiated the total reorganization of the Ottoman navy. The work was part of a larger naval strategy that transformed the Ottoman empire from a land-based power into a formidable naval one. The reformed Ottoman navy was instrumental in halting Portuguese expansion in the Red Sea and the Persian Gulf and in the conquest of Mamluk Egypt under Selim I in 1517. Following this, the Ottomans set about eliminating all hostile bases in the eastern Mediterranean. Appointing Hayreddin 'Barbarossa' governor of Algiers (1519) and grand admiral of the Ottoman navy (1533), and co-opting the corsairs of the Barbary States of Algiers and Tunis, was a smart and economically efficient way to further strengthen the Ottoman navy and extending Ottoman influence westwards.

The Mediterranean fleet, under the command of the grand admiral, formed the core of the Ottoman navy. Operating independently of this main fleet, there were smaller squadrons under the command of the captain of Kavala, who patrolled the northern Aegean; the governors of Lesbos and Rhodes, the latter commanding the sea routes between Egypt and Constantinople; the admiral of Egypt, who controlled both the Egyptian fleet based in Alexandria and the Suez fleet; and the captain of Yemen, who guarded the entry to the Red Sea. In addition, smaller flotillas operated on the rivers Danube, Tigris and Euphrates.

Gallipoli (in the Dardanelles) – the first naval arsenal – remained an important shipyard for the construction and repair of Ottoman ships. Nevertheless, by the start of the 16th century the naval arsenal on the shore of the Golden Horn, inherited from the Genoese of Galata and expanded in the reign of Selim I, had become the principal centre of Ottoman shipbuilding and maintenance. In the 1550s, 250 ships could be constructed or repaired there at a time. In addition to Gallipoli and Constantinople, there were arsenals at Izmit on the Sea of Marmara, at Sinop and Samsun on the Black Sea, at Suez in the Red Sea and at Birecik and Basra on the Euphrates and the Shatt al-Arab, respectively. If the smaller shipyards are included, the number of Ottoman shipbuilding sites is close to seventy for this period.

IDEOLOGY, LEGITIMIZATION AND WARFARE

The early Ottomans have often been presented as fighting 'Holy Wars against the infidels'. However, the early Ottoman military activity described thus in Ottoman chronicles is now thought to have been a much more fluid undertaking, sometimes referring to actions that were nothing more than raids, and sometimes referring to a deliberate holy war – but most often combining a mixture of the two.

The Ottomans fought numerous campaigns against fellow Muslim Turks, subjugating and annexing the neighbouring Turkoman principalities. In accordance with their portrayal of the early Ottomans as 'holy warriors', 15th-century Ottoman chroniclers often ignored these conflicts, claiming that the Ottomans acquired the territories of the neighbouring Turkic principalities through peaceful means (purchase and/or marriage). When they did mention the wars between the Ottomans and their Muslim Turkic neighbours, Ottoman chroniclers tried to legitimize these conquests by claiming that the Ottomans acted either in self-defence or were forced to fight, for the hostile policies of these Turkic principalities hindered the Ottomans' holy wars against the infidels. This latter explanation was used repeatedly by Ottoman legal scholars to justify their wars against their Muslim Turkoman neighbours, such as the Karamans and Ak Koyunlus (1473).

The justification of the wars against the Mamluks was more problematic. Mamluks followed Sunni Islam, as did the Ottomans, and the descendant of the last Abbasid caliph al-Mustansir (r. 1226–42) resided in Cairo. The Mamluk sultans were also the protectors of Mecca and Medina and guarantors of the haj, the pilgrimage to Mecca. To justify his attack against the Mamluks, Selim advanced several pretexts and secured a legal opinion (fatwa) from the Ottoman religious establishment. This accused the Mamluks of oppressing Muslims and justified the war against them with reference to the alleged Mamluk–Safavid alliance, declaring that 'who aids a heretic [i.e. the Safavids] is a heretic himself'.

Ottoman victory over the Mamluks between 1516 and 1517, and the subsequent introduction of Ottoman rule in these Arab lands, had major ideological and political consequences, in addition to the economic and strategic ones discussed above. With his conquests, Selim became the master of Mecca and Medina, 'the cradle of Islam', as well as of Damascus and Cairo, former seats of the caliphs. Selim and his successors duly assumed the title of 'Servant of the Two Noble Sanctuaries' (namely Mecca and Medina), and with this the task of protecting and organizing the annual haj pilgrimage to Mecca, which gave the Ottomans unparalleled prestige and legitimacy in the Muslim world.

This is not to state that the Ottomans did not use the ideology of the 'holy war'. In the 1300s, the spirit of the holy war was alive on the Turco-Byzantine frontier. Situated in the vicinity of Byzantium, the seat of eastern Christianity, the Ottomans were strategically positioned to wage such wars, and served as a magnet for the mighty warriors of the Anatolian Turco-Muslim emirates. By defeating repeated crusades, conquering Constantinople and subjugating the Balkan Christian states, the Ottomans emerged as champions of anti-Christian wars. Their successes against the Venetians in the Aegean and the western Balkans under Mehmed II and Bayezid II, and against the Habsburgs in the Mediterranean and Hungary under Süleyman I, further enhanced the Ottomans' prestige as holy warriors and defenders of Islam.

In their rivalry against the Habsburgs, Ottoman ideologues and strategists used religion, millenarianism and universalist visions of empire to strengthen the legitimacy of the sultan within the larger Muslim community. Similarly, Ottoman victories against Habsburg Catholicism and Safavid Shi'ism formed an integral part of Ottoman propaganda. In the early years of Süleyman's reign, the grand vizier Ibrahim Pasha consciously propagated the sultan's image as the new world conqueror, the successor of Alexander the Great. In his latter years the sultan viewed himself as the 'lawgiver', a righteous ruler in whose realm justice and order reigned.

MILITARY STRENGTH, WEAPONRY AND TACTICS

Although recent research with regard to the size of European armies has shown that the popular figures quoted in the literature are unreliable, it is obvious that the Ottomans had numerical and logistical superiority over their enemies until roughly the end of the 17th century. The campaign of Mehmed II in 1473 against Uzun Hasan mobilized 100,000 men-at-arms, a body of men which included 64,000 fief-based Sipahis, 12,000 Janissaries, 7,500 cavalry of the Porte, and 20,000 'unmarried' infantrymen. The central imperial budget of 1528 numbered some 120,000 to 150,000 members of the regular units, including 38,000 provincial fief-holders, 20,000 to 60,000 men-at-arms brought to the campaigns by the fief-holders, and 47,000 mercenaries. These figures do not include the various auxiliary troops, some of whom repaired the roads and bridges in front of the marching armies, others who helped to transport cannons, or who collected the draught animals and cast cannon balls in the mines, or who performed various engineering work or were raiders, and finally the Tatar troops.

This sword was made from steel, ivory and gold for Mehmed II.

Janissary Guns

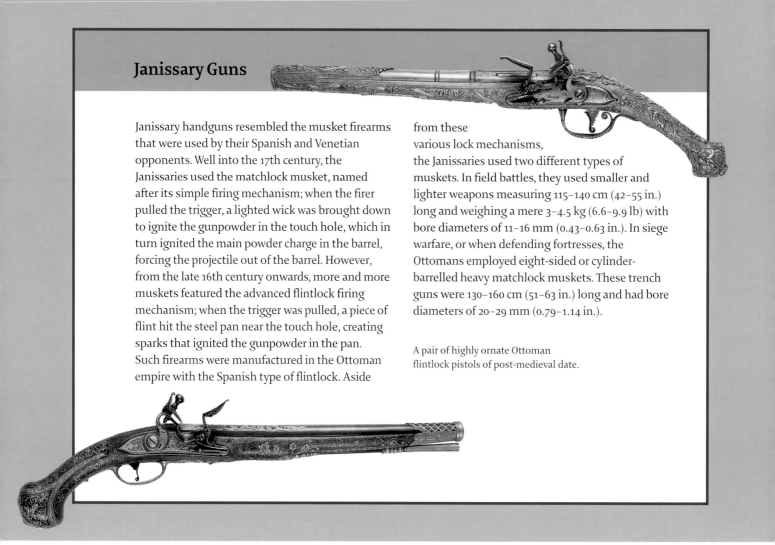

Janissary handguns resembled the musket firearms that were used by their Spanish and Venetian opponents. Well into the 17th century, the Janissaries used the matchlock musket, named after its simple firing mechanism; when the firer pulled the trigger, a lighted wick was brought down to ignite the gunpowder in the touch hole, which in turn ignited the main powder charge in the barrel, forcing the projectile out of the barrel. However, from the late 16th century onwards, more and more muskets featured the advanced flintlock firing mechanism; when the trigger was pulled, a piece of flint hit the steel pan near the touch hole, creating sparks that ignited the gunpowder in the pan. Such firearms were manufactured in the Ottoman empire with the Spanish type of flintlock. Aside from these various lock mechanisms, the Janissaries used two different types of muskets. In field battles, they used smaller and lighter weapons measuring 115–140 cm (42–55 in.) long and weighing a mere 3–4.5 kg (6.6–9.9 lb) with bore diameters of 11–16 mm (0.43–0.63 in.). In siege warfare, or when defending fortresses, the Ottomans employed eight-sided or cylinder-barrelled heavy matchlock muskets. These trench guns were 130–160 cm (51–63 in.) long and had bore diameters of 20–29 mm (0.79–1.14 in.).

A pair of highly ornate Ottoman flintlock pistols of post-medieval date.

The Ottomans also showed genuine interest and great flexibility in adopting European weaponry and tactics. The Ottomans became acquainted with firearms in the second half of the 14th century, probably during their conquests in the Balkans. Firearms in the Ottoman empire gained tactical significance in the 1440s, when the Ottomans fought several wars against the Hungarians who had used various types of cannons for generations. These wars forced the sultan's soldiers to emulate their opponents' weaponry and tactics. It was also during these wars that the Ottomans became acquainted with the *wagenburg* or 'wagon fortress' system (see Chapter 8) – defensive arrangements of war carts, chained together wheel to wheel, and protected by heavy wooden shielding and equipped with firearms.

The Ottomans not only adopted firearms at an early stage of the development of their armed forces, but were also successful in integrating gunpowder weaponry into their military by establishing a separate artillery corps as part of the sultan's standing army. By the 1390s the Ottoman government had, on a permanent basis, employed gunners who manufactured and handled firearms. A separate corps of gunners was established under Murad II. These artillerymen were aided by the corps of gun-carriage drivers, established in the latter part of the 15th century. The gunners and the gun-carriage drivers, along with the armourers, formed the Ottoman artillery corps, which was an integral part of the sultan's standing army. Numbering about

Opposite below In the 15th and 16th centuries the Ottomans were known for their use of gigantic cannons. While they continued to use some of these great weapons longer than their European rivals, especially in their forts, medium and small cannons, cast in the Constantinople foundry, composed the majority of the Ottoman ordnance.

1,110 in 1514, the size of the corps almost doubled in the 1520s, and reached 6,500 by the end of the 16th century. In Europe, artillerymen remained a transitory category between soldiers and craftsmen well into the 17th century.

Initially the Janissary corps was equipped with bows, crossbows and javelins. Under Murad II they began to use firearms, probably matchlock harquebuses (see box opposite). It was not, however, until around the mid-16th century that most of the Janissaries carried firearms. Their firepower, especially in the early 16th century, often proved fatal for their adversaries.

The Ottomans had a long-lasting superiority in making especially strong and reliable musket barrels, using flat sheets of steel, similar to materials used for the Damascus swords that were famous for their strength and sharpness. These sheets were coiled into a spiral, producing great strength in the barrel and thus enabling it to withstand higher explosive pressure. Ottoman musket barrels were less likely to burst than European ones, which were constructed with longitudinal seams. In addition to their handguns, the Janissaries' traditional weapon – the recurved bow – remained an important and formidable weapon well into the 17th century.

Like some of their European opponents in the 15th century, the Ottomans were also capable of casting several giant cannons, which were some of the largest guns known to contemporaries. While these large bombards were clumsy, difficult to manoeuvre, had a very low rate of fire (a couple of shots per day) and were of questionable usefulness, the production of such monsters required unusual technical and organizational skills that only the most advanced European states possessed. Unlike most of their European adversaries, who had abandoned the production of such gargantuan cannon by the beginning of the 16th century, the Ottomans continued to use a handful of these monstrous weapons. However, they

Above Ottoman quiver and bow case from the 17th century. The Ottomans, like other Turks before them, were expert archers both on horseback and as infantrymen. The Janissaries continued to use their composite bows well into the 17th century, although by this time they had been armed with muskets. Janissary bows were known and feared for their long range and armour-piercing capability.

produced and employed all three main classes of guns used in early modern Europe: parabolic-trajectory mortars and howitzers, flat-trajectory, large-calibre siege and fortress guns of the cannon class and medium- and small-calibre pieces of the culverin type. Contrary to the common European theory that Ottoman ordnance was dominated by gigantic cannons, archival sources suggest that the overwhelming majority of the guns cast in Ottoman foundries and deployed in their battles consisted of small- and medium-calibre pieces.

Although large-scale military uniformity and technical standardization was nowhere accomplished in the early modern period, the Ottomans lagged behind the most advanced western European nations in terms of standardization. The Ottoman arsenal included a perplexing variety of artillery pieces, a deficiency that was shared by some of the sultan's adversaries, most notably by the two Mediterranean nations Venice and Spain.

THE WEAPONS INDUSTRY AND OTTOMAN MILITARY SELF-SUFFICIENCY

Before the establishment of the imperial cannon foundry in Constantinople by Mehmed II, the most important foundry was in Edirne, where most of the guns used during the 1453 siege of Constantinople were made. From the mid-15th century onwards, the Ottomans cast cannon in their provincial capitals and mining centres, as well as at Constantinople and in temporary foundries established during campaigns. The production output of some of these foundries could easily match that of the Constantinople foundry, especially in the late 15th and early 16th centuries. During the Ottoman–Venetian war of 1499–1503, the Ottomans cast 288 cannons in Vlorë for the imperial navy in just ten months between late 1499 and mid-1500. Despite the temporary importance of local foundries, Constantinople remained the centre of Ottoman cannon casting, producing hundreds of pieces each year.

The early centralization of the Ottoman weapons industry was instrumental in the advancement of military technology. Furthermore, this military industrial complex in the capital, supplemented by cannon foundries, gunpowder workshops and arsenals of smaller scale in the provinces, enabled the Ottomans to establish long-lasting firepower superiority in eastern Europe, the Mediterranean and the Middle East. At Çaldıran (1514) the Ottomans had some 500 cannons, whereas the Safavids had none. At Mohács (1526) the Ottomans employed between 240 and 300 cannons, whereas the Hungarians used only 53. However, the technologically driven approach should not be taken too far. Even in the most oft-cited cases in respect of the effectiveness and decisiveness of firearms – Çaldıran, Marj Dabik (1516), Raydaniyya (1517) or Mohács – other factors such as numerical superiority, the deployment of cavalry, better logistics and tactics or profiting from terrain and the mistakes of the enemy, to name but a few, proved to be as crucial as firepower superiority.

Ottoman cavalrymen (Sipahis) were protected by helmets, similar to this 16th-century steel example. The earliest extant Ottoman helmets in Turkish collections date from the first decades of the Ottoman state. Helmets for sultans and other dignitaries were decorated in gold with quotations from the Quran. The most elaborate ones were worn only on parade.

This representation of the battle of Mohács is from Arifi's *Süleymanname* ('Book of Süleyman', 1558), which narrated and illustrated Süleyman's conquests. The miniature clearly shows the importance of Ottoman cannon and Janissaries using hand firearms. Ottoman and European accounts agree that cannon fire and the Janissaries' volleys were decisive in the Ottomans' overwhelming victory. The battle sealed the fate of medieval Hungary, whose central parts were conquered and incorporated into the Ottoman empire in 1541.

CONCLUSION

By the early 16th century the Ottoman empire had emerged as one of the most important powers in Europe and the Middle East. Their empire could be compared to the illustrious Roman and Byzantine models, the similarly multi-ethnic neighbouring Habsburg empire and to the other great Islamic empires of the Abbasids, Safavids and the Indian Mughals. The Ottoman military and bureaucracy and the fiscal systems that supported and financed them played crucial roles in the emergence of the empire. However, as we have seen, the early Ottoman sultans were practical, and in addition to sheer military force they also used marriage alliances, flexible administrative practices, ideology and propaganda to further their territorial expansion. From the reign of Mehmed II onwards, the Ottomans became part of European power politics. This was never more obvious than under Süleyman, who was an important player in the 16th-century struggle for European supremacy between the Habsburgs and Valois. Although the first half of the 16th century saw both the Habsburgs and the Ottomans occupied with multiple policy commitments, the Habsburg–Ottoman rivalry would remain a major theme in international politics for the following two centuries.

T. A. Heathcote, Peter Lorge,
Matthew Bennett and Karl Friday

10 The Wider World: Warfare in India, China, Korea and Japan, 500–1500

Opposite A group of 12th-century Japanese horsemen and foot soldiers on their way to battle. The warriors on horseback wear the *ōyoroi* style of armour, while the foot soldiers are clad in the more economical *haramaki*.

The term 'medieval' is usually associated with western Europe and the countries around the Mediterranean that had originally formed part of the Roman empire. More recently it has been extended to include the Islamic lands of the Fertile Crescent and the Eurasian steppe. However, in a book of this nature it would be remiss to ignore military developments further afield, despite the fact that history in other parts of the world was taking a different course from that in Europe. As the Roman empire was collapsing, China was being reunited after a period of rule by warlords, first under the Sui dynasty and then the more powerful Tang dynasty (618–907). Indeed it is important to remember that during the Justinianic revival of the mid-6th century, there is evidence of trade contact with the Far East (including the famous story of Byzantine monks smuggling silkworms out of China). It is even possible to speak of a globalization of trade in this era.

The century of Islamic conquests between 630 and 730 disrupted contacts between the western powers and those beyond the Caspian Sea. Although trade was still possible, it was heavily mediated by Muslim control of routes to the East. The declining power of Byzantium from 1100 onwards meant that only the entrepreneurial activities of the Italian mercantile city-states maintained contacts across this barrier. This was the driving force behind the attempt to find routes to China and other eastern countries by sailing westwards around the globe in the 15th century (especially after Constantinople's conquest by the Ottoman Turks in 1453).

It was, though, the Mongol conquests of the 13th and 14th centuries that entirely reframed the global strategic situation. Chingiz Khan and his talented successors conquered China, northern India, the Muslim lands as far west as Syria and Russia, as well as making short-lived incursions into Europe, southeast Asia and Japan (see box on p. 247). The impact of the Mongols persisted until the end of the era covered in this volume, when native dynasties began to reassert themselves, although the Mughals continued to rule in India into the 18th century.

Outside this period, events in India, China and the Far East were unconnected with those of medieval Europe, and their nations developed very different styles of warfare from those found in the West. It would take another book to cover these developments in detail, but this chapter contains case studies of India, China, Korea and Japan in order to provide insights into how warfare was managed. As the section on China explains, warfare was far more advanced than in Western Europe owing to the early development of gunpowder and low, earthen-walled bastion-style fortifications in the 13th century, some 300 years before equivalent developments in the West. Why, then, did China not conquer the world and become a superpower half a millennium before the modern world? One reason is certainly that the Chinese imperial structure was so monolithic and inward-looking as to not seek such dominion. The extensive Chinese naval expeditions of the early 15th century famously resulted in the conclusion that there was nothing to be gained by such expansion. In contrast, the European exploration of Africa and the New World led eventually to western societies building up a momentum of conquest and a technological superiority that had become irresistible by around 1700.

INDIA

Warfare in medieval India had much in common with that in the contemporary West. Cavalry, composed of men of high social status using close-quarter weapons that demanded skill, strength and courage, was the most prestigious and decisive arm. The quasi-feudal military system produced independently minded princes and nobles for whom war was a natural occupation, but also gave them private armies whose existence, as in Christendom, encouraged continual rebellions and civil wars.

Throughout the 6th century, the last great Hindu empire of northern India, that of the Guptas, was invaded by Central Asian invaders, the Hunas, known to the Byzantines as Hephthalites or White Huns. Successor states emerged, most of which were unified by the campaigns of Harsha (r. 606–47), a prince who, like Alfred the Great of Wessex, had intended to become a monk, and came to the throne only through the death of his brother. He attempted to invade southern India, but the Chalukya king Pulikesi II held the passes of the Vindhya Mountains, where Harsha's conventional army, composed of elephants (see box on p. 230), cavalry and infantry in accordance with classical Hindu theories of war, could make no progress.

On Harsha's death, his realm was replaced by smaller kingdoms under Rajput princes who continually fought against each other and their southern neighbours. As they did so, a new religion, Islam, spread from Arabia to Central Asia. Between 1001 and 1027 a Muslim Turkish prince, Sultan Mahmud of Ghazni, called 'the Iconoclast' owing to his zeal in destroying idols, descended the passes from Afghanistan and conducted seventeen great raids deep into India. The Rajputs set aside their differences and gathered their forces to oppose him. Rich women sold their jewels to pay the troops, poor women spun cotton for uniforms, but almost always the invaders won the day and returned to their hills laden with booty and so many captives as to cause a collapse in the price of slaves throughout Central Asia.

A century later, Sultan Muhammad of Ghor led his own army over the mountains. The

The Pallavas, with their capital at Kanchi (Conjeeveeram), ruled in southern India from 350 to 900. They were great temple builders, favouring images of the legendary hero Rama, here depicted in a 9th-century granite relief with the longbow used in ancient Hindu armies. This bow, made of bamboo, shot cane arrows, and the longer variants were steadied in use by the archer's foot resting on the ground.

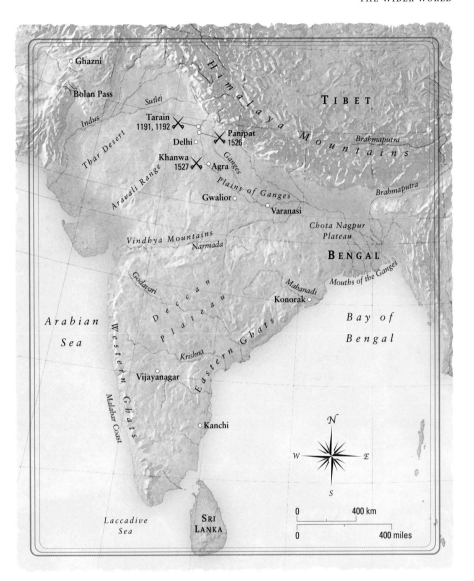

Map of India, showing the main sites
and regions discussed in this section.

Rajputs, led by the warrior-king Prithvi Raj, again gathered a huge army, and in 1191 at Tarain (Taraori) Muhammad was wounded and defeated. The following year he returned and at the second battle of Tarain his fast-moving army of armoured cavalry and horse-archers from the steppes routed the ponderous Rajput forces, which were still organized on the long-outdated traditional Hindu model. The heroic Prithvi Raj was captured and killed. The battlefield was covered with countless slain, along with the flags, jewelled swords, plumed helmets, damascene armours and gaily dyed scarves of the defeated Rajputs. The rich Indo-Gangetic plains lay open and by 1200 almost all of northern India was under Muslim rule.

In 1206 Muhammad of Ghor was assassinated, and his leading general, Qutb al-Din Aibak, took over his Indian domains as the first sultan of Delhi. Qutb's successor Iltutmish (r. 1211–36) had to face the initial Mongol invasion, but the horde turned back into Central Asia and swept on through Iran to eastern Europe. A series of wars between rivals for the throne of Delhi ended with the reign of the aged general Balban (r. 1266–86), who ruthlessly stamped out domestic rebellion while resisting Mongol raiders. A further time of troubles ended in 1294 with the

The War Elephant

India's unique contribution to warfare was the use of elephants. These animals are first mentioned as being trained for war around 480 BC. Armoured with leather, bamboo, metal plates or mail, they carried a driver (*mahut*) and two or three warriors, armed with long spears, darts and bows, and were deployed like modern tanks to break the enemy line and smash down defences. Their height, speed and cross-country performance made them ideal mobile command posts. Theorists recommended that each fighting elephant had its own infantry detachment for close protection. Smaller bulls and cows were used as pack or draught animals.

Against men and horses unfamiliar with them, charging elephants were a terrifying prospect. Nevertheless, elephants could easily be panicked and might then turn into a common enemy, trampling friend and foe indiscriminately, and carrying commanders off the field. Well-disciplined armies had little to fear from elephants, but successive conquerors in India invariably succumbed to the prestige of this impressive arm, only to find their confidence in it misplaced in their turn.

Above War-elephants served primarily as weapons platforms, carrying crews who fought in shock action with long lances or in missile action with darts and bows. This statue from Konorak, northern India, shows an elephant holding a man in its trunk.

accession of Ala al-Din Khalji, following his victory over the Hindu raja Ramchandra in central India.

Ala al-Din's general, Malik Kafur, defeated the remaining Rajput kingdoms and in 1310 invaded the Tamil lands of southern India. Ethnically and linguistically distinct from the Indo-European peoples of the north, the Tamils shared their Hindu culture and established great empires of their own. During the 11th century, kings of the Chola dynasty mastered India and controlled the Bay of Bengal with their navies. Like the Rajputs, the Tamil kings fought constantly among themselves and all were defeated by Malik Kafur, so that by 1329 the Muslim conquest of India was complete.

In 1398, with the sultanate of Delhi weakened by civil wars, Sultan Timur of Samarkand led his armies from Central Asia into India. His aims, he said, were spiritual, to punish unbelievers and heretics, and worldly, to gain booty for the faithful. At Delhi the defenders waited for him with a large army including war-elephants, whose appearance unsettled his men and horses alike. However, faith in this arm proved misplaced. With their charge broken by caltrops and a line of wagons, the dreaded elephants were driven from the field like cows, and when Timur's horsemen attacked from both flanks and the rear, the army of Delhi dissolved in ruin.

In time Delhi recovered, under a line of Afghan or Pathan (Pashtun) sultans, but the weakening of central power allowed outlying provinces to become separate sultanates. In the north, many Rajput princes regained their independence. In the south, a new Tamil empire, that of Vijayanagar, was founded as early as 1336, and the five neighbouring Muslim sultanates fought against it and each other until it was finally destroyed in 1565. The same fate awaited the sultanates in the following century, when the Mughal emperors marched south.

In 1524, a prince of the house of Timur, Zahir al-Din Muhammad, known as Babur ('the Tiger'), followed the example of his famous ancestor and 'placing my foot in the stirrups of resolution and my hand on the reins of confidence in God', marched down the passes from Kabul into Hindustan. On 21 April 1526, at Panipat, the cockpit of India, he was met by Sultan Ibrahim Lodi of Delhi, who had an army

The battle of Panipat, 1526. The Mughal army consisted mostly of horse-archers, but also included trained matchlock men and field artillery, both then novel in Indian warfare. The inexperienced Ibrahim Lodi marched against Babur with a vast host and was tempted into an attack on a narrow front against the Mughals' field defences. In the counterattack by Babur's horsemen, Ibrahim was killed and his army dispersed.

of 100,000 men and 1,000 war-elephants. Ibrahim, however, was an inexperienced commander who, in Babur's words, 'marched without order, halted or retired without method, and engaged without foresight'. Babur, who had known war since boyhood, defended his position with a line of wagons, trenches and stockades. Between them he placed his force of matchlocks and field artillery, the first significant use of this arm in Indian warfare. These broke the charge of Ibrahim's infantry and elephants, while Babur's horse-archers galloped round their flanks and shot into the struggling mass at will. Ibrahim and over 15,000 of his men (three times the number of Babur's whole force) were killed. The following year, the whole chivalry of the Rajputs, hoping to restore their former glory, gathered with 80,000 men and 800 war-elephants at Khanua, and repeated the tactic of a frontal attack on Babur's field works, only to be defeated in the same way. Babur was a Turk, not a Mongol, but to Indians all invaders from Central Asia were Mongols. The Mughal empire that he founded led India from the medieval into the modern period.

INDIAN CONDUCT IN WAR

Hindu convention prescribed rules of war broadly similar to those of western chivalry. Women, priests, non-combatants and soldiers fleeing, wounded or seeking quarter were to be spared. A mounted man should not strike a man on foot. Places of worship were respected. Poisoned weapons were forbidden. Heralds and ambassadors were sacrosanct. A guest given shelter must be protected at all costs. Honour was everything, death was nothing. The battlefield was where a warrior fulfilled his destiny. To abandon one's lord was to incur lasting disgrace. In practice, these ideals were rarely achieved. The *Arthashastra*, an early treatise on statecraft, taught that they could all be ignored if military necessity so demanded, and that a live dog was better than a dead lion.

Warfare was the sport of kings and it was the ambition of every great king to perform the *asvamedha* or horse sacrifice, by which a horse, attended by a group of

Gwalior Fort is among the most famous in India, known as 'the pearl in the necklace of the castles of Hind'; it stands on a sandstone hill with walls around 3 km (2 miles) in circumference and 10 m (33 ft) high. Founded in the 6th century, it defied Mahmud of Ghazni in 1021 but was captured by Qutb al-Din Aibak in 1196. It subsequently changed hands between Rajput, Mughal, Maratha, Jat and British conquerors, until it was restored by the British to their ally, the Maharaja Sindhia, in 1886.

heroes, was allowed to wander freely. Any neighbouring ruler into whose lands it went had to submit or give battle. The doctrine of *mandala* (circles) was equally disruptive. Each king was encouraged to conquer his neighbour while forming alliances with the kings beyond him, with the consequence that if the neighbour was defeated, former allies automatically became enemies. These practices fatally weakened the kingdoms of India before the Muslim invasions.

A further weakness lay in the separation of Hindu society into four great, divinely ordained classes, of which only one, the *kshatriyas*, provided the warriors. Medieval Hindu armies, sometimes half a million strong, were composed mostly of non-combatants, each performing logistic or supporting tasks according to a caste system by which everyone was born to his special calling. In northern India, late in the first millennium AD, successful invaders from Central Asia were absorbed into the Hindu system as new *kshatriyas*. Calling themselves Rajputs, 'the sons of kings', they eagerly embraced every aspect of Hindu military tradition. Proud, haughty, fiercely devoted to their clan chiefs, and liable to quarrel over quixotic points of honour, it fell to the Rajputs to defend Hindustan against the Muslim onslaught.

Many Islamic texts call for compassion and mercy after victory, especially over other Muslims. India, however, full of idolaters and polytheists, was judged a 'land of war', which by God's command it was right for Muslims to pillage and conquer. Believers waging jihad were assured that if they fell in battle they would go straight to paradise. The rich treasuries of Indian princes, intended as evidence of wealth and power, only served to attract gold-hungry adventurers. Defeated Hindus were given the choice of conversion or death, though they might be spared if they paid a poll tax in lieu of the military service theoretically incumbent on Muslims. Practical rulers often came to terms with those whose lands lay in difficult or unprofitable regions. Most Muslim conquerors were more concerned with enjoying their newly won wealth than with destroying those who produced it, and even bigots employed Hindu contingents when it suited them.

THE MILITARY SYSTEM OF MEDIEVAL INDIA

As with all newly conquered lands, the problem for the conqueror was one of dividing up the spoils and then retaining control. In medieval India, the system was based on military tenure, much as it was in medieval Europe. Apart from a small core of household troops and specialists (artillery, elephants, etc.), reliance was placed on contingents, originally provided by the participants in a successful invasion. Those who supported the new ruler were rewarded not by the assignment of land, as in Europe, but the land revenue (the government's share of the crop) of a specified area. From this, the assignee was required to maintain a given number of cavalrymen for service, for a limited period of time. Usually he lived in the area assigned to him and was expected to lead his contingent in person, though problems arose when the original commanders grew too old for war. A more serious weakness was that assignees sometimes did not maintain the required number of troops, and instead pocketed the revenues that had been assigned for their upkeep. A common practice was to hire men and horses who went from muster to muster ahead of the periodic inspections. Thus, when an army was needed, it was not to be found.

CHINA

Warfare in medieval China was entirely unlike that of the contemporary West. Although cavalry was an important part of Chinese armies, and almost the only kind of force deployed by steppe armies, China itself was conquered and ruled by vast infantry armies supported by complex, bureaucratic logistics systems. The goal of ambitious men in medieval China was to rule a unified, centralized empire. Where medieval Europe experienced continual upheaval among the decentralized and dispersed local warlords who took warfare as their defining characteristic, China was politically and militarily unified by relatively short, intensely violent periods separated by much longer periods of overall peace.

In 500 China was politically divided between north and south, as it had been since the fall of the Han dynasty in AD 220. For much of that time the divisions had been even greater, with small power-holders competing for local influence across what had been the Han empire, while one regime after another rose and fell in the north and south. All this would change when a new dynastic house, the Sui, conquered the Chinese ecumene in 589 and once again enforced the idea of imperial unity. The Sui dynasty was short-lived, however, overreaching itself both militarily and politically.

The rise of the Tang dynasty (618-907), which conquered the territory of the Sui and established a longer lasting Chinese empire, was a signal event in East Asia. Tang culture would set a standard for imperial culture and ideology throughout the region. Its armies reached into Korea itself, and the possible threat of a Tang invasion stimulated military reform in Japan. The Tang imperial family was partly Turkic, and it inherited a considerable measure of steppe culture. At the same time, some of the great clans that had arisen in the tumultuous centuries preceding the Tang perceived themselves as above the imperial family. These aristocratic families initially saw domination of the imperial government as an inherited right. It would take nearly a century and a half, as well as a cataclysmic rebellion, to pry loose their control.

In 755, a Turkic border general named An Lushan rebelled against the central government. An Lushan rose to power during a period in which the powerful border commands were gradually shifted over to non-Han Chinese officials. The new generals were more effective in securing the border, but they also commanded armies of professional soldiers whose loyalty was directed more towards their immediate superiors than the court. When the political winds at court shifted against An he rebelled, and quickly swept down from the north to capture the capital. Members of the most prominent aristocratic clans were slaughtered along the way. It would take until 763 for the central government to finally put down the rebellion. Yet, in regaining control the government was forced to cede considerable authority to the generals and regional officials who had remained loyal.

The nominal authority of the Tang government continued until 907, but the reality was rather different. Not only did the various powers on the Tang border, like the Tibetans, take advantage of the Tang's weakened situation, but the relevance of the central government to local affairs was limited. The Tang government gradually increased its internal authority without ever regaining its former strength. These gains were erased with the Huang Chao rebellion (875-84), and the trend toward provincial and local power increased.

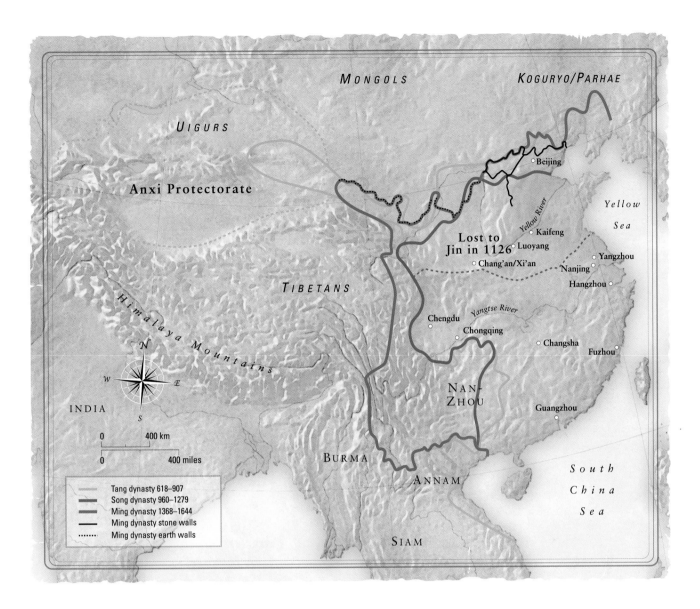

Map of China showing the extents of the main dynasties covered in this section.

The Five Dynasties and Ten Kingdoms Period (907–60) saw a series of five regimes in northern China, and a number of other regimes, variously enumerated, in southern and western China. To the north, the Kitan developed a partially Sinified empire that would last until 1125. Turkic, or partly Turkic, military men continued to be influential in the struggle for power in northern China until about 950, when a new group of Chinese generals overtook the enervated remnants of the previous factions and began to consolidate power. Meanwhile, in the south and west a number of other regimes, often ruled by emperors, flourished in the ruins of the Tang territories. The foundation of most of the high culture of the Song dynasty (960–1279) would, in fact, come from these regimes.

It took the Song dynasty some four decades from its official founding to eliminate every regime within the Chinese ecumene and to clearly establish a military balance of power with the Kitan. The Shanyuan treaty agreed with the Kitan in 1005 marked the end of the Song conquest, and created a stable northern border that remained at peace for over a century. The 11th century marked a high point in Chinese civilization in almost every sphere. Yet the Shanyuan treaty continued to rankle, and hostility to

A Tang-dynasty wall painting from the Mogao caves, Dunhuang, showing a Tang expeditionary force under the command of Zhang Yichao setting out to attack the Tibetans. Most of the troops for such a campaign would have been cavalry.

the Kitan empire ran deep. Despite a century of peaceful relations, the Song court allied itself to the rising Jurchen power north of the Kitan to destroy its hated enemy. This was accomplished in 1125, though poor Song military performance, and a dispute over the distribution of the spoils, led to a Jurchen invasion of the Song. Although it reached the capital, Kaifeng, the Jurchen were bought off, but a second invasion the following year resulted in the capture of not only the capital in 1127, but also the emperor, the retired emperor and a large proportion of the imperial clan.

The Song dynasty regrouped in the south, placing a brother of the emperor, who had fortunately been outside the capital when it fell, on the throne. Although the Jurchen were able to overrun northern China, they repeatedly failed in their invasions of the south. The Song, for its part, was similarly incapable of retaking the north. This stalemate continued until the rise of Chingiz Khan. By 1234 the Mongols had destroyed the Jurchen, but it would take them another fifty years to breach the Song's naval defences on the River Huai. In the interim, the Mongols conquered much of Eurasia and established the largest land empire in the history of the world. It proved short-lived, however, and by the 14th century the Mongol Yuan dynasty was disintegrating.

Once again, regional warlords emerged to vie for overall power. This time the conquering regime started not in the north, but in the south. Zhu Yuanzhang's Ming dynasty (1368–1644) emerged victorious from the contest between two other regimes along the River Yangtse, where naval battles were critical. From the beginning of the

The Great Wall, built in the 15th century on the northern frontier, was intended to hold the steppe armies at bay, but neither this line of defence nor the deployment of advanced weapons, developed from the 13th century, was able ultimately to protect China against the Mongol threat.

Ming until well after 1500, the Mongol threat from the steppes would remain an ever-present concern. By the late 15th century Ming military orientations were primarily defensive, marked most clearly by the construction of what is today known as the Great Wall.

CHINESE MILITARY SYSTEMS

The military systems used by the major Chinese dynasties between 500 and 1500 varied quite widely, and even changed within the timespan of a single dynasty. There was no single, consistent pattern, though a few generalizations can safely be made. First, Chinese (or Mongol) armies were always large: individual forces usually ran into the tens of thousands, and overall campaign armies often numbered over 100,000 soldiers, dwarfing their European counterparts. These armies were supported by complex, literate and numerate bureaucracies, well-developed economies and robust logistical systems.

The early Tang military was based upon the *fubing* system, which David Graff has described in detail. This system had been inherited from the Sui dynasty, if not before, but it had to be revitalized at the beginning of the Tang. Several hundred locally recruited and locally based units of about 800 men each served rotations in the capital under one of twelve imperial guard commands for one month each, with the possibility of serving up to three years on the border. When not on military duty these men worked the land, and were expected to maintain their skills and supply

A Tang-dynasty statuette of a Tang soldier. Standard armour included protection for the head, neck, torso, shoulders and arms. Figurines like this were included in many tombs.

their own military equipment in return for reduced taxes. Underlying the entire system was the general distribution of plots of land to all farmers based in the empire. The *fubing* troops were supplemented by paid steppe tribesmen, who supplied most of the cavalry for the army, and drafts of able-bodied men from areas without *fubing* units when extra troops were needed.

Although the *fubing* system worked extremely well at the beginning of the Tang, it began to fail in the late 7th century. The military activities of the mature empire required lengthy posting to border garrisons, rather than short-term service, and the land distribution system had been eroded as more and more fields were collected into the manors of powerful families. A new system of full-time soldiering was put in place by the end of the first half of the 8th century, still supplemented by steppe cavalry. In the final phase of Tang military evolution, military governors began to control frontier garrisons as well as the financial and other governmental powers of the surrounding territory. An Lushan was just such a military governor, and it was his control of troops and resources that allowed him to defend the border effectively and to temporarily overthrow the central government.

Military governors continued to be major regional strongmen until the second half of the 10th century, and from the 8th century until the end of the Song dynasty Chinese armies consisted of professional soldiers. Although the Song centralized military authority, this was done at an immense cost to the state. The Song army, which reached a paper strength of nearly 1.7 million men in the 11th century, always maintained half its strength in the capital to prevent any regional rebellion. The imperial army itself was recruited from local militias and provincial soldiers and was based upon minimum height requirements and performance standards. These professional soldiers were fully armed and supported by the state, much to the distress of Confucianized government officials who looked back to the *fubing* system and earlier expedients of farmer-soldiers.

The Song army never produced enough cavalry to fight steppe armies effectively in the open field. Despite far greater economic and industrial power, the Song were unable to defeat the Kitan empire to the north, and barely managed to drive back the Tanguts to the northwest by the end of the 11th century. The latter came at great cost, and enervated rather than stimulated the Song army. Its losses were never made up, and it failed against the Jurchen in the 1120s, before being more effectively concentrated under four military commands along the new border with the Jurchen.

The Jurchen and Mongols, for their part, functioned partly on a system of universal conscription of adult males who brought their own horses and equipment to the battlefield. Mongol units were organized in 5,600-man guard units. Chinese soldiers from captured areas were used for infantry and naval purposes, as well as Koreans, Uigurs and any other subject populations with useful skills. Chinese warlords ruled most of northern China under the Mongols until they rebelled in the late 13th century. After the destruction of the Song, the Mongols extended their very loose control over the rest of China. Mongol garrisons were placed at strategic points to keep the population quiet.

Ming practice was structurally similar to the Mongol system of guard units, and was based upon a hereditary military. The founding emperor's troops were given land for their maintenance, which they were to farm when not on duty, and their descendants were expected to continue this system. This had largely broken down by 1500.

TECHNOLOGICAL CHANGE IN CHINA

The most important change in Chinese warfare in this period was the development of first gunpowder and then guns, bombs and rockets. But it is important to note that another technological change of similar momentousness was introduced a century or two before 500, namely the stirrup. Its place of origin is still unclear, but by the beginning of the 6th century it had increased the importance of cavalry, both light and heavy, and brought various steppe groups more firmly into the north Chinese military forum.

Cavalry remained the main reconnaissance and striking arm of Chinese armies until perhaps the late 18th century, but Chinese armies were predominantly infantry forces. The importance of infantry, and the extensive Chinese use of fortifications and naval forces, was an important precondition for the development of gunpowder weapons. A substance that we might call gunpowder is first mentioned in 808, though well outside the military context. The next notice of gunpowder, this time very directly in a military context, comes in 1044, with the inclusion of its recipe in a government military encyclopedia. By this time the Song government had a regularly established arsenal to produce gunpowder and related weapons, though not yet guns.

Below left A 6th- to 7th-century Chinese bronze stirrup. The earliest representation of a mounting stirrup in China is from 302, and a pair of stirrups are known from about 20 years later.

Below right Relief representation of Saluzi, one of the six battle chargers of Li Shimin (later emperor Tang Taizong), commemorated for his tomb in 637.

This Yuan-dynasty bronze firearm has multiple barrels to enhance its firepower. Many portable firearms and larger pieces became a regular part of warfare in the 12th and 13th centuries in China.

Gunpowder's failure to dramatically reconfigure warfare, government and society in China, in contradistinction to its effects in Europe, has hitherto confused some people. Some have suggested, erroneously, that the Chinese did not use gunpowder for warfare, confining it to firework displays. This is entirely false, for the Chinese immediately and extensively used every kind of gunpowder weapon they could invent, up to and including the first guns. Long before the introduction of gunpowder and guns, however, China already featured cities protected by proportionally low, thick curtain walls of pounded earth, disciplined armies with articulated tactical units and a bureaucratic state to supply these forces. It would take until at least the 16th century before Europeans began to adopt these measures to exploit and manage the power of guns.

True guns were invented during the intense periods of warfare between the Song, Jurchen and Mongols in the 12th and 13th centuries. Since gunpowder is a propellant or even a low explosive it does not actually explode; it burns or deflagrates. Unsurprisingly, then, it was initially used to burn people or equipment. Tubes packed with gunpowder were attached to spears or poles, ignited, and used to fend off assailants trying to attack city walls. At some point shards of pottery and other particles were added to the mix, and the tubes also shifted from being made of paper or bamboo to iron. Finally, possibly before the end of the 12th century, but more likely in the early 13th, a single projectile that almost fully occluded the aperture of an iron tube was used, and the true gun was born.

Guns, along with many other gunpowder weapons, quickly moved from specialized tools of siege warfare into naval warfare, and then finally into the open field. These early weapons were not, however, capable of overcoming the power of steppe cavalry forces, or of battering down city walls. They nevertheless became quite ubiquitous in Chinese warfare, and were mass manufactured in fairly standard forms. By the 14th century guns had differentiated into cannons and handguns. Once the wars of the Ming founding had been concluded, gun development slowed. Special firearms training camps were organized near the capital, and between 1380 and 1488 the capital arsenals produced 3,000 cannon and 3,000 handguns annually. Even more firearms were produced by local blacksmiths. Although the Chinese started using cast-iron guns and solid iron shot in the 15th century, the forms of their guns were the same as those from the 13th century.

When Europeans arrived with new and improved guns in the 16th century, the Chinese eagerly adopted the technology. From then on, Chinese firearms were either purchased from foreigners or were copies of foreign designs. Still, nothing much had changed with the new weapons. Neither they, nor the 15th-century fortification on the northern frontier that we now call the Great Wall, could hold back the steppe armies of the 17th century. Guns changed warfare in medieval China, making it look very much like early modern European warfare – or, perhaps more fairly, European warfare in the 16th century started to resemble medieval Chinese warfare.

KOREA: KEY EVENTS

550 Three kingdoms in Korea: Koguryo, Silla and Paekche

590 Chinese invasion thwarted by storms

612 Chinese army of 300,000, led by Emperor Sui Yangdi, starves at Pyongyang

666 Chinese exploit internecine warfare and dominate Korea

675 Chinese withdraw from northern Korea

696 Korea united under Silla

918 Silla replaced by Koryo dynasty

993 Kitan invade and burn capital, but cannot consolidate rule

1018 Kitan invasion thwarted by flooding

1107 Jurchen Jin invasion defeated; northern Korea heavily fortified

1125 Peace with Jurchen

1225 Mongol ambassadors murdered

1231–55 Six Mongol invasions, ending in Korean defeat

1259 Koryo ruler becomes tributary to Mongols until mid-14th century

KOREA

Around 550, there were three kingdoms on the Korean peninsula: Koguryo in the north, Silla in the southeast and Paekche in the southwest. Inevitably, the independence of these kingdoms came under threat whenever China was united, as happened under the Sui dynasty in 589. The latter's attempt to demand tribute in 590 resulted in King Yongyang of Koguryo defiantly launching a raid across the River Liao in southern Manchuria. The Sui response was to send an invasion force of 300,000, supported by a fleet, against Pyongyang. However, storms dispersed the Sui navy and its land forces were destroyed by heavy rain, leading to a logistical collapse, starvation and disease before any battles were fought.

In 612, Emperor Sui Yangdi tried again. Several years of preparation produced a fleet of 300 great ships and an army of allegedly over a million men for the expedition. Certainly the entire resources of the empire were directed towards supporting the invasion, resulting in economic dislocation and mass starvation as food was directed towards the military operations. The army crossed the Liao in the spring using pontoon bridges, and signally defeated a Koguryo force, killing its generals. A siege of Yodong followed, with the Chinese army housed in a fortified camp 4 km (1.5 miles) square, but the city did not surrender. Meanwhile, the fleet landed 40,000 troops near Pyongyang, who swept aside Korean resistance and stormed the city. Once inside, though, order broke down and they were hurled back by a Korean counterattack. This force then remained on the coast awaiting the arrival of the main Chinese army. When this advanced on Pyongyang it was 300,000 strong, divided into nine contingents to ease the problems of supply. This precaution proved insufficient, and the Korean general Ulchi Mundok employed a Fabian strategy to wear down the invaders. By the time the Chinese reached Pyongyang they were too weak to conduct a proper siege. Forced into retreat, the Chinese army was destroyed by Korean harassing attacks. Subsequent campaigns in 613 and 614 were equally unsuccessful, and the defeats led to the downfall of the Sui dynasty.

With no serious external threat to face, the Korean kingdoms began to fight among themselves. In 645 Emperor Tang Taizong led another invasion of Koguryo in support of Silla. Once again the logistical preparations were impressive, with a fleet of over 400 ships, 60,000 Chinese troops and allegedly 200,000 Turkish and Kitan allies. The experienced Chinese general Li Shiji crossed the Liao secretly and, taking the Koreans by surprise, routed them in battle, seizing border forts and towns as a result. The fleet under Chiang Yang also achieved a signal success by storming the fortress of Pi-she-ch'eng at dusk, before the gates could be closed.

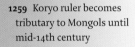

Statuette of a Sillan cavalryman in civilian dress, dating to the 5th or 6th century. The figure is a table vessel so the projection from the horse's chest (a spout) and the cup on its rump are part of this function and are not military features.

The main army moved to besiege Yodong. Koguryo sent an army of 40,000 to its relief. But after an initial success, the Koreans were drawn into a trap as the Chinese general Li Daozung first steadied the line and then sent an outflanking force around the enemy rear, inflicting heavy casualties. Yondong was captured when a strong wind was utilized by the Chinese to carry fire into the city. The Korean commander of Po-yench'eng surrendered the city after a relief force was driven off, and the rest of the campaign centred upon the epic siege of An-shih-ch'eng. Koguryo forces under Kao Yenshou advanced to relieve the siege, this time in formidable numbers, but once again they found themselves outmanoeuvred in battle by the Chinese. This may have been because the Korean troops were largely inexperienced while the Chinese army was a picked force raised from all over the empire. Despite a victory in the largest battle of the war, Tang Taizong was unable to take the city after a two-month siege, and as winter drew in was forced to withdraw, suffering losses on the way, including most of the army's horses. He could claim success on account of his victory in three battles, his capture of ten cities, and his taking of thousands of prisoners – but Koguryo remained resistant.

It was only when China sought to exploit the rivalry between the three kingdoms that the situation changed. Silla sought Chinese aid in these conflicts, and in 660 invaded Paekche; its allies provided a large fleet and army to ensure success. Koguryo took advantage of the fact that Silla troops were otherwise occupied to attack the country, but terrible storms destroyed their siege equipment, forcing them to withdraw. The following year the Chinese general Su Dingfang landed troops from a fleet near Pyongyang and invested the city, but the promised reinforcements did not arrive and the siege continued into the winter. As a result, King Munmu of Koguryo and his general Kim Yushin led their troops across mountain passes in bitter weather to join them; exhausted by the conditions, the Chinese withdrew.

Meanwhile, Paekche called upon its Japanese allies, numbering 27,000 strong, who succeeded in occupying two Silla cities in 663. Combined Silla and Chinese forces counterattacked, with the Chinese fleet performing the key role. After three indecisive encounters the Chinese navy achieved the upper hand, surrounding and burning the Japanese fleet. Despite continued resistance from Paekche loyalists for another two years, the flight of their king to Koguryo was the writing on the wall. When civil war broke out in that country in 666, the Chinese seized the opportunity they had been seeking for half a century. The eighty-year-old veteran general Li Shiji was given command and quickly seized the key fortress of Xinzheng; its citizens had imprisoned their garrison commander and surrendered. Despite a failed landing near Pyongyang, wrecked by severe storms, Li persisted, preferring the strategy of mopping up towns and fortresses in the north to a direct approach to the capital, and defeating a Koguryo relief force in the process. Joined by Silla forces, the Chinese conducted a final and successful siege of Pyongyang, which was captured and burned to the ground.

Silla's rulers had no intention of being absorbed into the Chinese empire, though, and over the next decade secured Koguryo as Korean. Even the death of King Yushin in 673 did not end a conflict in which the balance of success swayed

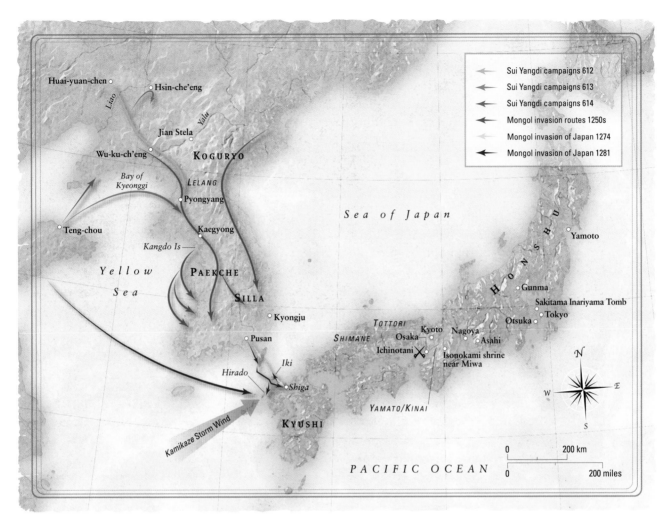

Map of Japan and Korea showing Sui Yangdi's campaigns and the later Mongol invasions of Japan.

both ways. A treaty in 675 resulted in the Chinese withdrawing from northern Korea over the next couple of years, although they retained their Liao territories. Even these were lost in 696, when a revolt broke out against Chinese rule; the imperial government, distracted by problems elsewhere, conceded. Korea was now effectively unified under Silla, although it owed nominal obedience to the emperor.

THE KOREAN MILITARY SYSTEM

The military forces of Korea seem to have been organized very much on the Chinese model. The smallest unit was of ten men, called a *huo* after the campfire they shared. Four companies of fifty men made up a *tuan*, and four to six *tuan* formed a *fu* of 800 to 1,200 men. The core of the army, following reorganization in the mid-7th century, were the 'banner units' of the royal bodyguard based in the Silla capital of Kumsong. The first unit was raised in 583 and the second in 625, with another seven in the 670s and 680s from the Koguryo, Paekche and Malgal troops of the unification period, achieving a total of about 10,000 men, all or mostly heavy cavalry. Another type of predominantly cavalry forces was the *chong*, up to 1,000 strong and drawn from each of Silla's nine provinces. The emphasis certainly seems to have been placed on the mounted retinues of lords, and the management of bow, lance and sword on horseback were key aristocratic pursuits. Numbers are difficult to gauge and are often exaggerated in the sources. In the late 7th century it is possible to make a case for about 25,000 trained troops, with half of them cavalry and half of them (mostly household troops) with armour for man and horse. Details of the rest of the infantry forces are less certain, and this may mean that they were recruited as levies only in emergencies. It is certain that maritime matters played a major role in the Korean economy as the country became rich through trade, but, apart from the establishment of an office for marine affairs under King Munmu of Koguryo in 583, evidence is scarce.

THE KITAN WARS

In 918, Silla was succeeded by the Koryo dynasty, which soon found itself threatened by the Kitan (or Liao), who were trying to take over China. Despite an invasion in 946, they failed to achieve this and the Chinese consolidated under the Song dynasty in 960. A generation later the Kitan were unified enough to attempt further expansion, but then Korea was subject to three serious invasions over a twenty-five-year period.

In 993 King Seonjong was ruling Koryo, with the able support of his minister Kang Kam-chan, who became the hero of the period. The invasion of that year, after initial Kitan successes, was eventually halted by dogged resistance along the Ch'ong-ch'on river line. This enabled Korea to negotiate a peace with the Kitan general Xiao Sunning who withdrew his forces over the River Yalu. In 1004 the Kitans finally defeated the Song and forced them to pay tribute, leaving Koryo as the sole state standing against them. In a political coup in 1009 the general Gang Jo deposed and murdered Emperor Mokjong of Koryo, and placed Emperor Hyeonjong on the throne; this gave the Kitan emperor Shengzong a pretext to invade once more. The next year, leading an army that some have claimed to be 400,000 strong, Shengzong quickly defeated and executed Gang Jo. Emperor Hyeonjong was persuaded not to surrender but to withdraw into the hills and conduct a guerrilla war. Despite capturing and burning the capital, the Kitan were unable to conquer the countryside and were forced to withdraw without enforcing imperial rule.

The Kitan regime was not prepared to allow this situation to continue, though, and in 1018 launched another invasion under General Xiao Baiya. Korean forces under the seventy-year-old general Kang opted not to face the invaders in battle. At Heunghwajin Kang directed his troops to block a river and flood out the Kitan. Xiao continued to lead his forces south to capture the capital of Kaesung, but when this proved impossible he staged a withdrawal. This time Kang attacked the retreating and dishevelled enemy near the fortress of Kwiju, scattering the Kitan army. Once again, Korean independence had been maintained by a clever utilization of geography.

A period of peace with their northern neighbours followed for Korea, allowing prosperity to grow and cultural life to flourish. The Koreans were also threatened by the Jurchen Jin dynasty from Manchuria, which replaced the Kitan around 1100. The main outcome of this threat was the work of General Yun Kwan in raising an army to repel invasion in 1107 and in developing a heavily fortified region in the northeast to hold other attackers at bay. This region

Korean cavalry helmet, 16th century. It is of the spangenhelm type, made up of a conical frame with four segments and large pendant leather flaps to protect the face.

featured nine fortresses and possibly encouraged a sense of complacency after peace was made with the Jurchen in 1125, for a greater danger was to arise a century later.

THE MONGOL INVASIONS, 1231–59

By 1170 the Koryo kings had become mere figureheads, and were effectively replaced in 1196 by a dynasty of hereditary military regents founded by Ch'oe Ch'ung-hon. In 1217, a sudden irruption of 90,000 Kitans, including some 20,000 warriors, in flight from the Mongols, broke through the northern borders. Towards the end of the following year, just as the Koreans were bringing this invasion under control, a force of 10,000 Mongols proper, with 20,000 Jurchen subject allies, appeared in pursuit, and established an annual tribute. In 1225 the Mongol ambassador coming to claim this tribute was assassinated whilst crossing the Yalu; this was an insult that the Mongols could not tolerate. The succession of Great Khan Ögödei in 1229 initiated a strategy of global conquest in which the inhabitants of Koryo would find themselves caught up. In early September 1231 the Mongol general Sartai crossed the frontier, surprising the Korean defenders. The following month he brought Korean forces to battle, inflicting a heavy defeat on them outside the important fortress of Anbuk-ku. King Kojong (r. 1213–59) was quick to sue for peace, and paid a heavy tribute in January 1232. Later that year, at the instigation of the regent Ch'oe U, the royal court was moved from Kaegyong to Kangwha Island in the Bay of Kyeonggi to make it more secure. The Mongols considered this provocation, so another attack was launched and their forces deeply penetrated the peninsula. Lacking a fleet, however, they were unable to capture Kangwha. Moreover, the Koreans fell back on guerrilla warfare and when the Mongol general Sartai was killed by a warrior monk, the Mongols withdrew without achieving their objectives.

An early gun tube, dating to the 14th century; it would have been fixed to a pole by the tang behind the barrel. The Mongols were precocious in using gunpowder, which initially shocked their opponents, though many, like the Koreans, rapidly learned to use the technology themselves.

They returned again for a lengthy campaign known as the Third Invasion (1235–39), this time supported by Korean renegades, advancing as far as Kyongju. These operations caused untold destruction to Korean religious sites and cultural artefacts, but only served to stiffen resistance. An uneasy peace was brokered, which lasted until 1248 when the Mongols returned in force. Again they blockaded Kangwha without success, and on the death of the Great Khan Güyük the invaders left Korea to elect his successor. Ch'oe U died in 1249 and diplomatic negotiations followed, but his son and successor as military regent Ch'oe Hang continued to lead the resistance. The new Great Khan Möngke demanded homage from King Kojong of Koryo in 1251, and when this was refused a fifth invasion was launched in 1253. This time the attack was on two fronts, with a parallel attack along the coast of the Sea of Japan. They also brought with them puppet rulers, Koreans who had gone over to the Mongol cause, chief amongst them Hong Pog-won. A combination of systematically reducing the fortresses and inflicting signal massacres on the population broke the morale of the Koryo forces. Once again, though, civilian resistance halted the invaders. The key event in this was the defence of Ch'ungju under the inspirational leadership of Kim Yun-hu; after sixty-six days, the Mongols were forced to abandon the siege in mid-December.

The Sixth Invasion, beginning in 1254, turned out to be the final, successful attempt by the Mongols to conquer the Korean peninsula. The Mongol general Jalairtai and Hong Pog-won advanced along the line of the River Han. Although repulsed at several fortifications, the Mongols devastated the countryside, and are recorded as having taken over 200,000 prisoners (though this number – some ten per cent of the population – may be understood to refer to those brought under Mongol dominion). Retreating in the winter, they returned in October 1255, and, despite suffering an initial defeat, pressed south into the province of Kyongsangdo. Jalairtai also concentrated on the coast and islands of Sohaedo in an attempt to undermine the Koreans' defensive strategy. By mid 1257, the pressure of these attacks forced the Koryo government into negotiation. The crown prince was sent to the Mongol court, with the intention of delaying the inevitable outcome, although without success. In June 1258 the end game began, as the Mongols dominated the south. By December, fifteen fortresses of the eastern territories had also surrendered. In 1259 King Kojong and the Great Khan Möngke died within a few months of each other. When Crown Prince Wonjong arrived at the Mongol court on another embassy he was greeted by the new ruler, Kublai Khan, and sent home with the title of king of Koryo, in return for submission and regular tribute. Dissident Koreans continued to fight on, and it took a combined campaign by royalist troops and Mongol allies from 1270 to 1274 to eventually end hostilities. Korea remained a tributary state of the Mongols until the mid-14th century, when King Gongmin began to assert renewed independence.

JAPAN

Medieval Japanese warfare was in every respect the product of its times. Its early tactical paradigms arose apace with the warrior order itself, and waxed and waned with the changing circumstances of the later medieval age, all in response to a complex sequence of interacting political, social, strategic and technological imperatives.

By the middle decades of the 6th century, much of Japan had been bound together into a loose confederation of regional chieftains, among which one – the royal, or Yamato, house – stood as first among equals. A few of the other houses were entirely dependent upon the Yamato for their positions, but the majority had their own geographical bases of power, within which they were largely autonomous; their positions were permanent, hereditary and only nominally related to the king's authority. All of this changed rapidly and dramatically during the 7th century, as this polity gave way to a centralized imperial regime.

The changeover accelerated after the sixth month of 645, when radicals led by the future emperor Tenji seized power by hacking their political opponents to pieces with swords and spears, in the midst of a court ceremony. In the wake of this spectacular coup d'état, Tenji and his supporters introduced a series of centralizing measures collectively known as the Taika Reforms, after the calendar era in which the first were launched. Over the next several decades, the great regional powers were stripped of their independent bases and converted to true officials of the state, while the Yamato sovereigns were restyled in the image of Chinese emperors. The result was what historians have come to refer to as the 'imperial' state.

The Mongol Invasions of Japan

In the late 1260s the Mongol potentate Kublai Khan turned his eye on Japan, perhaps as a base for his quest to conquer the Southern Song. After eleven diplomatic overtures failed, Kublai ordered the construction of an expeditionary fleet of ships, which departed from Koryo on the third day of the tenth month of 1274, arriving in Hakata Bay, in Kyushu, on the twentieth.

Yuan chronicles describe an enormous force of 23,000 troops, but modern estimates are closer to 2,000 or 3,000 Mongol, Chinese and Korean soldiers, who were met on the beaches by a slightly larger number of samurai. Fighting from behind temporary fortifications, Japanese archers effectively pinned down the invaders on the coast, and eventually forced them to withdraw.

A second invasion force, launched in 1281 – reported by Japanese and Mongol chroniclers to have numbered over 100,000, but probably consisting of around 10,000 – fared little better. Blocked at their landing sites in Kyushu by newly built stone walls, the Mongol troops were forced to retreat to their ships each evening. Samurai raiders commandeered fishing boats and rowed in to cut anchor lines, board ships and kill those on board. As Mongol losses mounted and supplies dwindled, a dramatic coup-de-grâce, in the form of an out-of-season typhoon, sank much of the Mongol fleet at anchor.

While both invasion attempts failed, they did have lasting effects on subsequent Japanese history, particularly the fate of the Kamakura shogunate. By assuming complete responsibility for national defence during the crisis, Kamakura significantly enlarged the formal scope of shogunal authority. But the costs of the defence, and the long cold war of continued vigilance that followed, strained its resources, while the regime's inability to reward its vassals for their efforts – there being no lands or other spoils that could be confiscated from the enemy and redistributed – strained their allegiance.

Mongol forces arrayed in battle formation during Kublai Khan's attempted invasion of Japan in 1274. From the *Mokō shūrai ekotoba* ('Picture Scroll of the Mongol Invasions'), commissioned by Takezaki Suenaga.

Warriors under Minamoto no Yoshitomo attack the Sanjō Imperial Palace in 1159, during the opening rounds of the Heiji Incident. From the *Heiji monogatari emaki* ('Picture Scroll of The Tale of Heiji').

The reformers prevailed through cajolery, cooptation and coercion, aided in no small measure by widespread apprehension over the growing might of Tang China, which had been engaged since the early 600s in one of the greatest military expansions in Chinese history. Centralization and restructuring of the military constituted a major element of the reformation process.

The imperial codes placed the whole of the state's martial resources under the direct control of the newly emergent emperor and his court, prescribing an elaborate military apparatus centred on a militia composed principally of subjects conscripted as part of their corvée (forced labour) tax obligations, and enrolled into provincial regiments. Troops spent most of their year tilling their own fields, and were called up in rotation for training or service. In time of war, expeditionary forces were formed from temporarily mobilized regiments under staff officers holding temporary commissions.

These arrangements were modelled on those of Tang China, but the Japanese system was neither technologically nor organizationally a duplicate of its archetype. The Japanese showed little interest, for example, in adopting handheld crossbows, a key weapon of Chinese armies. Nevertheless, like its Tang epitome, the imperial military was a force that featured a mixed weapons system. This predominantly comprised light infantry augmented by heavily armoured light cavalry, and by a mysterious artillery piece called an *ōyumi* or *dō*, which appears to have been some sort of platform-mounted, crossbow-style catapult.

An army of this sort was formidable in pitched battles, particularly on the defensive, but it was logistically ill-suited to long offensive campaigns, owing to its

size and to the fact that it drew its manpower from the same farmers who produced its food and other supplies. It was even less appropriate to domestic peacekeeping functions – which had, by the mid-700s, replaced foreign defence as the court's military priority.

THE WAY OF THE HORSE AND BOW

The imperial state avoided the logistical difficulties involved in training peasant conscripts to fight from horseback through the simple expedient of staffing its cavalry units only with men who had acquired the basic skills of mounted archery on their own – the upper echelon of provincial society and the lower-ranked members of the central aristocracy. One largely unintentional result of this policy was to institutionalize the identification of mounted archery as the weapons system of the elite, marking cavalrymen as a class apart from their foot-soldier comrades.

From the mid-8th century both the prominence and the tactical importance of this elite technology expanded exponentially. By this time the threat of invasion from the continent had evaporated, and with it the value of large field armies, prompting the court to begin restructuring its military apparatus. The most dramatic step in this direction came in 792, when the infantry-centred regiments were abolished everywhere except on the frontiers and in other 'strategic' provinces. Henceforth, the court focused its attention on developing small, highly mobile squads that could be assembled with a minimum of delay and sent out in pursuit of criminals and on similar policing tasks.

By the mid-10th century the state no longer trained or maintained armies of its own, depending instead on the members of an emerging order of privately trained warriors commissioned with new titles that legitimized their use of personal martial resources on behalf of the court. Acquisition of a monopoly over the means of armed force did not, however, lead quickly or directly to warrior autonomy in the application of force.

During the first three centuries of their existence samurai were essentially mercenaries, offering their skills and services in exchange for long-term patronage of their careers by court powers or for immediate rewards. Such rewards most often took the form of ranks and posts in the government or private estate system hierarchy. While these often included perquisites over lands and peoples, and sometimes involved the transfer of lands hitherto administered by warriors on the losing side of a conflict, samurai were rarely, if ever, able to specify the size or the particulars of the rewards for themselves, and any transfers of land were accomplished indirectly, through the agency of the court and in accord with the niceties prescribed by the court-centred legal system.

Thus, the missile cavalry tradition the samurai inherited from their forebears was exceedingly well matched to the social and political circumstances and tactical needs of the age. Already long associated with elite socio-economic status, mounted archers could also be effective in relatively small numbers, and without extensive large group drill. The superior mobility of cavalry, both on and off the battlefield, moreover, made it the natural arm of attack and pursuit – an important consideration for warriors whose functions centred on law enforcement.

In urban skirmishes and other situations that circumscribed the arena of combat, samurai often fought on foot. They also conscripted or hired foot soldiers and deployed them in most sorts of battles. Such troops were active combatants, not just grooms and attendants to the mounted warriors (as they have often been portrayed). At the same time, they were considerably less than an infantry.

Technological circumstances were perhaps the key factor that shaped samurai cavalry tactics, which differed remarkably from those of other celebrated light cavalry traditions, such as the horseriding peoples of the continent. To begin with, the boxy *ōyoroi* style of armour (see box on p. 258) favoured by the first samurai was heavy, unevenly balanced and fitted loosely at the waist (so that it could hang over the saddle without pushing up the plates of the skirt) thereby exposing the wearer's thighs. It therefore shifted readily, like a bell around its clapper, complicating a warrior's efforts to maintain his balance in the saddle. Japanese warhorses were, moreover, stout, short-legged beasts, incapable of carrying more than about 90 kg (200 lb) – including rider, saddle and weapons – and lacking the endurance to run about for long periods or distances. They were also unruly and difficult to control – especially when both hands were occupied with a task like archery.

Japanese bows, fashioned from plain wood or, from the 13th century onwards, from laminates of wood and bamboo, further limited samurai tactical

'Stay calm as the enemy approaches. Keep the shoulder plate that faces incoming arrows opposite your helmet. Close the gaps in your armour – keep shaking and hiking it up so that you do not let an arrow through. Do not let your armour open as you move.'
Advice to warriors in the Genpei war, from *The Tale of the Heike*

options. Wood lacks the flexibility and springiness of horn and tendon, forcing samurai to contend with very long weapons – about 2.5 m (8.2 ft), making them impossibly awkward to use from horseback – that were of limited range and lacked penetrating force.

This combination of weak bows, sturdy armour and arrows carried in numbers too few to permit any to be wasted, forced early samurai to shoot only at very close range – usually 10 m (30 ft) or less – and to target with precision the gaps and weak points in the armour of specific opponents. Accordingly, they developed a peculiar form of light cavalry tactics that involved individuals and small groups circling and manoeuvring around one another in a manner that bore an intriguing resemblance to dogfighting aviators.

In this sort of combat, horsemanship counted for as much as marksmanship. The angle at which warriors closed with opponents was crucial, because their bows and armour permitted them to shoot comfortably only to their left, along an arc of roughly 45°, from the ten or eleven o'clock to about the nine o'clock position. Canny warriors, therefore, attempted to approach the enemy from his right, where he could not return fire, while keeping him on their own left. All such manoeuvring was, of course, further complicated by the presence of other horsemen and foot soldiers, and by the terrain and particular circumstances of the battle site.

Early medieval warriors seldom attempted large-scale tactical manoeuvre, but neither did they fight as individuals, independent of their comrades. Instead, tactical cooperation devolved to smaller units and components, with troops working together in small teams of varying numbers and make-up. The fighting men who

A Heian-period warrior clad in ōyoroi ('great armour'), the premier armour of the early medieval era, which appeared at some time between the mid-10th and the early 11th centuries; it was initially worn without leg armour, but plated shin guards (suneate) were introduced during the late 12th century, and lower-cut fur shoes replaced calf-high bearskin boots.

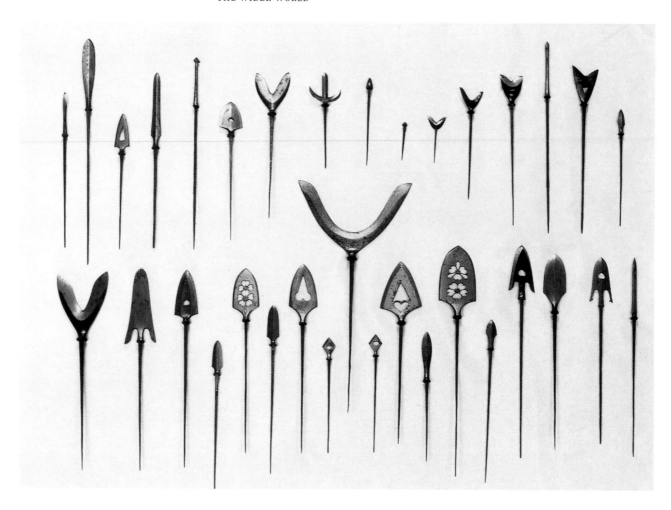

Japanese arrowheads. The arrows in use from the mid-Heian period onward averaged between 86 and 96 cm (34 and 38 in.), and were usually made of bamboo. Arrowheads were mounted into the shafts by long, slender tangs, in the same manner as sword blades were mounted into hilts, and assumed a bewildering variety of shapes and sizes: narrow, four-sided heads; flat, leaf-shaped broadheads; forked heads; blunt, wooden heads (used for practice); and whistling heads (used for signalling).

composed these monadic organizations lived and trained in close proximity to one another, honing their skills through a variety of regimens and competitive games. Hence they were able to coordinate and cooperate, harmonizing their actions to those of close associates with an impressive degree of discipline and fluidity. Battles, therefore, tended to be aggregates of lesser combats: mêlées of archery duels and brawls between small groups, punctuated by general advances and retreats, and by volleys of arrows launched by bowmen on foot, protected by portable walls of shields.

RAIDS AND BARRICADES

The samurai of the Heian period (794–1185) legitimately took to the saddle only to chastise lawbreakers, as agents of the court or of the noble houses that comprised it. Their right to 'self-help' – to the pursuit of private ends through violence – was closely circumscribed under law and precedent. Consequently, military campaigns of the era – even private ones – defined victory in terms of the destruction or apprehension of opposing warriors, not the capture of territory.

Faced with an often thorny challenge of running elusive foes to ground, 10th- and 11th-century warriors on the offensive favoured night attacks and other raids on the homes and fields of the enemy, his allies and dependents. Raids of this sort were tactical expedients whose underlying strategic objectives were not the real estate itself, but the humans whose livelihoods were tied to it; their purpose was

Takezaki Suenaga leads his warband past a command post established by Kikuchi Jirō Takefusa, en route to engage Mongol forces during their second invasion attempt, in 1281. From the *Mokō shūrai ekotoba*.

destruction, not seizure – raiders burned fields, plundered houses, killed inhabitants and then moved on. Attacks on an opponent's home or economic base threatened his long-term survival, and forced him to stand and fight. Seizure of land, on the other hand, offered no long-term gain within the political framework of the times, inasmuch as title over the lands was still subject to the confirmation and approval of central authority.

By the 12th century, as the scale of samurai military and socio-economic resources grew, and the costs attendant on raiding, evasion and refusal of battle became less and less bearable, tactics began to centre on entrenchments and barriers. 12th- and 13th-century fortifications were defensive lines, not castles or forts intended to provide long-term safe haven for armies ensconced within. Many were simply barricades erected across important roads or mountain passes. Others were transient wartime modifications to temples, shrines or warrior residences. Their purpose, in either case, was to concentrate campaigns and battles, by slowing enemy advances, thwarting raiding tactics, controlling selection of the battleground, and restricting cavalry manoeuvre. Such breastworks were temporary, and rudimentary in comparison to the castles of the later medieval period, but they were not always small in scale. Some, like the famous Taira defence works erected in 1184 at Ichinotani, near Naniwa on the border of Settsu province, could be quite impressive.

THE FIRST SHOGUNATES

Most warfare between the 10th and 12th centuries was localized and of small scale, involving just a few dozen troops on either side. Even conflicts of major status – the insurrections of Taira Masakado (935–39) and Taira Tadatsune (1028–31) and the like – were contested by forces numbering only in the hundreds. But the Genpei war (1180–85) represented a significant departure from even the very recent past, with troops involved in individual battles often ranging into the thousands – even exceeding 10,000 in some.

Above Takezaki Suenaga (pictured at the bow of the ship) and his followers attack a Mongol ship at anchor and take prisoners on the fifth day of the seventh intercalary month of 1281. From the *Mokō shūrai ekotoba*.

Below Portrait of a 14th-century warrior leader, long assumed to be Ashikaga Takauji, the founder of the Muromachi shogunate, now generally believed to be Kō no Moronao, one of Takauji's senior retainers.

The regime that this conflict established – the Kamakura shogunate – was a kind of government within a government, both part of and distinct from the court in Kyoto. Initially, it acted as the main military and police agency of the court, exercised broad governing powers in eastern Japan and held special authority over the warriors, scattered countrywide, that it recognized as its formal vassals. By the end of the 13th century, however, the shogunate had assumed control of most of the state's judicial, military and foreign affairs.

In the meantime, Kamakura vassals across the country had discovered that they could manipulate the insulation from direct court supervision the regime offered them, to lay ever stronger and more personal claims to lands – and the people on them – they ostensibly administered on behalf of the powers in the capital. Bit by bit, real power over the countryside spun off steadily from the centre to the hands of local figures, and a new warrior-dominated system of authority absorbed the older, courtier-dominated one. By the second quarter of the 14th century, this evolution had progressed to the point where the most successful of the shogunate's provincial vassals had begun to question the value of continued submission to Kamakura at all.

The Kamakura regime fell in 1333, as a result of events spawned by an imperial succession dispute that led to the short-lived Kemmu Restoration (1334), the inauguration of a new shogunate under Ashikaga Takauji (1338) and the six-decade-long 'Southern and Northern Court' era (1336–92), the longest and most significant dynastic schism in Japanese history. Warfare between the two courts broke out immediately, and rapidly spread across the country. Leading warriors shifted sides again and again, in response to advantages and opportunities of the moment, playing each court off against the other in much the same way that the court had once kept warriors weak by pitting them against one another. Such developments took a predictably heavy toll on imperial authority.

By the time the third Ashikaga shogun, Yoshimitsu, tricked the southern pretender, Go-Kameyama, and his followers into returning to Kyoto, whatever remained of centralized power in Japan was in the hands of the shogunate.

Fifteen Ashikaga shoguns reigned between 1336 and 1573, when the last, Yoshiaki, was deposed; but only the first six could claim actually to have ruled the country. By the late 1400s, while both the court and the shogunate remained nominally in authority, real power in Japan had devolved to a few score regional barons called *daimyō*, whose authority rested first and foremost on their ability to hold lands by military force.

CHANGE AND CONSERVATISM

The Genpei and 'Southern and Northern Court' wars were momentous events, that ushered in profound changes to the place of warriors in Japan's social, political and economic order. Both are, moreover, celebrated in epic war tales whose vivid descriptions of battle have shaped the imaginations of scholars and popular audiences alike for centuries. Nevertheless, the methods of war remained much what they had been in earlier centuries. While the weaponry, recruitment, deployment, organization and articulation of 14th-century armies advanced in sophistication, battle continued to revolve around skirmishes between clusters of warriors wielding bow and arrow from horseback.

This pertinacity of hoary tactical paradigms reflects the survival of key socio-cultural imperatives at the eye of a swirling maelstrom of change. Foremost among these were the samurai's identity and self-image within the social hierarchy, and the belief in the existence of a centralized, national power structure. Together, these ideological constructs stayed warriors from fully exploring the possibilities being opened up by advances in weapons technology and military organization.

Between the late 12th and late 14th centuries, samurai political power progressively displaced that of the imperial court, but the idea that a centre existed continued to dominate political – and therefore strategic – thinking. The evolving realities of power on the land notwithstanding, warrior leaders persistently clung to status defined in terms of hierarchies averring possession of countrywide authority. These circumstances provided little incentive to seek out new strategic or tactical models.

Nevertheless, the relatively sudden appearance of armies numbering in the thousands – a product of the countrywide scope of the Genpei conflict – introduced new tactical problems, which were intensified by the use of field fortifications. The combination concentrated battles and battlefields, rendering the former longer and the latter more crowded. These factors, in turn, limited the mobility of both attacking and defending troops, enhancing the role and value of foot soldiers.

While the battles of the 'Southern and Northern Court' period were, in the main, much smaller in scale – in terms of the numbers of men actually in the field at any one time – than those of the Genpei era, fighting was general and endemic throughout most of this sixty-year span, and involved warriors from every province in the country and battles fought in every region. The need to prosecute this enduring conflict translated into an imperative towards enhanced ability to control and extract surplus from the countryside, in order to better raise, equip, feed, transport and

'Men and horses tumbled down one upon
another from the eastern and western slopes
surrounding the fortress, filling the deep
valleys and choking the roads with corpses.
The River Kozu ran with blood, as if its
waters reflected the crimson of autumn
leaves. After this, though the besieging forces
swarmed like clouds and mist, none
dared assail the fortress.'
Siege warfare in the 'Southern and Northern
Court' era, 1336–92, from the *Taiheiki* epic

direct soldiers and armies. Provincial warrior leaders were able to expand ostensibly temporary commissariat rights and powers into a more comprehensive local political authority than had existed in Japan since the advent of the imperial state at the turn of the 7th century.

The battles of the 1330s also introduced a new form of siege warfare, as imperial loyalist forces looked to fortifications not just as tactical barricades but as rallying points, sanctuaries and symbols of resistance. While 12th- and 13th-century defensive works had been constructed across or adjacent to roads, beachheads and other travel arteries, 14th-century commanders ensconced themselves in remote mountain citadels, whose purpose and presence defied Kamakura authority and served as a beacon to other recruits. Fortresses were now

Opposite Himeji castle, in Hyogo prefecture, established in the mid-14th century and rebuilt by Toyotomi Hideyoshi in the 1580s.

fully enclosed and often reinforced with wooden palisades and turrets erected at various points along the walls. Compact enough to be easily defended on all exposures, and located on terrain sufficiently treacherous to render them difficult to approach quickly or in large numbers, the new fortresses enabled relatively small numbers of warriors to tie up sizeable enemy forces for long periods, buying time and credibility for their cause, and whittling away at the morale of Kamakura's troops.

Unlike the easily abandoned defensive lines favoured by 12th- and 13th-century warriors, 14th-century citadels allowed the defenders no rapid means of escape or retreat; indeed, they invited encirclement and siege. Nevertheless, such citadels were not readily taken by direct onslaught – even if besieging forces did not actually have to contend with the collapsing sham walls, decoy armies of mannequins, and other imaginative tactics described in literary accounts of the battles. Most often, mountain castles fell to attrition – sometimes hastened by cutting off the garrison's water or food supplies. Others were captured by infiltration or stealth.

Weapons technology was changing as well. By the late 1300s the Japanese had evolved new forms of straight-bladed thrusting spears and pikes that gradually supplanted the heavy glaives (polearms) favoured since the 11th century; lighter, more flexible styles of armour that fitted more closely at the waist and permitted greater freedom of movement on horseback and on foot; and more powerful, laminated-wood-and-bamboo bows that extended the effective killing range of arrow shots.

THE COUNTRY AT WAR

In the end, the Ashikaga-led polity did not endure. Power continued to devolve steadily and decisively from the capital to the countryside until, by the closing decades of the 15th century, only the thinnest pretext of local rule drawing its legitimacy from a central governing authority remained. The province-wide jurisdictions defined by the imperial codes broke apart into smaller territories controlled by a new form of local hegemon. These *daimyō* ruled all-but autonomous satrapies whose borders coincided with the lands that they – and the lesser warriors whose loyalties they commanded – could dominate by force.

One effect of this new political reality was a shift in the underlying purpose of war. For the first time in the history of the samurai the primary strategic objective of warfare became the capture or defence of territory. At the same time, tighter organizational structures built upon local power rather than authority delegated from the centre dramatically enhanced the ability of *daimyō* to collect revenue from the land, which in turn enabled them to forge and sustain much larger armies, and to keep them active in the field for much longer periods than ever before.

The armies fielded by the emerging warlords were increasingly composed of contingents of fighting men bound to their leaders by standing obligations of service, rather than by short-term, contractual promises of rewards. Changing the make-up and goals in turn made increasingly disciplined group tactical manoeuvre possible for late medieval armies, although samurai did not immediately grasp the tactical possibilities that were emerging for them – the sporadic conflicts of the early 14th century were contested in much the same way those of earlier eras had been.

In the fifth month of 1467, however, a shogunal succession dispute erupted into

Japanese Armour

There were five principal styles of armour to be seen on medieval Japanese battlefields (*ōyoroi, haramaki, haramaki-yoroi, dōmaru* and *hara-ate*). All five were constructed from the same fundamental components: tiny plates, or lamellae, fashioned from iron or rawhide. Individual lamellae were stacked with each overlapping the one to its right, and laced together with leather or braided silk cords through the bottom three holes, to form plates, which were lacquered to protect them from moisture, and then laced together in rows that overlapped downward, like shingles on an upside-down roof.

Above Construction of Japanese armour. Individual lamellae (*sane*) of iron or leather were laced together into plates, called *saneita*, which were then lacquered and laced together in overlapping rows.

Lamellar armour is more flexible, easier to move in, easier to store and transport and requires less customization to fit than plate armour, and it offers better protection than chain mail. Its principal defensive advantage over other types of armour is its capacity to absorb shock, by diffusing the energy of blows landing against it through the layers formed by the overlapping scales and lacings.

The premier armour of the early medieval era, the *ōyoroi* ('great armour'), featured a boxy cuirass; a four-piece lamellar skirt to protect the wearer's hips, abdomen and thighs; and large, flat, rectangular shoulder plates that served mounted archers (who needed both hands to ride and shoot) as substitutes for hand shields. Foot soldiers were outfitted with simpler forms of armour that were better suited to their needs.

Left A *haramaki-yoroi* of late 13th- or 14th-century design. *Haramaki-yoroi* was a hybrid armour, compiled by adding the distinctive shoulder pieces (*ōsode*), shin guards (*suneate*), gauntlets (*kote*) and other key ornaments of the much more expensive *ōyoroi* to the armours of the *haramaki* design, originally developed for foot soldiers.

full-scale warfare in the capital. The early weeks of the fighting saw both sides engaged in wholesale burning of large areas of the city, in an effort to create open spaces in which their horsemen could manoeuvre. But commanders quickly discovered that the larger, better disciplined infantry units they had been forging for the past half century – now armed with better bows, spears and armour – could readily hold their ground against mounted samurai.

By the early months of 1468, both sides had begun constructing barricades and digging trenches in strategic parts of the capital, and the Onin war (named after the calendar era in which it began) settled into a stalemate that dragged on for ten long years. Fighting centred on night raids during which small bands of foot soldiers attempted to set fire to enemy fortifications and lodgings, and on forays against enemy villages intended to disrupt supply lines.

In 1473 both the original protagonists, Yamana Sozen and Hosokawa Katsumoto, died within a few months of one another. The subordinates and allies who remained grew increasingly restive, frustrated with the tactical stand-off on the front and concerned with conflicts developing in their home territories. One by one, commanders began to desert. The last, Ouchi Yoshihiro, burned his position and slipped away in the eleventh month of 1477, bringing the war in the capital to an end.

There followed a century and a half of near-continuous warfare as *daimyō* contested with *daimyō*, and with those below them, to maintain and expand their domains. The spirit of this Sengoku (literally, 'country at war') age is captured in two expressions current at the time: *gekokujō* ('the low overthrow the high') and *jakuniku kyōshoku* ('the weak become meat; the strong eat').

Faced with a new strategic imperative to capture or defend specific geographic areas, and armed with new tools and enhanced organizational powers, commanders began to incorporate the lessons of the Onin war into their tactical conceptualization, and rapidly discovered that archers (and later gunners) on foot were just as effective at harassing and breaking enemy formations, and far more successful at holding ground, than their mounted counterparts. Cavalry became relegated to a supportive role, used for reconnaissance and small-scale skirmishing, while battles centred on the effective coordination of light and heavy infantry.

Further Reading

Introduction

Bartlett, R., *The Making of Europe: Conquest, Colonization and Cultural Change, 950–1350* (London, 1993)

Bradbury, J., *The Medieval Siege* (Woodbridge, 1992)

Contamine, P. (trans. M. Jones), *War in the Middle Ages* (Oxford, 1984)

Holmes, R., *The World Atlas of Warfare: Military Innovations that Changed the Face of Warfare* (London, 1998)

Hooper, N., and M. Bennett, *Cambridge Illustrated Atlas of Warfare: the Middle Ages, 768–1487* (Cambridge, 1996)

Keen, M. (ed.), *Medieval Warfare: a History* (Oxford, 1999)

Nicholson, H., *Medieval Warfare: Theory and Practice of War in Europe, 300–1500* (Basingstoke, 2004)

Nicolle, D., *Medieval Warfare Source Book*, vol. 1: *Warfare in Western Christendom*; vol 2: *Christian Europe and its Neighbours* (London, 1996)

——, *Crusader Warfare*, vol 1: *Byzantium, Western Europe and the Battle for the Holy Land*; vol 2: *Muslims, Mongols and the Struggle against the Crusades* (London, 2007)

Prestwich, M., *Armies and Warfare in the Middle Ages: the English Experience* (New Haven, CT, and London, 1996)

Riley-Smith, J., *The Atlas of the Crusades* (London, 1991)

Rose, S., *Medieval Naval Warfare 1000–1500* (London, 2002)

Sawyer, R. D., *The Seven Military Classics of Ancient China* (New York, 1993)

Chapter 1

Beaucamp, J., F. Briquel-Chatonnet and C. J. Robin, 'La persécution des chrétiens de Nagran et la chronologie himyarite', *ARAM*, 11: 1 (1999), pp. 15–83

Cameron, A., *Agathias* (Oxford, 1970)

——*Procopius and the Sixth Century* (London, 1985)

Greatrex, G., *Rome and Persia at War, 502–532* (Leeds, 1998), pp. 122–47

——and S. N. C. Lieu, *The Roman Eastern Frontier and the Persian Wars, Part II: AD 363–630: A Narrative Sourcebook* (London and New York, 2002), pp. 62–228

Howard-Johnston, J., 'Procopius, Roman Defences North of the Taurus and the New Fortress of Citharizon', in D. H. French and C. S. Lightfoot (eds.), *The Eastern Frontier of the Roman Empire*, BAR International Series, 553 (Oxford, 1989), pp. 203–29

——'Heraclius' Persian Campaigns and the Revival of the East Roman Empire, 622–630', *War in History*, 6 (1999), pp. 1–44

Lillington-Martin, C., 'Archaeological and Ancient Literary Evidence for a Battle near Dara Gap, Turkey, AD 530: Topography, Texts and Trenches', in A. S. Lewin and P. Pellegrini (eds.), *The Late Roman Army in the Near East from Diocletian to the Arab Conquest*, BAR International Series 1717 (Oxford, 2007), pp. 299–311

Rance, P. R., 'Tactics and Tactica in the Sixth Century: Tradition and Originality' (PhD, University of St Andrews, 1994)

Sabin, P., H. van Wees and M. Whitby (eds.), *The Cambridge History of Greek and Roman Warfare*, vol. 2: *Rome from the Late Republic to the Late Empire* (Cambridge, 2007)

Tomlin, R., 'A. H. M. Jones and the Army of the Fourth Century', in D. Gwynn (ed.), *A. H. M. Jones and the Later Roman Empire* (Leiden, 2008), pp. 143–65

Whitby, M., 'Procopius and the Development of Roman Defences in Upper Mesopotamia', in P. Freeman and D. Kennedy (eds.), *The Defence of the Roman and Byzantine East*, BAR International Series 297, ii (Oxford, 1986), pp. 717–35

——*The Emperor Maurice and his Historian: Theophylact Simocatta on Persian and Balkan Warfare* (Oxford, 1988)

Chapter 2

Bachrach, B. S., *Merovingian Military Organization, 481–751* (Minneapolis, 1972)

——'Charles Martel'; 'Mounted Shock Combat'; 'The Stirrup and Feudalism', in *Armies and Politics in the Early Medieval West* (Aldershot, 1993)

——*Early Carolingian Warfare* (Philadelphia, 2001)

Barford, P. M., *The Early Slavs* (London, 2001)

Carver, M. (ed.), *The Age of Sutton Hoo* (Woodbridge, 1992)

Christie, N., *The Lombards* (Oxford, 1995)

Collins, R., *The Arab Conquest of Spain, 710–797* (Oxford, 1989)

——*Visigothic Spain, 409–711* (Oxford, 2004)

Davidson, H. E., *The Sword in Anglo-Saxon England* (Woodbridge, 1994)

DeVries, K., and J. France, *Warfare in the Dark Ages* (Aldershot, 2008)

Evans, S. S., *The Lords of Battle* (Woodbridge, 1997)

Fauber, L. H., *Narses Hammer of the Goths* (Gloucester, 1990)

Fouracre, P. *The Age of Charles Martel* (Harlow, 2000)

——*The New Cambridge Medieval History*, vol. 1, 500–700 (Cambridge, 2005)

Geary, P. J., *Before France and Germany* (Oxford, 1988)

Halsall, G., *Warfare and Society in the Barbarian West, 450–900* (London, 2003)

——*Barbarian Migrations and the Roman West, 376–568* (Cambridge, 2007)Marren, P., *Battles of the Dark Ages* (Barnsley, 2006)

McCormick, M., *Eternal Victory* (Cambridge, 1986)

Schutz, H., *The Germanic Realms in Pre-Carolingian Central Europe, 400–750* (New York, 2000)

Wood, I., *The Merovingian Kingdoms, 450–751* (London, 1994)

Chapter 3

Bowlus, C. R., *The Battle of Lechfeld and its Aftermath, August 955* (Aldershot, 2006)

Franklin, S., and J. Shepard, *The Emergence of the Rus, 750–1200* (London, 1996)

Gardiner, R. (ed.), *The Earliest Ships* (London, 1996), especially pp. 72–88

Graham-Campbell, J., *The Viking World* (London, 2001)

Griffiths, P., *The Viking Art of War* (London, 1995)

Haldon, J., *Warfare, State and Society in the Byzantine World 565–1204* (London, 1999)

——*The Byzantine Wars* (Stroud, 2001)

Kennedy, H., *The Armies of the Caliphs* (London, 2001)

——*The Prophet and the Age of the Caliphates* (Harlow, 2004, 2nd edn)

Leyser, K. J., 'The Battle at the Lech, 955', in *Medieval Germany and its Neighbours 900-1250* (London, 1982), pp. 43–67

McGeer, E., *Sowing the Dragon's Teeth: Byzantine Warfare in the Tenth Century* (Washington, DC, 2005)

Sawyer, P. H., *Kings and Vikings* (London, 1982)

Chapter 4

France, J., *Victory in the East: a Military History of the First Crusade* (Cambridge, 1994)

——'Crusading Warfare and its Adaptation to Eastern Conditions in the Twelfth Century', *Mediterranean Historical Review*, 15 (2000), pp. 49–66

Hamilton, B., *The Leper King and his Heirs: Baldwin IV and the Crusader Kingdom of Jerusalem* (Cambridge, 2000)

Jotischky, A., *Crusading and the Crusader States* (Harlow, 2004)

Mayer, H. E., *The Crusades* (Oxford, 1965)

Phillips, J., *The Second Crusade* (New Haven, CT, 2007)

Powell, J. M., *Anatomy of a Crusade, 1213–21* (Philadelphia, 1986)

Riley-Smith, J., *The First Crusade and the Idea of Crusading* (London, 1986)
——*The Crusades: a Short History* (London, 1987)
Smail, R. C., *Crusading Warfare, 1097–1193* (Cambridge, 1956), pp. 161–65

Chapter 5
Amitai-Preiss, R., *Mongols and Mamluks: the Mamluk–Ilkhanid War, 1260–1281* (Cambridge, 1995)
Barfield, T. J., *The Perilous Frontier: Nomadic Empires and China, 221 BC to AD 1757*, Studies in Social Discontinuity (Cambridge, MA, 1989)
Buell, P. D., *Historical Dictionary of the Mongol World Empire* (Lanham, MD, 2003)
Chambers, J., *The Devil's Horsemen: the Mongol Invasion of Europe* (Edison, NJ, 2003)
Hookham, H., *Tamburlaine the Conqueror* (London, 1962)
Manz, B. F., *The Rise and Rule of Tamerlane* (New York, 1991)
Marozzi, J., *Tamerlane: Sword of Islam, Conqueror of the World* (New York, 2004)
May, T., *The Mongol Art of War* (Barnsley, 2007)
Morgan, D. O., *The Mongols* (2nd edn, Cambridge, MA, 2007)
Nicolle, D., *The Mongol Warlords* (Poole, 2004)
Ratchnevsky, P. (trans. T. Nivison), *Genghis Khan: his Life and Legacy* (Cambridge, MA, 1991)

Chapter 6
Christiansen, E., *The Northern Crusades: the Baltic and the Catholic Frontier, 1100–1525* (Minneapolis, 1980; 2nd edn, New York, 1998)
Maier, C., *Preaching the Crusades: Mendicant Friars and the Cross in the Thirteenth Century* (Cambridge, 1994)
Murray, A. (ed.), *Crusade and Conversion on the Baltic Frontier, 1150–1500* (Aldershot, 2001)
Urban, W., *Tannenberg and After* (2nd edn, Chicago, 2002)
——*The Teutonic Knights* (London, 2003)

Chapter 7
Ayton, A., and P. Preston, *The Battle of Crécy, 1346* (Woodbridge and Rochester, 2005)
Barker, J., *Agincourt: the King, the Campaign, the Battle* (London, 2005)
Bennett, M., *Agincourt, 1415* (Oxford, 1991)
Contamine, P. (trans. M. Jones), *War in the Middle Ages* (Oxford, 1984)
Curry, A., *The Hundred Years War* (Basingstoke, 1993)
——and M. Hughes (eds.), *Arms, Armies and Fortifications in the Hundred Years War* (Woodbridge, 1994)

——*Agincourt: a New History* (Stroud, 2005)
DeVries, K., *Infantry Warfare in the Early Fourteenth Century* (Woodbridge, 1996)
Jones, M. K., *Agincourt 1415* (Barnsley, 2005)
Keen, M. (ed.), *Medieval Warfare: a History* (Oxford, 1999)
Prestwich, M., *Armies and Warfare in the Middle Ages: the English Experience* (New Haven, CT, and London, 1996)
Rogers, C. J. (ed.), *The Wars of Edward III: Sources and Interpretations* (Woodbridge, 1999)
——*War Cruel and Sharp: English Strategy under Edward III, 1327–1360* (Woodbridge, 2000)
Strickland, M., and R. Hardy, *The Great Warbow* (Stroud, 2005)
Wright, N., *Knights and Peasants: the Hundred Years War in the French Countryside* (Woodbridge and Rochester, 1998)

Chapter 8
Bartoš, F. M., *The Hussite Revolution 1424–1437* (Boulder, CO, 1986)
Boffa, S., *Warfare in Medieval Brabant* (Woodbridge, 2004)
Bonjour, E., H. S. Offler and G. R. Potter, *A Short History of Switzerland* (Oxford, 1952)
Caferro, W., *John Hawkwood: an English Mercenary in Fourteenth-Century Italy* (Baltimore, 2006)
DeVries, K., *Medieval Military Technology* (Peterborough, Ontario, 1992)
Heymann, F. G., *John Žižka and the Hussite Revolution* (Princeton, 1955)
Mallett, M., *Mercenaries and their Masters: Warfare in Renaissance Italy* (London, 1974)
Miller, D., and G. Embleton, *The Swiss at War, 1300–1500* (Oxford, 1979)
Nicolle, D., *Fornovo, 1495: France's Bloody Fighting Retreat* (Oxford, 1996)
Smith, R. D., and K. DeVries, *The Artillery of the Dukes of Burgundy, 1363–1477* (Woodbridge, 2005)
Trease, G., *The Condottieri: Soldiers of Fortune* (London, 1970)
Vaughan, R., *Charles the Bold* (London, 1973)
——*Valois Burgundy* (London, 1975)

Chapter 9
Ágoston, G., *Guns for the Sultan: Military Power and the Weapons Industry in the Ottoman Empire* (Cambridge and New York, 2005)
Babinger, F. (trans. R. Manheim), *Mehmed the Conqueror and his Time*, ed. W. C. Hickman (Princeton, 1992)
Brummet, P., *Ottoman Seapower and Levantine Diplomacy in the Age of Discovery* (New York, 1994)
Finkel, C., *Osman's Dream: the Story of the Ottoman Empire, 1300–1923* (New York, 2005)

Har-El, S., *Struggle for Domination in the Middle East: the Ottoman–Mamluk War, 1485–91* (Leiden, 1995)
Imber, C., *The Ottoman Empire, 1300–1650* (New York, 2002)
Inalcik, H., and C. Kafadar (eds.), *Süleyman the Second and his Time* (Istanbul, 1993)
Kunt, M., and C. Woodhead (eds.), *Süleyman the Magnificent and his Age: the Ottoman Empire in the Early Modern World* (London, 1995)
Murphey, R., *Ottoman Warfare* (New Brunswick, NJ, 1999)
Perjés, G., *The Fall of the Medieval Kingdom of Hungary: Mohács 1526 – Buda 1541* (Boulder, CO, 1989)

Chapter 10
India
Barua, P. P., *The State at War in South Asia* (Lincoln, NB, 2005)
Basham, A. L., *The Wonder that was India: a Survey of the Culture of the Indian Subcontinent before the Coming of the Muslims* (London, 1954)
Bhatia, H. S., *Rival Hindu Kingdoms and Sultans: Fusion of Hindu and Muslim Civilisations* (New Delhi, 1984/86; repr. 2001)
Edwardes, M., *A History of India from the Earliest Times to the Present Day* (London, 1961)
Fass, V., *The Forts of India* (London, 1986)
Goyal, S., *Harsha: a Multidisciplinary Political Study* (Jodhpur, 2006)
Haig, W., *The Cambridge History of India*, vol. 3: *Turks and Afghans* (Cambridge, 1928)
Kumar, R. (ed.), *Survey of Medieval India*, vol. 1 (New Delhi, 1999)
Mansingh, S., *Historical Dictionary of India* (Lanham, MD, 1996)
Rawlinson, H. G., *India: a Short Cultural History* (London, 1937)
Rizvi, S. A. A., *The Wonder that was India*, vol. 2: *1200–1700* (London, 1987)
Sandhu, G. S., *The Military History of Medieval India* (New Delhi, 2003)
Smith, V. A., *The Oxford History of India* (Oxford, 1953)
Thapur, R., *A History of India*, vol. 1 (London, 1966)

China
Dien, A. E. (ed.), *State and Society in Early Mediaeval China* (Palo Alto, 1991)
Ebrey, P. B., *The Cambridge Illustrated History of China* (Cambridge, 1996)
Graff, D., *Medieval Chinese Warfare, 300–900* (London and New York, 2002)
Lorge, P., *War, Politics and Society in Early Modern China* (London, 2005)
——*The Asian Military Revolution* (Cambridge, 2008)
Mote, F., *Imperial China, 900–1800* (Cambridge, 2003)

Peers, C. J., *Medieval Chinese Armies, 1260–1520* (London, 1992)

Standen, N., *Unbounded Loyalty* (Honolulu, 2007)

Korea

Franke, H., and D. Twitchett (eds.), *The Cambridge History of China*, vol. 6: *Alien Regimes and Border States, 907–1368* (Cambridge, 1994)

Kim, C., *The History of Korea* (Westport, CT, 2005)

Seth, M. J., *A Concise History of Korea: from the Neolithic Period through the Nineteenth Century* (Lanham, MD, 2006)

Shultz, E. J., *Generals and Scholars: Military Rule in Medieval Korea* (Honolulu, 2000)

Japan

Adolphson, M. S., *Teeth and Claws of the Buddha: Monastic Warriors and Sohei in Japanese History* (Honolulu, 2007)

Berry, M. E., *The Culture of Civil War in Kyoto* (Berkeley, 1994)

Bottomly, I., and A. P. Hopson, *Arms and Armour of the Samurai: the History of Weaponry in Ancient Japan* (New York, 1988)

Conlan, T., *In Little Need of Divine Intervention: Scrolls of the Mongol Invasions of Japan* (Ithaca, NY, 2001)

——*State of War: the Violent Order of Fourteenth Century Japan* (Ann Arbor, 2003)

Farris, W. W., *Heavenly Warriors: the Evolution of Japan's Military, 500–1300* (Cambridge, MA, 1992)

Friday, K., *Hired Swords: the Rise of Private Warrior Power in Early Japan* (Stanford, 1992)

——'Pushing Beyond the Pale: the Yamato Conquest of the Emishi and Northern Japan', *Journal of Japanese Studies*, 23:1 (1997), pp. 1–24

——*Samurai, Warfare and the State in Early Medieval Japan* (London, 2004)

——'Off the Warpath: Military Science and Budō in the Evolution of Ryūha Bugei', in A. Bennett (ed.), *Budo Perspectives*, vol. 1 (Auckland, 2005), pp. 249–68

——'Lordship Interdicted: Taira Tadatsune and the Limited Horizons of Warrior Ambition', in M. Adolphson, E. Kamens and S. Matsumoto (eds.), *Centers and Peripheries in Heian Japan* (Honolulu, 2007), pp. 329–54

——*The First Samurai: the Life and Legend of the Warrior Rebel, Taira Masakado* (New York, 2008)

Goble, A. E., 'War and Injury: the Emergence of Wound Medicine in Medieval Japan', *Monumenta Nipponica*, 60:31 (2005), pp. 297–338

Hurst, G. C., 'The Warrior as Ideal for a New Age', in J. P. Mass (ed.), *The Origins of Japan's Medieval World: Courtiers, Clerics, Warriors, and Peasants in the Fourteenth Century* (Stanford, 1997), pp. 208–33

McCullough, W., 'Shōkyūki: an Account of the Shōkyū War of 1221', *Monumenta Nipponica*, 19:1–4 (1964), pp. 163–215

——'Azuma Kagami Account of the Shōyū War', *Monumenta Nipponica*, 23 (1968), pp. 102–55

Robinson, H. R., *Japanese Arms and Armor* (New York, 1969)

Varley, H. P., *The Onin War: History of its Origins and Background, with a Selective Translation of the Chronicles of Onin* (New York, 1967)

——*Warriors of Japan as Portrayed in the War Tales* (Honolulu, 1994)

——'Warfare in Japan 1467–1600', in J. Black (ed.), *War in the Early Modern World, 1450–1815* (London, 1999), pp. 53–86

List of Contributors

Matthew Bennett is a Senior Lecturer at The Royal Military Academy Sandhurst, where he has taught for twenty-five years. A military historian with a particular interest in pre-modern war he specializes in medieval warfare. His publications include the *Cambridge Illustrated Atlas of Medieval Warfare*; the *Dictionary of Ancient and Medieval Warfare*; *Campaigns of the Norman Conquest*; and *Agincourt 1415*. He is the author of two dozen academic articles on the ethos and practice of warfare with a focus on chivalry and the Crusades, and the General Editor of the 'Warfare in History' series of monographs for the Boydell Press, which has published twenty-five volumes since its inception in 1996.

Gábor Ágoston is Associate Professor at the Department of History of Georgetown University. His research focuses on Ottoman economic and military history from the 15th to 18th centuries, early modern Hungarian history, and the comparative study of the Ottoman and Habsburg empires. In addition to his five Hungarian–language books and numerous articles, he is the author of *Guns for the Sultan: Military Power and the Weapons Industry in the Ottoman Empire* and with Bruce Masters of *The Encyclopedia of the Ottoman Empire*.

Roy Boss graduated in history from Southampton University many years ago. He has maintained a lifelong interest in late antique and early medieval warfare, has contributed to several publications on the warfare of the period and is the author of *Justinian's Wars in the West*.

John France is Professor Emeritus at Swansea University. His academic interest is in crusading and warfare, and as a result he has travelled extensively in the Middle East. His books include *The Crusades and the Expansion of Catholic Christendom, 1000–1714*; *Western Warfare in the Age of the Crusades, 1000–1300*; and *Victory in the East: a Military History of the First Crusade*.

Karl Friday is Professor of Japanese History at the University of Georgia. A specialist in early medieval social history, he has written extensively on samurai history and culture. His major publications include *Hired Swords: the Rise of Private Warrior Power in Early Japan*; *Legacies of the Sword: the Kashima-Shinryu and Samurai Martial Culture*; *Samurai, Warfare & the State in Early Medieval Japan*; and *The First Samurai: the Life and Legend of the Warrior Rebel, Taira Masakado*.

T. A. Heathcote is an alumnus of the University of London's School of Oriental and African Studies, with a BA in South Asian history and a PhD in the history of Baluchistan. He spent his Civil Service career as curator of the Royal Military Academy Sandhurst, retiring in 1997 as the principal curatorial officer in the MOD. His publications include five books on the military history of British India, including Afghanistan. He served for thirty years as an officer in the Reserves.

James Howard-Johnston is a Fellow of Corpus Christi College, Oxford, and University Lecturer in Byzantine Studies. His main academic interests lie in international relations and Byzantine institutional history. Military matters have loomed large in his research and writing, from his doctoral thesis ('Studies in the Organization of the Byzantine Army in the Tenth and Eleventh Century', Oxford, 1971) to the present. Currently he is working on a history of the last great war of antiquity, between the Byzantines and Persians (603–30).

Peter Lorge is Senior Lecturer in Chinese and Military history at Vanderbilt University. He specializes in 10th- and 11th-century Chinese history, with a particular interest in military history and thought. He is the author of *War, Politics and Society in Early Modern China, 900–1795* and *The Asian Military Revolution: From Gunpowder to the Bomb*.

Timothy May is the Associate Professor of Middle Eastern and Central Eurasian History at North Georgia College and State University. He is the author of *The Mongol Art of War* and several articles on the Mongol Empire and the medieval Middle East.

Michael Prestwich took his first degree and his doctorate at the University of Oxford. He taught first at the University of St Andrews, and then at Durham, where he is now Professor Emeritus, having retired in 2008. His books include *War, Politics and Finance under Edward I*; *The Three Edwards*; *Edward I*; *Armies and Warfare in the Middle Ages: the English Experience*; and *Plantagenet England, 1225–1360*.

William Urban is Lee L. Morgan Professor of History and International Studies at Monmouth College in Illinois. Author of several books on the Baltic Crusade, including *Tannenberg and After*, and co-translator of several chronicles, he has studied in Germany and taught in Italy, Yugoslavia and the Czech Republic. He is a corresponding member of the Historische Kommission für Ost- und Westpreußische Landesforschung and the Baltische Historische Kommission in Germany.

Sources of Illustrations

t: top, b: bottom, c: centre, r: right, l: left

1 Topkapi Sarayi Museum, Istanbul; **2–3** Collection the Earl of Leicester, Holkham Hall, Norfolk/Bridgeman Art Library; **4–5** Tapestry Museum, Bayeux; **6** Dallas and John Heaton/ Free Agents Limited/Corbis; **7** Gianni Dagli Orti/Corbis; **8** Steve Irwin/www.istockphoto.com; **9** The Royal Library, Windsor; **10** Bibliothèque de l'Ecole des Beaux-Arts, Paris/Giraudon/ Bridgeman Art Library; **11** British Library Board. All Rights Reserved/Bridgeman Art Library; **12** British Library, London; **14** akg-images/Jérôme da Cunha; **16** Metropolitan Museum of Art, New York; **17** Musée du Louvre, Paris; **19** Musée du Louvre, Paris; **20** San Francesco Chruch, Arezzo, Italy; **21** Photo David Nicolle; **22–23** Werner Forman Archive/Biblioteca Nacional, Madrid; **24** Ann Ronan/HIP/Scala, Florence; **25** Bridgeman Art Library; **26t** Fitzwilliam Museum, University of Cambridge; **26b** Photo Michael Whitby; **29** Art Archive/Gianni Dagli Orti; **30** Biblioteca Vaticana, Rome; **32** Museum für Islamische Kunst, Berlin; **34** Zühmer/Rheinische Landesmuseum, Trier; **38** Landesamt für Denkmalpflege und Archäologie Sachsen-Anhalt, Juraj Lipták; **41** epa/Corbis; **43** Museo Nazionale del Bargello, Florence; **44** Historisches Museum, Bern; **45** Time & Life Pictures/Getty Images; **49** Württembergische Landesbibliothek, Stuttgart. Cod. bibl. 2° 23; **50–51** Drazen Tomic © Thames & Hudson Ltd, London; **52** akg-images/Erich Lessing; **53** Abbey de Saint-Denis, Paris; **55** Archivo Iconografico, S.A./Corbis; **56t** Württembergische Landesbibliothek, Stuttgart. Cod. bibl. 2° 23; **56b** Württembergische Landesbibliothek, Stuttgart. Cod. bibl. 2° 23; **57** Germanisches Nationalmuseum, Nuremberg/ Bridgeman Art Library; **59** Umberto Tomba, Museo di Castelvecchio, Verona; **60** Kunsthistorisces Museum, Vienna; **61** Viking Ship Museum, Oslo/Giraudon/Bridgeman Art Library; **62–63** National Museum of Iceland, Reykjavík; **63** Giant Screen Films; **64** Museum of Cultural History - University of Oslo; **65b** Historiska Muséet, Stockholm; **66** Glydendal, Copenhagen; **67** Universiteitsbibliotheek Leiden, Per F 17, fol. 22r; **68** Wuttembergisch Landesbibliothek, Stuttgart. Cod. bibl. 2° 23; **70** Historiska Museet, Stockholm; **71** British Museum, London; **72–73** V&A Images/Victoria and Albert Museum, London; **74** Werner Forman Archive/ Biblioteca Nacional, Madrid; **75t** Biblioteca Nacional de Madrid, Skylitzes Matritensis. Archivo Oronoz; **75b** Biblioteca Nacional de Madrid, Skylitzes Matritensis, fol. 33. Archivo Oronoz; **77l & r** V&A Images/Victoria and Albert Museum, London; **78** Nick Jakins © Thames & Hudson Ltd, London; **81** Bibliothèque Nationale, Paris; **82** Tapestry Museum, Bayeux; **83** Courtauld Institute of Art, University of London; **84** Bibliothèque Nationale, Paris; **85** British Museum, London; **87l** Bibliothèque Nationale, Paris; **88** Tapestry Museum, Bayeux; **89** © Museum of London; **90** British Museum, London; **91** Bibliothèque Nationale, Paris; **92** The Art Archive/Alfredo Dagli Orti; **93** The Royal Library, The Hague Ms. 69; **94** Bibliotheque Nationale, Paris/Bridgeman Art Library; **95b** Photo John France; **96** Basilica di San Marco, Venice; **97** Michael Major/www.istockphoto.com; **98–99** Scala Florence/HIP; **98bl & br** Photo Sally Nicholls; **99br** Photo Sally Nicholls; **101** Museum of Islamic Art, Cairo; **102l** Bodleian Library, University of Oxford, Ms. Huntington 264, fol.117; **102r** Bodleian Library, University of Oxford, Ms. Huntington 264, fol.102v; **103** akg-images/Erich Lessing; **104** Bibliothèque Nationale, Paris/Giraudon/Bridgeman Art Library; **105** Photo © The British Library Board. All Rights Reserved 2009; **106** British Museum, London/Bridgeman Art Library; **108** Bodleian Library,

University of Oxford, Ms. Laud Misc 587, fol.1; **109t** Corpus Christi College, Cambridge; **109b** British Library, London; **110** akg-images/VISIOARS; **111** British Museum, London; **112** British Museum, London; **113** National Palace Museum, Taipei, Taiwan; **115** Corpus Christi College, Cambridge, Ms. 16, fol.166r; **116** Bibliothèque Nationale, Paris; **117** Pauline Taylor/Alamy; **118** Leonid Katsyka/ www.istockphoto.com; **119** Österreichische Nationalbibliothek, Ms. Codex 2623, fol. 29r; **120** Bibliothèque Nationale, Paris, Ms. Persan Suppl. 1113 fol.180v; **121** National Palace Museum, Taipei, Taiwan; **122** Yann Arthus-Bertrand/Corbis; **123** Furusiyya Art Foundation Collection, Liechtenstein; **124** © The Board of Trustees of the Armouries; **126** British Library, London; **127** Art Archive/Musée du Louvre Paris/Gianni Dagli Orti; **128tl** Furusiyya Art Foundation Collection, Liechtenstein; **128bl** Furusiyya Art Foundation Collection, Liechtenstein; **128r** Furusiyya Art Foundation Collection, Liechtenstein; **130** Gur-e Mir Mausoleum, Samarkand; **131** British Library, London, Johnson Album 1, no. 2; **132** Staatsbibliothek, Berlin; **133** Victoria and Albert Museum, London/Stapleton Collection/Bridgeman Art Library; **134** Edinburgh University Library, Orms 20, fol. 124v; **136-37** Private Collection/Bridgeman Art Library; **138** Victoria & Albert Museum, London/Bridgeman Art Library; **139** Private Collection/Bridgeman Art Library; **140** WoodyStock/Alamy; **141** Courtesy Museum of the Polish Army, Warsaw, Poland; **143** British Film Institute, London; **145** Albert Speelman/ www.istockphoto.com; **146** University Library, Heidelberg, Codex Manesse, Cod. Pal. Germ. 848; **147** Staatsarchiv Königsberg, Göttingen; **148** Courtesy Museum of the Polish Army, Warsaw, Poland; **149t** Photo William Urban; **149b** Courtesy Museum of the Polish Army, Warsaw, Poland; **150** Courtesy Military Museum of Vytautas the Great, Kaunas, Lithuania; **151** Czartoryski Museum, Cracow/Bridgeman Art Library; **152** The Granger Collection, New York; **153** Courtesy Museum of the Polish Army, Warsaw, Poland; **154** Biblioteka Jagiellonksa, Cracow; **155** SMPK, Geheimes Staatsarchiv; **156t** Courtesy Museum of the Polish Army, Warsaw, Poland; **160** British Library, London; **161** Bodleian Library, University of Oxford, Ms. Bodl. 264; **162** Jon Tarrant/www.istockphoto.com; **163l** Duomo, Florence; **163r** © Museum of London; **165** Bibliothèque Nationale, Paris; **166** British Museum, London/ Bridgeman Art Library; **167** Sandro Vannini/Corbis; **168** Art Archive/Biblioteca Nazionale Marciana, Venice/Alfredo Dagli Orti; **169** British Museum, London; **170** British Library, London; **171** British Library, London, Ms. Add. 47682, fol.40; **173** British Library, London; **174** Biological Anthropology Research Centre, Archaeological Sciences, University of Bradford; **174b** British Library, London; **175t** akg-images/Erich Lessing; **175b** Photo courtesy Renaud Beffeyte/Armedieval; **176** Lambeth Palace Library, London/Bridgeman Art Library; **177** Photo © British Library Board. All Rights Reserved 2009. Cotton Caligula D V, fol.43v; **178** British Library, London; **179l, c, tr** & **br** Warwick Castle, Warwick; **180** British Library, London; **181** Bibliotheque Nationale, Paris/Bridgeman Art Library; **182** British Museum, London; **183** British Library, London. Photo Scala Florence/HIP; **185t** Staatliche Museen zu Berlin; **185b** akg-images/ullstein bild; **186** Burgerbibliothek, Berne, Mss. Hist Helv 1. 16, S. 456; **187** Tschantlanchronik, Zürich, Zentralbibliothek; **188** akg-images/ Erich Lessing; **189t** Bibliothèque Municipale. Photo akg-images/ Erich Lessing; **189b** Photo Zdenek Prchlik jun. Husitske muzeum v Tabore, Czech Republic; **190** Art Archive; **191t** Bibliothèque Nationale, Paris, Ms. Italien 372, fol.4v;

Sources of Quotations

191b Santi Giovanni e Paolo Church, Venice; **192** Rosenwald Collection. Image courtesy Board of Trustees, National Gallery of Art, Washington; **195t** Biblioteca Capitolare, Padua, Italy/ Giraudon/ Bridgeman Art Library; **195** Photo © British Library Board. All Rights Reserved 2009. Royal 14 E. IV, fol.59v; **196b** Photo © Crown copyright reproduced, courtesy of Historic Scotland; **197** Antonio Ovejero Diaz/ www.istockphoto.com; **198t** Art Archive/Museo Correr, Venice/Alfredo Dagli Orti; **198b** Photo © Culture and Sport Glasgow (Museums); **199t** akg-images/Rabatti-Domingie; **199b** Atlantide Phototravel/ Corbis; **203t** Palazzo Vecchio (Palazzo della Signoria) Florence, Italy/ Bridgeman Art Library; **203b** Science Museum, London; **204** National Gallery, London; **207** Art Archive/Corbis; **208t** akg-images/Erich Lessing; **208b** Edinburgh University Library, Special Collection Department, Or Ms. 20, fol.119r; **210** Photo © The Trustees of the British Museum. All Rights Reserved; **211** State Hermitage Museum, St Petersburg; **212** Hazlan Abdul Hakim/ www.istockphoto.com; **213t** Istanbul University Library; **213b** Art Archive/ Moldovita Monastery Romania/Alfredo Dagli Orti; **215t** British Museum, London; **215b** Topkapi Sarayi Museum, Istanbul; **216** Art Archive/Bodleian Library Oxford; **217t** Gemäldegalerie, Kunsthistorisches Museum, Vienna; **217b** Topkapi Sarayi Museum, Istanbul; **218t** Private Collection; **218b** Ljiljana Pavkov/ www.istockphoto.com; **219** Topkapi Sarayi Museum, Istanbul; **221** Topkapi Sarayi Museum, Istanbul; **222** Wallace Collection, London; **223t** Furusiyya Art Foundation Collection, Liechtenstein; **223b** Scala Florence/HIP; **224** Furusiyya Art Foundation Collection, Liechtenstein; **225l & r** Topkapi Sarayi Museum, Istanbul; **226** Seattle Art Museum/Corbis; **228** National Museum of India, New Delhi/ Bridgeman Art Library; **230** Adam Woolfitt/Corbis; **231** National Museum of India, New Delhi; **232** Michael Freeman/ Corbis; **236** Mogao Caves, Dunhuang, Gansu Province, NW China; **237** Keren Su/Corbis; **238** Art Institute of Chicago. Gift of Russell Tyson; **239l** Ashmolean Museum, University of Oxford/ Bridgeman Art Library; **239r** University of Pennsylvania Museum of Archaeology and Anthropology, Philadelphia; **240** Shaanxi History Museum, Xi-An, China; **241** National Museum of Korea, Seoul; **247** Art Archive/Laurie Platt Winfrey; **248-49** Museum of Fine Arts, Boston, Massachusetts; **251** © The Board of Trustees of the Armouries; **252** Honda Museum/ Courtesy ISEI, Tokyo; **253** Art Archive/Laurie Platt Winfrey; **254t** Sakamoto Photo Research Laboratory, Tokyo; **254b** Agency for Cultural Affairs, Tokyo; **256** Hiroyuki Yamaguchi/ amanaimages/ Corbis; **258b** Kagoshima Jingū, Kagoshima Prefecture

All maps and 3-d battle plans: Red Lion Prints © Thames & Hudson Ltd, London

19 H. Turtledove (trans.), *The Chronicle of Theophanes ... (A.D. 602–813)* (Philadelphia, 1982); **20** Nicephorus Phocas, *De velitatione*, in G. T. Dennis (ed. and trans.), *Three Byzantine Military Treatises* (Washington, DC, 1985), 9; **24** G. T. Dennis (trans.), *Maurice's Strategikon: Handbook of Byzantine Military Strategy* (Philadelphia, 1984), Book XI, 1; **37** H. Turtledove (trans.), *The Chronicle of Theophanes ... (A.D. 602–813)* (Philadelphia, 1982); **44** W. D. Foulke (trans.), *History of the Lombards*, new edn, ed. E. Peters (Philadelphia, 1974), Book V, 11; **46** L. Thorpe, *Gregory of Tours: the History of the Franks* (Harmondsworth, 1974; repr. 1977), Book VII, 24; **49** Agathias Scholasticus, *Histories*, Book I, 22; **52** Royal Frankish Annals, 789; **58** G. T. Dennis (trans.), *Maurice's Strategikon: Handbook of Byzantine Military Strategy* (Philadelphia, 1984), Book XI, 3; **59** J. M. Pizarro (trans.), *The Story of Wamba: Julian of Toledo's Historia Wambae regis* (Washington, DC, 2005), Book 18; **76** G. T. Dennis (trans.), *Maurice's Strategikon: Handbook of Byzantine Military Strategy* (Philadelphia, 1984); **77** A.-M. Talbot and D. F. Sullivan (ed. and trans.), *The History of Leo the Deacon* (Washington, DC, 2005); **86** F. Gabrieli (trans.), *Arab Historians of the Crusades* (New York, 1957), 73; **94** A. C. Krey, *The First Crusade: the Accounts of Eye-Witnesses and Participants* (Gloucester, MA, 1958), 261; **100** Odo of Deuil, *De profectione Ludovici VII in orientem: the Journey of Louis VII to the East*, ed. and trans. V. G. Berry (New York, 1948), 21; **104** F. Gabrieli (trans.), *Arab Historians of the Crusades* (New York, 1957), 138; **111** M. R. B. Shaw (trans.), *Chronicles of the Crusades* (Harmondsworth, 1963), 225; **116** G. T. Scanlon (ed. and trans.), *A Muslim Manual of War* (Cairo, 1961); **118** J. A. Giles (trans.), *Matthew Paris's English history*, 3 vols. (1852–4; repr. New York, 1968), vol. 1, p. 30; **121** J. A. Giles (trans.), *Matthew Paris's English history*, 3 vols. (1852–4; repr. New York, 1968), vol. 1, p. 312; **129** M. R. B. Shaw (trans.), *Joinville and Villehardouin: Chronicles of the Crusades* (Harmondsworth, 1983); **131** H. Yule (trans.) and H. Cordier (ed.), *The Travels of Marco Polo*, 2 vols. (New York, 1993), vol. 1, p. 263; **135** C. Dawson (ed.), *The Mongol Mission: Narratives and Letters of the Franciscan Missionaries in Mongolia and China in the Thirteenth and Fourteenth Centuries* (London, 1955), p. 17; **142** J. A. Brundage (trans.), *The Chronicle of Henry of Livonia*, 2nd edn (Madison, WI, 1961), pp. 106–7; **143** Pope Innocent IV, grant of plenary indulgences, Lyons, 7 May 1245; *Preussisches Urkundenbuch*, vol. 1 (Königsberg, 1882; repr. 1961), 124; **151** K. Koppmann and F. Bruns (eds.), *Die Chroniken der niedersächsischen Städte*, vol. 1: *Lübeck* (Leipzig, 1884); **163** D. Rollason and M. Preswich (eds.), *The Battle of Neville's Cross, 1346* (Stamford, 1998), 135; **171** T. Johnes (trans. and ed.), *Chronicles ... by ... Froissant*, 2 vols. (London, 1839), vol. 1, p. 225; **174** A. Curry (ed.), *The Battle of Agincourt: Sources and Interpretations* (Woodbridge, 2000), 160; **181** C. Rogers (ed.), *The Wars of Edward III: Sources and Interpretations* (Woodbridge, 1999), 194; **188** F. G. Heymann, *John Žižka and the Hussite Revolution* (Princeton, 1955); **190** Enea Silvio Piccolomini [Pope Pius II], *De Bohemorum origine ac gestis historia* (1457); **194** D. M. Schullian (trans.), *Diary of the Caroline War* (New York, 1967); **201** P. de Commines, *Memoirs*, Book I, 3; **207** K. F. Neumann (ed.) and J. B. Telfer (trans.), *The Bondage and Travels of Johann Schiltberger ... in Europe, Asia, and Africa, 1396-1427* (London, 1879), chapter 2; **208** J. Black (ed.), *The Seventy Great Battles in History* (London and New York, 2005), 78; **211** A. H. Lybyer, *The Government of the Ottoman Empire in the Time of Suleiman the Magnificent* (Cambridge, MA, 1913), 249; **212** J. Black (ed.), *The Seventy Great Battles in History* (London and New York, 2005), 85; **250** K. Yasuo, K. and O. Eiichi (eds.), *Heike monogatari (Engyōbon)*, 4 vols. (Tokyo, 1990), vol. 2, p. 246; **256** Tadashi, H. (ed.), *Taiheiki (Tenshōbon)*, 4 vols. (Tokyo, 1994), vol. 1, p. 133.

Index